Finance for Freelancers

Finance for Freelancers

Money, Taxes, and Savings When the Rules Don't Fit

Jonas Wilder

Mindful Pages

Published in 2025

ISBN: 9789371779111 (PB)
ISBN: 9789371779371 (eBook)

Published by

Mindful Pages
Imprint of Alpha Editions LLC
312 W. 2nd St #1834
Casper, WY 82601, USA

Content

Introduction
The Invisible Money Problem

Freelancers are celebrated in rhetoric and overlooked in practice. The modern economy extols their virtues—flexibility, creativity, autonomy—but its infrastructure lags behind. The popular narrative frames freelancing as liberation from corporate confines, a life of self-direction and imagination. Behind that glittering veneer, however, lies a quieter, more complicated truth: income is erratic, responsibilities multiply, and systems designed for traditional employment often undermine the independence they purport to support.

This book opens with a simple, urgent premise: most financial advice assumes you are someone you are not.

If you freelance, contract, create independently, or earn outside the salary system, you know this intimately. The world presumes regular paychecks, automatic tax withholding, employer benefits, and a clear separation between work and personal life. It presumes you know next month's—or next week's—earnings, that your job comes with boundaries, that your retirement is organised by HR. You live beyond these assumptions.

The consequence is daily navigation through a maze built for others. Every aspect of finance—income, taxes, budgeting, insurance, retirement, debt—assumes predictability you rarely enjoy. Independence without structure, though alluring, is simply vulnerability disguised as freedom.

The Fallacy of Conventional Financial Advice

Much of mainstream personal finance is not wrong—it's irrelevant. Budget 50% of income for essentials? Which month? Set aside 15% for retirement? From which client payment? Automate savings every payday? Which paydays? Each rule silently relies on an assumption: regularity.

Freelance earnings are rarely predictable. Payments surge, pause, or disappear. Projects vanish. A successful quarter can be followed by drought. This is not mismanagement; it is structural. Yet financial systems treat such volatility as a moral failing rather than a design reality. They propose discipline over design, overlooking that uncertainty is a feature, not a flaw.

This book does not attempt to squeeze freelancers into a salaried mould. It does not offer generic templates or platitudes about working harder. Instead, it begins with the reality you inhabit—and works from there.

Money When the Rules Don't Fit

Freelancers live a life of contradictions. You are employer and employee, CEO and janitor, salesperson and service provider. You deliver the work, find the work, price the work—and then wrestle with the money when it arrives. There is no HR, no payroll, no IT desk. Every financial decision rests on your shoulders, often under ambiguity and pressure.

Your tools must be active, intelligent, adaptive. You do not need rigid rules; you need a resilient system that flexes with income flows, handles unpredictability, and enables planning as a self-financed enterprise—because that is what you are. This book proposes precisely such a system: a philosophy rooted in adaptability, clarity, and control. Financial stability emerges not from steady income alone, but from thoughtful design and disciplined practice. Security is not a fixed bank balance; it is a structure that bends without breaking.

The Psychological Toll of Uncertainty

Beyond numbers and regulations lies a subtler burden: uncertainty drains mental energy. Not knowing next month's earnings—or whether expenses can be met without touching your tax fund—makes simple decisions fraught. Each postponed invoice, unopened budgeting app, or ignored retirement plan compounds stress. Behavioural science confirms it: humans make poor decisions under uncertainty, and freelancers exist in it by default. Without containment, emotional exhaustion grows. Stress spikes. Impulsive choices replace strategy. Alone, it feels like personal failure rather than a systemic gap. This book exposes that gap—and begins to fill it.

The Role You Didn't Apply For

Choosing freelancing means assuming an unspoken role: Chief Financial Officer of You Incorporated. Cash flow, taxes, budgets, pricing, insurance, long-term planning—all fall to you. There is no safety net, no corporate cushion. This responsibility is structural, not optional. Acknowledging it does not simplify the work, but it clarifies the path forward.

The problem is not intelligence or willpower; it is that you were handed a complex role with no training. This book offers that guidance—not as a textbook, but as a field-tested framework built from lived experience.

The Framework Ahead

This work is more than advice; it is a system designed for how freelancers actually earn and live. We begin by dismantling myths: that freelancing is always freedom, that traditional structures suffice. We then explore real earnings, not just what lands in your account. We construct a budgeting model suited to irregular paydays. We design account structures separating taxes, expenses, and savings, removing guesswork and guilt.

You will learn to set aside money when it is available, not merely when convenient. You will understand why a three-month emergency fund is insufficient—and what to build instead. Insurance will be reframed as income protection, and we will show how to pay yourself a steady salary despite volatile earnings. We address pricing, client selection, and designing a sustainable income mix. By the end, the goal is not a number—it is a system. Real wealth is confidence, clarity, and choice; not richness, but resilience.

A Different Kind of Freedom

Freelancing promises freedom, yet unstructured freedom becomes chaos, and chaos erodes autonomy. The opportunity is not to replicate salaried life, but to build something stronger: a financial system that adapts, bends, and grows with you.

If you've felt overwhelmed, you are not alone. If you've felt behind, you are not broken. If the rules never fit, that is not a flaw in you—it is a flaw in the system. You do not need to work harder. You need to work differently.

Welcome to the financial playbook for those the old rules forgot.

Chapter 1
The Money Myth of Freelancing

The allure of freelancing is seductive, wrapped in the rhetoric of liberty: no boss, no timecard, no office dress code. You are, ostensibly, the master of your schedule, the curator of your projects, the sovereign of your creative output. In a culture that prizes autonomy, freelancing presents itself as the ultimate upgrade—a departure from nine-to-five monotony and the bureaucracy of corporate life. It promises control, flexibility, and purpose. Yet, beneath the glossy narrative lies a subtler, more intricate reality—one that often only becomes visible when experience collides with expectation.

Time may be yours, but financial certainty rarely is. Freed from office politics, you are simultaneously untethered from the institutional scaffolding that makes money intelligible and manageable. Working in pyjamas sounds idyllic until 11 p.m. finds you wrestling with quarterly tax calculations. No one advertises the unpaid administrative work, the ghosted invoices, or the months when revenue dwindles to a trickle. The myth of freelancing celebrates sovereignty; the lived experience, for many, is systemic neglect.

This disconnect warrants close examination. The assumption that freelancing automatically equates to financial empowerment is not only misleading but perilous. It suggests that talent or hustle alone guarantees success, glossing over the structural imbalances baked into every freelance engagement. Systems built to manage income, tax, benefits, and savings remain calibrated for the salaried model, leaving independent workers to navigate gaps with improvisation and anxiety.

The money myth persists through selective visibility. It highlights autonomy, mobility, and work-life balance, while erasing the cognitive and logistical burdens of unpredictability. This is not merely inconvenient—it actively erodes financial wellbeing. Freedom, without a supporting framework, is conditional at best.

Consider the contemporary landscape. Self-employment has surged across sectors: graphic designers, yoga instructors, journalists, software developers, online educators—the independent workforce is no longer peripheral; it is central. Yet institutions lag behind. Banks struggle to verify freelance income for mortgages. Governments expect stable quarterly taxes from volatile monthly earnings. Health insurance, retirement planning, and credit assessments all favour regularity. The fault lies not with freelancers but with systems misaligned to reality.

Available tools are often retrofitted from salaried assumptions. Budgeting apps assume fixed monthly pay, payroll software presumes automatic tax withholding, and financial advice extols "living below your means" without acknowledging that "means" may fluctuate dramatically. The result is confusion, stress, and chronic cognitive load.

The psychological weight of uncertainty is profound. Traditional employment carries predictable timing; freelancing does not. Even high earners can feel insecure because unpredictability drains mental resources. Behavioural science demonstrates that uncertainty impairs decision-making. Late client payments or project cancellations trigger constant vigilance: hoarding liquidity, delaying long-term investments, second-guessing spending. Everyday choices—buying equipment, enrolling in courses, or taking a holiday—become fraught calculations. Volatility fatigue sets in, affecting strategy and mental clarity alike.

Many freelancers internalise this as a personal shortcoming, oscillating between avoidance in lean months and micromanagement during high-earning periods. Emotional whiplash compounds, undermining confidence and clarity. The solution is not moral discipline but structural reorientation.

To transcend the money myth, freelancers must adopt a new mental model: seeing themselves as full-spectrum financial operators. This is rarely intuitive. Writers wish to write, designers to design, therapists to heal—not to wrestle with tax codes or cash flow models. Yet recognising the dual role of practitioner and strategist is essential to regaining agency over finances.

Freelancing is, in essence, running a business. And like any business, it requires a finance department. That department is you. You are the CFO.

This does not demand accounting degrees or MBAs. It requires thinking in systems: anticipating cycles, smoothing income spikes and droughts, calculating net earnings, separating business and personal expenditures, and constructing a reliable salary from irregular inflows. Risk becomes an operating condition, not an abstract concept.

Another persistent illusion is that clarity comes with higher earnings. Many freelancers assume that disorganisation stems from insufficient income and that success alone brings order. In reality, greater revenue without a framework intensifies chaos. Financial resilience is not about income magnitude—it is about managing what exists.

This chapter provides the foundational lens for the book. It is a reframe, not a how-to: a confrontation with inherited assumptions and a recalibration of your role in financial life. Subsequent chapters will explore practical strategies—calculating real hourly rates, structuring accounts, preparing for taxes, budgeting without fixed paydays, and building savings and retirement plans from irregular income. Yet none of these tools will be effective if the mindset remains trapped in myth. Tools serve a system. The system supports a mindset. That mindset begins with acknowledging that old rules were never designed for you.

This recognition is liberating. Clarity frees you from mimicking salaried behaviours that do not fit. It allows you to design your financial life around reality rather than fantasy. Freelancing is not a flawed form of employment—it is a distinct mode of work requiring a bespoke financial framework, one that integrates volatility rather than hiding from it.

You are not merely the labour—you are the infrastructure. And that makes all the difference.

The Fantasy vs. the Reality

To declare oneself a freelancer is, in the cultural imagination, to step into a kind of professional enlightenment. The phrase "be your own boss" is wielded like a badge of honour—emblematic of autonomy, creative liberty, and escape from bureaucratic constraint. It conjures visions of café laptops, midday gym sessions, and work pursued purely on one's own terms. The traditional office fades into obsolescence. The freelancer ascends, untethered, unburdened. And yet, this fantasy, while emotionally seductive, is financially myopic. It conceals as much as it reveals—chief among the omissions being the complex, often invisible architecture that salaried employment quietly provides. What is celebrated in theory becomes far more entangled in practice.

The myth of freelancing's freedom has endured because it is not entirely untrue. There *is* autonomy. You can often choose your clients, projects, even the style and schedule of your work. But freedom in one domain often comes at the cost of structure in another. The same liberty that allows a freelancer to reject a bad brief also demands that they chase invoices, track quarterly tax obligations, and weather dry spells with little external support. The fantasy assumes that independence brings clarity. In truth, it often introduces complexity, especially where money is concerned.

The most persistent blind spot in this fantasy is its silence on *cash flow volatility*. In salaried employment, income is rhythmic, reliable, and planned. Taxes are withheld at source, benefits are administered by someone else, and your net pay arrives on a fixed schedule. The very infrastructure of daily financial life is designed to accommodate predictability. When you freelance, you are effectively removed from that infrastructure and dropped into open terrain. You may earn £2,000 one month and £6,000 the next—followed by a month with nothing at all. Client payments are often late, sporadic, or subject to dispute. Meanwhile, your rent, utilities, and groceries do not share your clients' flexibility. The mismatch between irregular income and fixed expenses creates not only logistical strain, but a continuous undercurrent of financial tension that is rarely acknowledged in the freelance narrative.

This tension becomes acute during moments of financial whiplash—when a high-revenue quarter is followed by an unexpected drought, or when a project ends abruptly without renewal. Because there is no default structure to buffer these shocks, freelancers must build one themselves—or face a kind of economic vertigo. It is not simply a matter of earning more, but of designing systems that accommodate unpredictability. Yet this need is often masked by the myth that creative freedom automatically equates to financial fluency.

Another invisible tax on freelance life comes in the form of *administrative labour*. The very act of earning requires layers of additional work unrelated to one's core skill. The writer must become an accountant. The designer, a contract negotiator. The consultant, a compliance officer. Tasks that are handled by departments in traditional firms—legal, finance, HR—now fall entirely to the individual. These are not optional extras; they are fundamental to sustaining a freelance income. They consume time, attention, and emotional bandwidth. And because they rarely produce immediate income, they are easily neglected—until the neglect becomes costly.

Consider the reality of taxes. A salaried worker rarely needs to consider them beyond checking their annual P60 or T4. A freelancer must not only calculate and remit their own taxes but also anticipate their liabilities months in advance. In the UK, this often includes payments on account—advance tax payments based on the prior year's income, due before the current year's returns are even filed. The U.S., Canada, and Australia all have similarly complex mechanisms. These systems are logical only when viewed through the lens of stable income. For freelancers, they create a paradox: the more you earn in a good year, the more you owe before you even know how your current year will unfold.

These are not just bureaucratic inconveniences. They are structural mismatches that penalise volatility. When traditional financial systems encounter freelance earnings, they often default to suspicion or rejection. Mortgage lenders, for instance, typically demand several years of documented self-employment income, often applying stricter affordability thresholds than they would for salaried applicants. Credit card providers may reject freelance applicants due to irregular deposits, despite robust annual earnings. Insurance companies may lack products suited to the unique risks of self-employment. The freelance economy has grown in scale, yet remains largely unrecognised by the financial institutions that govern access to stability.

This mismatch extends beyond logistics and into the realm of psychology. Behavioural economists have long documented the corrosive effects of uncertainty on cognitive functioning. When the timing and quantity of income are unpredictable, financial planning becomes a series of educated guesses, often tinged with anxiety. Each financial decision—whether to invest in new equipment, take a holiday, or simply go out for dinner—becomes a risk assessment. The absence of regular paydays creates not only economic strain but emotional erosion.

Uncertainty demands attention. It monopolises mental bandwidth. The freelancer, unsure of whether next month will bring abundance or scarcity, often oscillates between feast and famine behaviours: overspending during windfalls, hoarding or panic cutting during dry periods. Even high-earning freelancers may live with a persistent background noise of financial insecurity—not because they lack money, but because they lack *predictability*. Without the calming rhythm of consistent cash flow, money becomes a source of cognitive noise rather than clarity.

This is compounded by social perception. Because freelancing is culturally framed as a choice, its challenges are often dismissed as consequences of personal mismanagement rather than systemic design. If a freelancer struggles, the assumption is that they are not marketing well enough, managing time efficiently, or charging appropriately. But rarely is the conversation expanded to include the institutional void that surrounds freelance work. There is a subtle but pernicious narrative that says: if you chose freedom, you must also choose fragility. This framing is not only unjust—it is intellectually lazy.

Freedom and structure are not opposites. In fact, they are co-dependent. The freelance life, to be sustainable, must be underpinned by a financial architecture as intentional and robust as any company's. What freelancers lack in built-in systems, they must replicate by design. This includes creating segmented accounts to separate taxes, operating expenses, and personal income; modelling cash flow scenarios across variable income tiers; automating savings and buffer contributions during high-earning periods; and adopting financial planning habits that embrace flexibility without sacrificing foresight.

Such practices do not emerge spontaneously. They require a mindset shift—from seeing oneself as merely a service provider to understanding oneself as the *financial steward of an independent enterprise*. This is the hidden truth of freelancing: every invoice you send is a business transaction, and every pound that enters your account brings with it a cluster of secondary responsibilities—tax, savings, reinvestment, personal pay. The structure behind the scenes is not optional; it is foundational.

The reality is that many freelancers do not fail due to lack of talent, demand, or dedication. They fail because they believed the fantasy. They assumed that creative freedom would naturally produce financial freedom. But freedom is not a by-product of creativity; it is a product of design. And design, in this context, means *building systems that work when the rules don't fit*.

The myth of freelancing is alluring precisely because it contains a partial truth. Autonomy is real. Flexibility is powerful. But without the accompanying structure to support them, these assets become burdens. The freelancer's true challenge is not to resist the myth entirely, but to reconstitute it—retaining its best elements while discarding the illusions that harm. This means seeing freedom not as the absence of systems, but as the *result of systems that match your reality*.

To build a financially viable freelance life, one must first tell the truth about what freelancing really is—not what it's marketed to be. It is not a utopia of passive income and café workdays. Nor is it an inevitable hustle of precarity and burnout. It is a professional mode that demands a distinct kind of intelligence: adaptive, self-directed, structurally aware.

This awareness is not a luxury. It is the first step towards a sustainable future. And it begins by discarding the fantasy—not out of cynicism, but out of respect for what freelancing can truly become when it is met with clarity, intention, and the courage to see its complexity as an invitation to build something better.

Why Financial Systems Fail Freelancers

Modern financial systems, in their most fundamental design, are calibrated for regularity. They presume not only consistent income but also institutional mediation—employers, payroll departments, benefit providers, and tax authorities working in synchrony to administer a predictable economic life. This model has proved remarkably effective for a workforce structured around stable employment. But the moment one steps outside the walled garden of salaried work, the cracks become unmistakable. Freelancers, whose earnings are characterised by variability, delays, and self-sufficiency, find themselves not only underserved by these systems, but frequently penalised by their very architecture.

The issue is not merely one of exclusion. It is one of misalignment. Most financial products and services are not overtly hostile to freelancers; they are simply constructed with entirely different use cases in mind. Consider the routine process of applying for a mortgage. A salaried worker presents a P60 or equivalent annual earnings summary, recent payslips, and an employer reference. The underwriter verifies the income and issues an offer. A freelancer, by contrast, is asked to furnish two or more years of tax returns, accountant-certified profit-and-loss statements, and a comprehensive list of retained clients—evidence not only of past income but of its perceived durability. The scrutiny is not incidental. It reflects an institutional suspicion of volatility itself.

This suspicion permeates more than just lending. It defines how banks structure their onboarding processes, how payroll apps define "income," and how insurance providers calculate risk. The idea of fluctuating earnings confounds systems designed to monitor consistency. Direct debit payments, credit scoring models, automatic bill-splitting services—they all assume not only the presence of money, but its reliable arrival. Freelancers who miss a utility payment due to an unpaid invoice are treated no differently from salaried workers who have mismanaged funds. The system does not ask *why* money is missing. It simply flags the irregularity.

This structural rigidity creates subtle but compounding penalties. A late payment fee here, a missed interest-free window there, a temporarily overdrawn account—all events triggered not by financial recklessness, but by the systemic refusal to accommodate lumpy cash flow. It is not that freelancers are inherently riskier borrowers, or less disciplined savers. It is that the systems tracking their financial behaviour are calibrated to reward regularity and punish deviation. In effect, freelancers are measured against a yardstick built for someone else.

The same dynamics emerge in tax collection. Tax codes in most countries still reflect assumptions forged in the industrial age: that income is earned in stable, monthly increments, subject to employer withholding. In this framework, compliance is frictionless for employees—deductions are made at source, and the worker receives net pay with taxes already handled. Freelancers, by contrast, are expected to function as their own tax authority. They must estimate their liabilities, set aside appropriate amounts, and remit payments on a quarterly or annual basis—often with little guidance or support.

In the UK, for example, the system of Payments on Account requires freelancers to make advance payments towards the *next* tax year based on earnings from the *last*. For someone whose income fluctuates significantly year to year—a freelance writer landing a lucrative contract one year and modest gigs the next—this can result in tax bills wildly out of sync with current earnings. The logic is internally consistent, but externally divorced from the freelancer's lived reality. The system assumes consistency even when the taxpayer cannot guarantee it.

The effect is not only logistical complexity but psychological burden. For many freelancers, the administrative work required to simply remain compliant—tracking expenses, forecasting income, calculating tax buffers—is itself a part-time job. And yet this labour is invisible to the systems around them. Financial platforms still offer default budgeting tools tied to monthly paycheques. Accounting software designed for SMEs often includes payroll modules irrelevant to sole traders but lacks features suited to ad-hoc project invoicing. Tax calculators presume a regular income stream when building estimated payment schedules. The mismatch is consistent and profound.

One might ask: why haven't systems evolved? After all, freelancing is no longer fringe. In the UK, nearly five million people are self-employed, representing around 15% of the workforce. The US sees similar numbers. Platforms like Fiverr, Upwork, and Patreon have created entire ecosystems around independent work. Yet institutional inertia remains. Financial systems, especially those built at national or regulatory scale, change slowly. Their underlying data models, risk matrices, and process workflows are difficult to retrofit. More crucially, the freelancer's problem is *variability*, and variability is expensive to underwrite.

This explains why lenders and insurers continue to apply higher thresholds to freelancers—not out of personal bias, but because their algorithms penalise unpredictability. A salaried worker earning £30,000 per year appears more "secure" than a freelancer whose income fluctuates between £2,000 and £6,000 per month, even if the latter ends the year with a higher gross. Predictability, not prosperity, is the coin of the realm.

This has real-world consequences. A freelance videographer who secures a high-value project in January might face three months without income thereafter. During that lull, cash on hand becomes critical. But without a system that accommodates irregular revenue patterns, even well-compensated freelancers may face liquidity crises. Overdrafts, credit card reliance, short-term loans—all expensive tools used not because of overspending, but because the system failed to acknowledge income cyclicality.

Benefits systems, too, remain tied to an outdated conception of employment. Access to paid sick leave, employer pension contributions, and income protection insurance is still disproportionately routed through formal employment channels. While some countries have begun to offer parity—Australia's superannuation system and parts of Scandinavia offer models—the global norm remains exclusion. Freelancers must build their own safety nets, often with tools that are costlier, less efficient, and harder to access than those available to their salaried peers.

Moreover, this failure of systems is compounded by a failure of language. Much of the terminology used by financial institutions presumes a fixed income base. "Disposable income," "take-home pay," "salary sacrifice"—these are concepts that make sense when income is steady and expenses are planned. For freelancers, they are often abstractions. A payment for a three-month project may arrive in a lump sum, to be allocated across tax, savings, expenses, and personal income. To describe it as "take-home pay" is not just misleading—it is operationally useless. The freelancer must not only earn the income but then deconstruct it into parts that match institutional categories built for someone else.

This is where a new mental model becomes indispensable. Freelancers cannot afford to approach financial systems with passive compliance. They must *actively reinterpret and redesign* the structures around them. This involves creating proxy systems where none exist: segmenting income into distinct accounts to mimic payroll deductions; building rolling cash flow forecasts to replace monthly budgets; maintaining tax buffers as if they were mandatory withholdings. These are not luxuries—they are compensatory strategies designed to bridge the gap between how freelancers earn and how institutions assess.

Crucially, this new model must centre *resilience*, not rigidity. Traditional systems reward constancy; the freelancer must reward adaptability. This means tracking income trends over quarters, not weeks; understanding the lag between work performed and payment received; using average revenue, not peak months, to build spending baselines. It means understanding that the systems around you will not change fast enough—so you must build a micro-infrastructure that respects the volatility of your world without surrendering to it.

To do so requires not only technical skill but philosophical clarity. The freelancer is not merely a worker without a boss; they are an independent economic unit operating without institutional guardrails. The systems failing them are not malicious—they are just incomplete. The responsibility now falls to the freelancer to recognise this incompleteness and respond not with frustration, but with structural creativity.

That creativity will be tested repeatedly—by late payments, by tax demands that arrive mid-drought, by benefits systems that exclude or ignore. But with the right frameworks, it becomes possible not just to survive but to transcend the limitations of these systems. The goal is not to force volatility into stability, but to build a scaffolding strong enough to hold uncertainty without collapse.

Understanding *why* financial systems fail freelancers is not a theoretical exercise. It is the precondition for building a financial life that works on your terms. It begins by letting go of the idea that systems will adapt quickly to your needs—and ends with the conviction that you can design something better, smarter, and far more honest about how real work—and real income—actually functions today.

The Psychological Cost of Uncertainty

Few variables destabilise the human mind more quietly yet profoundly than unpredictability. In evolutionary terms, uncertainty once signalled danger—a rustle in the bushes that might be wind or predator. The brain evolved to resolve ambiguity quickly, erring on the side of caution to protect survival. In today's economy, that ancient wiring has not gone away. It has simply moved house. For freelancers and self-employed professionals, income unpredictability serves as the modern equivalent of rustling leaves. The ambiguity is persistent, socially sanctioned, and psychologically corrosive in ways still underappreciated by both policy-makers and financial educators.

The problem is not merely a logistical one. Irregular earnings complicate taxes, budgeting, and savings, yes—but the deeper damage is often cognitive and emotional. Behavioural science has consistently shown that human beings are profoundly sensitive to uncertain environments, and financial uncertainty is particularly potent. A study published in *Nature Communications* in 2016 revealed that the stress of *not knowing* whether something bad will happen activates more sustained anxiety than knowing it will. Freelancers live in that psychological limbo, not only wondering when the next invoice will be paid, but whether another one will ever be issued.

This state of ambiguity creates a kind of background noise in the psyche—constant, low-grade tension that undermines planning, focus, and decision-making. Even when cash is available, the *perceived insecurity* of future income generates what behavioural economists call "scarcity mindset." Scarcity, in this context, does not necessarily mean lack of funds, but rather the belief that there might not be *enough* soon. This belief narrows cognitive bandwidth. In their book *Scarcity: Why Having Too Little Means So Much*, Sendhil Mullainathan and Eldar Shafir illustrate how people under economic stress perform worse on tasks requiring sustained attention and long-term planning. The mere act of worrying about money—whether or not the situation is objectively dire—erodes mental capacity.

This erosion shows up subtly but pervasively. Freelancers may avoid reviewing their bank statements, delay invoicing, or fail to set aside money for taxes—not because they are irresponsible, but because each of these tasks represents an encounter with uncertainty. The mind, seeking to protect itself from discomfort, chooses deferral over exposure. What appears as disorganisation is often a form of *emotional triage*.

Avoidance behaviour, of course, compounds volatility. A late invoice results in a late payment, which results in a cash flow problem, which then prompts hasty financial decisions. This cycle is not unusual. It is structurally induced. Traditional employment systems are built to shield individuals from this loop—income arrives automatically, taxes are pre-withheld, and the burden of administrative foresight is externalised to the employer. The freelancer, by contrast, must face all of it head-on and alone.

This exposure creates *volatility fatigue*. The term is not clinical, but it captures an observable phenomenon: the cognitive and emotional exhaustion that accrues from managing unpredictable income over extended periods. Like chronic low-level inflammation in the body, volatility fatigue dulls responsiveness and motivation. It encourages short-termism—not because freelancers lack discipline, but because the brain, under stress, prioritises immediacy. Neurological studies have shown that people facing financial stress demonstrate increased activity in the amygdala, the brain's fear centre, and reduced activation in the prefrontal cortex, which governs planning and rational thought. The implication is sobering: *unrelieved uncertainty not only limits choices, it reshapes how we choose.*

One consequence of this neural recalibration is impulsivity. Behavioural drift becomes more common—whether through overspending during brief flush periods or under-investing in tools and education that would improve long-term prospects. These aren't moral failings; they are misfired survival mechanisms. The freelancer is not indulging in self-sabotage—they are responding, often subconsciously, to a world that refuses to stabilise.

There is also a social dimension to this. Freelancers rarely speak openly about the psychological toll of financial unpredictability. The cultural script celebrates their autonomy, so admitting to emotional strain can feel like confessing to failure. In traditional employment, there is shared language for stress—"burnout," "workload," "bad boss." In freelancing, the stress is often internalised: "I didn't plan well enough." "I should have saved more." "Maybe I'm just not cut out for this." The result is isolation layered atop anxiety, a mental state that few financial planners are trained to recognise, let alone address.

Yet recognising this cost is essential. Not for the sake of sympathy, but because clarity is the first precondition of change. If freelancers are to manage volatility well, they must first understand how it affects their cognition and behaviour. This awareness is not merely intellectual—it must become operational. That is, it must inform the way systems and habits are built.

The Counterweight: Designing for Stability Amid Instability

What freelancers require is not the illusion of control over income—because control is not always possible—but *structures that make unpredictability less punishing*. One of the most effective antidotes to volatility fatigue is habit design. In a world where the external environment cannot be fully regulated, internal systems become the anchor. The principle is straightforward: reduce decision-making load where possible so that cognitive energy can be preserved for essential judgements.

This starts with *automation*. When transfers to tax, savings, and personal pay accounts are automated immediately after a payment is received, the mental negotiation around "what to do with this money" is removed. The automation becomes a proxy for stability. It simulates the reliability of payroll by creating pre-committed flows, even when income itself is variable.

Another potent habit is *temporal reframing*. Many freelancers think in monthly terms because it mimics employment patterns. But monthly budgeting assumes consistent income, which freelance life rarely provides. A more effective approach is quarterly planning. This longer time frame accommodates fluctuations, reduces panic during low-income weeks, and allows for better pacing of expenses. The shift is not just logistical; it is psychological. It creates breathing room.

Equally important is *information hygiene*. When finances feel chaotic, the instinct is often to look away. But opacity breeds anxiety. Instead, freelancers benefit from regular, non-judgemental financial check-ins—short, scheduled sessions to review income, expenses, and upcoming obligations. These sessions are not about perfection; they are about visibility. The very act of looking reduces ambiguity, which reduces anxiety.

Of course, not every freelancer will respond identically. Financial personality, life stage, and the nature of one's work all shape the experience of uncertainty. But the universality of volatility across freelance sectors makes the broader principles clear: *the absence of predictability must be met with the presence of intentional systems*. Those systems should not aspire to eliminate uncertainty—that is impossible—but to insulate the individual from its most damaging psychological effects.

There is a parallel here to physical training. Athletes do not attempt to remove external pressure; they build bodies capable of withstanding it. Freelancers must do the same with their financial psychology. Building resilience means treating systems as scaffolding, not constraints. It means accepting that the work of managing money is not separate from creative or professional work—it is part of the infrastructure that sustains it.

Perhaps the most transformative realisation is this: *uncertainty is not a personal deficit—it is a design challenge*. When addressed head-on, with clarity and creativity, it can catalyse not just better financial outcomes, but a deeper sense of agency. The freelancer who builds habits that buffer volatility is not just managing money—they are reclaiming mental space, emotional bandwidth, and long-term decision-making capacity.

That reclamation is not trivial. In a world that asks freelancers to create value without providing structure, building one's own becomes not only a necessity but a profound act of self-leadership. It begins by confronting, without flinching, the true psychological cost of uncertainty—and then choosing to build anyway.

You're the CFO Now

In salaried employment, there is an entire ecosystem designed to shield workers from the full weight of financial decision-making. Your payslip arrives with taxes already withheld. Pension contributions are automatic, insurance coverage is often bundled in, and payroll departments ensure regulatory compliance with little to no input from you. The economic engine hums in the background while you focus on your job. But when you move into freelancing, that engine stops—unless you build it yourself. And in building it, you must assume a role you were likely never trained for: Chief Financial Officer of your own enterprise.

This is not a metaphor. It is a functional truth. Whether you call yourself a writer, designer, consultant, developer, coach, or independent researcher, your professional output is only one part of your work. The other part—the less visible but equally critical part—is managing the financial machinery that keeps your business solvent, resilient, and strategically sound. As a freelancer, you are simultaneously the product and the infrastructure, the workforce and the executive team. No one is coming to audit your books, run your cash flow projections, or prepare you for a tax bill. That is your job now.

And that job, candidly, is demanding. It involves roles that in a traditional firm would be divided across multiple departments. You are your own payroll officer, setting up systems to pay yourself consistently from inconsistent income. You are your own finance manager, tracking earnings, reconciling bank accounts, and analysing profit margins. You are your own tax advisor, calculating liabilities, tracking deductible expenses, and filing returns across relevant jurisdictions. You are your own risk analyst, identifying vulnerabilities—from health interruptions to client concentration risks—and building contingency plans. If you fail to embrace this reality, you are not delegating these roles—you are ignoring them. And ignored systems don't fail politely. They break catastrophically.

What makes this shift particularly challenging is that most freelancers enter their field out of a passion for the work itself, not for spreadsheets. The writer wants to write, not construct revenue maps. The developer wants to code, not forecast earnings. The therapist wants to help people, not estimate quarterly payments. But the skill that produces income is not the same as the skill that manages it. And over time, the latter becomes just as decisive in shaping the freelancer's quality of life. You can be talented and broke. You can be booked and stressed. Financial management is not ancillary—it is core.

One of the first mindset shifts required is seeing your income not as *personal money*, but as *business revenue*. When a client pays you, they are paying your business, even if that business is a sole proprietorship with no registered name. From that revenue, you must allocate money for taxes, business expenses, and savings before you even consider it available for personal use. This shift is crucial because it counters the common but hazardous instinct to treat every incoming payment as discretionary income. Without clear separation between business and personal funds, tax bills become emergencies, savings become aspirational, and expenses go unexamined.

Consider how traditional CFOs operate. Their job is not just to track money, but to interpret its patterns, manage its risks, and plan for its future deployment. They create dashboards, establish financial rhythms, prepare for audits, and stress-test assumptions. Their decisions are guided by visibility and foresight, not guesswork. The freelancer CFO must do the same—albeit at a smaller scale. This means building simple but robust systems: income accounts that segregate funds before they're spent, expense logs that clarify where money goes and why, and routine reviews that surface patterns before they become problems.

One of the most neglected aspects of this role is risk management. For salaried workers, risk is largely external—job loss, economic downturn, corporate restructuring. For freelancers, risk is internal as well. A single client represents 40% of your income. You get sick and can't bill hours for two weeks. A delayed invoice threatens your rent payment. These are not unusual events; they are routine structural risks. The CFO lens requires you to identify, quantify, and mitigate them.

This might involve building a buffer account large enough to cover three lean months without panic. It might mean securing insurance that covers loss of income during illness, or diversifying your client base so that no single relationship can collapse your revenue. It could also mean staging your work calendar in a way that reduces feast-and-famine cycles, replacing erratic project work with a blend of retainer contracts or recurring micro-services. The goal is not to eliminate risk—that's impossible—but to prevent it from becoming existential.

Another pillar of financial stewardship is data literacy. You don't need to be an accountant to understand cash flow—but you do need to stop ignoring the numbers. Many freelancers live with financial ambiguity because they fear what clarity might reveal. They suspect, rightly, that income is lower than expected or that spending is leakier than admitted. But opacity is not protection—it is paralysis. A functioning CFO seeks clarity not to shame the enterprise but to empower it. Even uncomfortable truths are easier to work with than illusions.

Practically, this means tracking not just revenue, but *net income after expenses*. It means logging admin hours and unpaid time to calculate your true hourly rate—not just what clients pay you, but what you keep. It means mapping income volatility across months and years, spotting patterns that allow for proactive planning. The freelancer who knows their peak revenue periods can save in high seasons to sustain the lows. The one who understands their operating cost baseline can avoid pricing work below sustainability. These are not abstract exercises. They are decisions with direct consequences.

There is also a broader ethical imperative in this role: *financial maturity sustains creative freedom.* Freelancers often choose their path to avoid bureaucratic entanglements, but without strong financial scaffolding, they find themselves shackled in subtler ways—accepting poor-fit projects to meet short-term needs, postponing breaks due to erratic income, or neglecting strategic growth because survival tasks always feel more urgent. A well-functioning internal CFO enables not just solvency, but discernment. With money managed, you can say no more often, invest when it matters, and think beyond this month's invoice. Autonomy, in this sense, is a by-product of discipline—not its replacement.

Critically, embracing the CFO mindset does not require perfection. It requires *intentionality*. Financial systems do not need to be complex to be effective—they need to be consistent. You can start with one day per week dedicated to financial tasks. You can build a personal dashboard using tools as simple as a spreadsheet or as robust as accounting software. You can schedule quarterly reviews where you assess savings, tax buffers, client concentration, and income distribution. What matters is not sophistication, but reliability. A mediocre system used consistently will outperform a perfect one you never touch.

There is also room here for delegation. Being the CFO does not mean doing *everything* yourself. It means knowing what needs to be done, understanding its implications, and choosing how to manage it—whether through automation, software, or outsourcing. Hiring a bookkeeper, working with an accountant, or using specialised tax tools can all be smart financial decisions *if* they are made with clarity. Delegation is a skill of leadership, not a sign of inadequacy.

Ultimately, this shift is about owning the full arc of your freelance life. Not just the work that brings in money, but the systems that protect, allocate, and optimise it. It means no longer treating finance as an afterthought or an occasional crisis. It means sitting at the metaphorical head of the table—not just doing the work, but directing its future.

The freelancer who understands they are the CFO now gains more than a title. They gain leverage. They stop reacting to money and start managing it. They make fewer decisions out of panic, and more out of design. And in a world that offers little stability by default, they create their own—with eyes open, systems in place, and authority fully assumed.

Chapter 2
Knowing What You're Really Earning

One of the most persistent misconceptions in freelance finance is the simple—but misleading—equation of income with earnings. A client pays £2,000 for a project, and it is tempting to record the full sum in your mental ledger, even before it clears. On the surface, it feels like a triumph. In practice, however, it is a dangerous illusion. That £2,000 is revenue, not pay. What you actually retain, after expenses, tax obligations, administrative overhead, and unpaid effort, often looks very different from the figure on the invoice.

This distinction is not theoretical; it is operational. The gravest threat to financial stability for freelancers is not insufficient income, but a skewed perception of it. Misjudging your true earnings leads to overspending, underpricing services, neglecting savings, and being continually surprised when the money runs dry. This is rarely a matter of discipline—it is a matter of clarity. You cannot manage what you have not measured, and measurement begins with dismantling the fallacy that gross income equates to personal wealth.

The problem is not naivety. It is structural. Systems around freelancers reinforce these misperceptions. Payment platforms highlight gross receipts, accounting software reports revenue before expenses, and even bank statements give a misleading sense of liquidity, overlooking taxes and outstanding costs. The very architecture of freelance finance encourages an inflated sense of security. Without conscious countermeasures, this becomes a persistent vulnerability.

The first step, therefore, is conceptual separation. Revenue is what comes in; net income is what remains after costs. Even net income can mislead if you fail to account for invisible labour—client acquisition, administration, revisions, unpaid research, professional development. The more meticulously these components are tracked, the more accurately you can assess the value of your time, price your services, and plan your finances. The objective is not obsession, but literacy.

Take, for instance, a freelance translator who earns £1,200 for a three-day project. At first glance, this appears a lucrative daily rate. But consider the hours spent negotiating the brief, reviewing client guidelines, formatting deliverables, managing revisions, and sourcing the client in the first place. Factor in transaction fees, software subscriptions, and a proportion of rent or co-working costs. What remains is not the headline number—it is the reality of what was truly earned, almost always lower than initial celebrations suggest.

Understanding your real hourly rate is foundational. It recalibrates your perspective on time, pricing, and capacity. It clarifies which projects are profitable, which clients are worth retaining, and which engagements should be declined—not from pride, but necessity. Freelancers are often exhausted not due to overwork, but inefficient work: calendars filled with low-value tasks that erode both financial and emotional bandwidth. Precision here is protection, not pedantry.

Achieving this precision begins with tracking total professional hours, not just billable ones. This includes proposals, invoicing, client communication, and business development. Dividing net income by this broader total often yields an initially disappointing figure—but that discomfort is useful. It punctures illusion and replaces it with actionable data. Once armed with this insight, you can raise rates, refine offerings, streamline administration, or enforce boundaries, transitioning from reactive earnings to deliberate income engineering.

Yet income is not only about time; the cost of being paid is equally critical. Transaction fees from Stripe, PayPal, or bank transfers accumulate. Platform commissions, from Upwork to Fiverr, can consume 20% or more of revenue before taxes and expenses. Some freelancers adjust pricing to accommodate this; others absorb it unconsciously, gradually eroding margins.

More insidious still are delayed payments. Thirty- or sixty-day cycles are common, and some clients default entirely, requiring follow-ups. Freelancers become de facto debt collectors, absorbing psychological labour rarely accounted for in profit calculations. Non-billable time—free consultations, speculative proposals, marketing—further diminishes capacity if left untracked. The result is calendars full of activity but thin bottom lines, where hidden labour outpaces pricing.

To manage this, freelancers must treat income like a season, not a stream. Earnings fluctuate by quarters, not months. Coaches, designers, or consultants experience predictable peaks and troughs, from which patterns emerge. Recognising these rhythms allows for smarter planning: buffer-building, holiday scheduling, and anticipating seasonal shortfalls. A dashboard or spreadsheet that maps income over time—when and how it arrives—offers a far more honest picture than fragmented records. It reveals dependency on clients, seasonal risk, and growth opportunities, enabling proactive financial management.

Ultimately, freelancers are not merely selling time—they are constructing a business model. That model must distinguish revenue from profit, busywork from high-value activity, and short-term wins from long-term sustainability. Above all, it demands clarity. Without it, freelancers operate in a fog, chasing numbers that impress but fail to deliver security or freedom.

This chapter clears that fog. It replaces instinct with insight, hustle with strategy. By understanding your true earnings, you create the conditions for intelligent growth, meaningful work, and financial resilience—not through ambition alone, but through measurement, reflection, and deliberate redesign. Once you see your numbers clearly, guessing becomes unnecessary. And frankly, you wouldn't want to return to it.

Why Gross Income Lies

The most dangerous number in a freelancer's financial life is the one that feels most exciting: gross income. It is the figure that flashes first in client contracts, payment notifications, and accounting dashboards. It offers the illusion of success, often delivered in clean, round digits—£3,000 for a project, £5,500 in monthly revenue, £68,000 for the year. These numbers are psychologically powerful. They reward effort, confirm viability, and provide a tangible sense of progress. But they are also profoundly misleading. Gross income is not what you earned. It is what your business received. And mistaking the two is one of the most persistent, costly errors in self-employment.

This confusion is understandable. In salaried work, the distinction between gross and net pay is handled for you. Your payslip delineates deductions—taxes, pension contributions, National Insurance—before your income reaches your account. You are given a final, usable number without needing to interpret it. Freelancers, by contrast, receive raw revenue. Nothing is pre-allocated. The £2,000 a client wires to your account feels like income, but it is not yet yours—not fully, not functionally. From it must come business expenses, tax withholdings, software subscriptions, transaction fees, and the cost of simply *keeping the operation going*. Treating gross income as available funds is not just financially inaccurate—it is behaviourally dangerous.

When freelancers base their lifestyle decisions on gross revenue, they build unsustainable systems. They overspend during high-earning months, under-save for tax and retirement, and develop pricing strategies disconnected from reality. The result is a pattern familiar to many in the self-employed world: feast and famine cycles, where periods of intense work and apparent prosperity are followed by cash flow stress, debt reliance, or sudden belt-tightening. But the instability often doesn't come from income variability alone—it comes from misreading the income entirely.

To correct this, one must start by reframing gross income as a *raw input*, not a financial outcome. It is the top line of the business, not the bottom line of your life. Between the two lies a chain of deductions and allocations that reflect the true structure of freelance work. This structure is not uniform. A freelance videographer may spend 30% of each project's fee on equipment rental, transport, and editing software. A freelance copywriter might spend only 5% on direct costs but invest heavily in ongoing training, client acquisition, or coworking space. What matters is not the absolute numbers, but the act of distinguishing them. *Revenue is not income until it passes through the logic of your business model.*

This is where the concept of *net income* becomes central. Net income, properly understood, is what remains after all business expenses have been accounted for—but before personal withdrawals. It is what your business generates in profit, not what you take home. Even then, it is not yet personal income. From net income must come personal taxes, long-term savings, and perhaps retained earnings to reinvest in the business. Without recognising this, freelancers risk drawing too much from their accounts, mistaking transient liquidity for sustainable earnings.

The distinction becomes even more significant when you consider fixed versus variable costs. Some expenses—like accounting software, professional insurance, or a domain name—must be paid regardless of workload. Others—like subcontractor fees, project-specific tools, or travel—scale with activity. A healthy freelance business knows both its baseline cost to exist and its marginal cost to produce. Only by understanding this split can you determine whether a given project is *profitable*, not just high-paying. A £1,500 gig that requires £300 in direct costs, 20 unpaid hours of prep, and a week of follow-up work may be less viable than a £750 retainer that arrives each month with minimal oversight. Gross income alone tells you nothing about this comparison.

Even within similar fields, margins can vary wildly depending on work structure. Consider two freelance graphic designers. One works through a platform that takes a 20% cut, pays for client leads, and absorbs PayPal fees. The other works by direct referral, accepts bank transfers, and has minimal third-party costs. If both invoice £50,000 annually, their financial realities are not remotely equivalent. One may net £35,000 before tax. The other, closer to £45,000. Yet both might present themselves as earning "fifty grand," a figure that shapes spending, planning, and self-assessment. Without a deeper accounting, that headline number becomes an optical illusion—confident on the surface, unstable underneath.

And then there's the question of *time*. Gross income says nothing about effort. Two freelancers may both earn £4,000 in a month. One works 50 hours a week to do so. The other works 15. One spends 30% of that time on unpaid admin, while the other has streamlined systems. One relies on intensive, one-off projects; the other enjoys recurring retainers. These differences compound. When you fail to account for *the labour behind the number*, you miss the true measure of your business: its efficiency.

This is why understanding operating costs isn't just about expense tracking. It's about strategic clarity. What does it cost you to deliver your services at the quality level your clients expect? How much are you spending to acquire new clients versus retain existing ones? Which tools, memberships, or subscriptions genuinely produce value, and which are legacy expenses carried forward out of habit or fear? These questions are operational, not philosophical. And they sit at the heart of knowing what you truly earn.

The issue is not that freelancers are failing to make enough money. It's that too many are failing to *see* what they're actually making. They confuse cash flow with income. They judge their financial health by gross receipts instead of retained earnings. They compare top-line numbers with salaried peers without factoring in the cost of self-employment. And the cultural environment doesn't help. Social media showcases revenue milestones without context. Business influencers flaunt six-figure incomes without disclosing ad spend, platform fees, or unpaid labour. In this landscape, misperception becomes normalised. Accuracy, by contrast, becomes a rare and radical act.

To resist this drift, freelancers must cultivate habits of financial visibility. Not perfection—visibility. This can start as simply as maintaining a single spreadsheet that logs revenue, expenses, and profit by month. Or using accounting software not merely to track receipts for tax season, but to review profitability trends. It means segmenting accounts so that taxes, operating capital, and personal income are clearly delineated. It means treating your freelance business *as a business*, not a side hustle with an improvised back-end.

Gross income will always have a role. It is a useful signal for market traction, capacity utilisation, and growth momentum. But it is not a measure of financial wellness. That requires depth. It requires understanding what you keep, what you spend to keep it, and how those dynamics evolve over time. Freelancers who ignore this distinction may find themselves working more and achieving less—running harder on a treadmill that never quite becomes a path. Those who embrace it, by contrast, unlock a more stable, transparent, and intentional financial life—one rooted not in projections, but in numbers that tell the truth.

The True Hourly Rate

Freelancers rarely sell time directly, yet time remains their most critical resource. It is the finite inventory from which all revenue must emerge, yet it is the least rigorously measured. When asked what they charge per hour, many freelancers respond confidently with a figure—£60, £100, £250—believing this rate reflects their value, expertise, or market positioning. But this rate often bears little resemblance to what they *actually* earn per hour. Why? Because the calculation almost never accounts for everything that eats into that time—non-billable work, client admin, unpaid labour, marketing, proposal writing, revisions, and internal operations. Nor does it account for the cost structure that underpins each hour worked. The result is a disconnect between what's charged and what's earned—a gap that leads to overwork, underpricing, and persistent fatigue disguised as hustle.

The concept of the *true hourly rate* is not about tracking time obsessively; it is about achieving clarity. It requires an honest reckoning with two variables: how much you truly take home, and how much time you truly invest. It asks not just what your clients pay you, but what remains once costs are deducted and time is fully accounted for. And it is in this reckoning that many freelancers discover an uncomfortable truth—they are earning far less than they assumed, often while working far more than they intended.

To calculate a meaningful hourly rate, you must first determine your *net income*. Not gross revenue, not what lands in your account after a single project, but what remains across a defined period—typically a month, quarter, or year—after subtracting business expenses. These expenses might include software, hardware, insurance, marketing, professional services, transaction fees, subscriptions, travel, and professional development. If you've billed £60,000 over the year but spent £15,000 operating your business, your net income is £45,000. This is your *real earnings pool*, from which tax must still be paid and personal needs met.

Next comes the more confronting exercise: counting your *total working hours*. Not just client-facing hours or billed project time, but the full scope of professional labour that supports your freelance practice. This includes onboarding new clients, issuing invoices, chasing payments, responding to emails, writing proposals, managing social media, handling your own bookkeeping, attending networking events, and learning new tools or systems. For many freelancers, these tasks represent between 30% and 50% of total work time. A graphic designer who bills 20 hours per week might actually work 35. A consultant charging £800 per day may spend a full day each week maintaining the engine that keeps those days billable.

When you divide your net income by your *total* working hours, you arrive at your *effective hourly rate*. This is the number that matters. It reflects the value of your time in reality, not in theory. And for many seasoned freelancers, it is an awakening. That £75 hourly rate you proudly quote to clients may, after costs and unpaid time, amount to £30 or £40 per hour. This does not mean you are failing. It means you are operating without full visibility. And visibility is what enables better decisions—about pricing, about project selection, about where to focus energy and where to set limits.

The true hourly rate also acts as a diagnostic tool. If your effective rate is lower than expected, there are only two variables to adjust: increase revenue or decrease time input. Sometimes the problem is underpricing—particularly common among those transitioning from salaried roles where hourly compensation was once abstracted behind a monthly wage. In other cases, the pricing may be sound, but time is leaking through inefficiencies: clients who demand too much communication, projects that expand without proper scope control, administrative systems that require too much manual labour. In either case, the solution begins with *awareness*.

The implications go beyond pricing strategy. The true hourly rate shapes how you make trade-offs between work and life. When you understand that your effective rate is £45 per hour, the decision to take a Friday afternoon off is not a vague indulgence—it is a deliberate cost-benefit choice. If that time could be monetised at £45, but you value the rest, you are making a conscious exchange. Without this information, work boundaries become porous, and guilt creeps in at the edges of leisure. Clarity replaces guilt with intent.

There is also a psychological cost to misjudging your time's value. Many freelancers report feeling chronically behind despite being constantly busy. Part of this stems from working long hours while believing they're earning more than they are. The discrepancy creates a feeling of failure—*I'm working so hard, why does it still feel like I'm not getting ahead?*—which corrodes motivation and encourages short-term decisions. But when the numbers are examined honestly, the paradox disappears. You're not failing. You're miscalculating.

Understanding your true hourly rate also reshapes how you evaluate opportunities. It helps you discern between high-revenue projects that drain time and low-maintenance engagements that offer higher margins. For instance, a £4,000 project that spans four weeks, includes six client meetings, two rounds of revisions, and constant communication might yield a lower effective hourly rate than a £1,800 package delivered in two focused days. A retainer client who pays £500 monthly but requires no meetings and consistent deliverables may outperform a more prestigious contract that demands constant customisation and unpredictable input. The headline number misleads; the hourly rate tells the story.

This clarity is particularly vital when planning for scale. If you intend to earn £80,000 annually and want to work no more than 30 hours per week, your effective hourly rate must be at least £51. If your current rate is £35, you either need to raise prices, reduce non-billable hours, or improve operational efficiency. There is no mystery—only arithmetic and implementation. But without confronting the true hourly rate, freelancers often remain stuck in cycles of high effort, low yield, and vague financial goals.

Some resist this level of calculation, worried that it reduces creative work to cold metrics. But the opposite is true. *When you understand the economics of your work, you can protect the space to do it well.* You can decline ill-fitting projects, pace your calendar, and carve out time for rest or innovation—because your decisions are grounded in a sustainable financial framework. The true hourly rate is not a tool of constraint. It is a mechanism of freedom.

It is worth noting that the true hourly rate will never be perfectly stable. It will fluctuate with seasonality, workload, and the structure of your pipeline. A high month may inflate your perceived rate, while a slow month deflates it. That's natural. The goal is not mathematical perfection, but meaningful orientation. You are not trying to fix your rate in stone, but to understand the forces shaping it—and use that understanding to build a practice that supports both your finances and your wellbeing.

To that end, the true hourly rate should become a routine point of reflection. Review it quarterly. Adjust your pricing and systems accordingly. Use it as a lens through which to examine clients, offerings, and working patterns. It is not just a number—it is a narrative, a signal, a benchmark of alignment between your effort and your reward.

In the freelance economy, where structure must be self-imposed, this kind of clarity is non-negotiable. The surface metrics—gross income, project fees, quoted rates—are useful, but they are not enough. It is only when you measure what remains, and what it cost you to create it, that you begin to see your work with the precision required to make it sustainable. The true hourly rate does not lie. It reveals. And in that revelation lies the power to price smarter, work saner, and live with a financial rhythm that respects both your ambition and your limits.

The Cost of Getting Paid

One of the quieter truths of freelance work is that earning income is not the same as *keeping* it. The process of converting professional expertise into cash in hand is riddled with micro-costs—some explicit, others obscured by complexity or delay. Freelancers often assume that the value of their work is reflected in the amount they invoice. But invoicing is not earnings, and payment received is not necessarily payment retained. Between gross project fees and actual usable income lies a chain of attrition: transaction fees, platform cuts, processing delays, currency conversions, administrative overhead, and the unpaid time it takes to chase, remind, and reconcile. The cost of getting paid is not merely a friction of doing business—it is a structural factor that can meaningfully shape your pricing strategy, business model, and long-term financial health.

What makes this cost particularly insidious is its fragmentation. No single fee seems dramatic. A 2.9% transaction charge here, a 20% platform commission there, a five-day clearing period, a £15 international wire fee. Each one is a small subtraction, easy to ignore in isolation. But they compound with scale and frequency. Across a year's worth of projects, they can erode a substantial portion of gross revenue—particularly for freelancers working across platforms, currencies, or client segments with slow payment cycles.

Consider a freelance designer earning £2,000 per month through Upwork. On the surface, that appears to be £24,000 annually—a viable income for a part-time solo operator. But Upwork's fee structure takes 20% of the first $500 billed per client and 10% thereafter. If the designer works with ten clients who never cross the $500 threshold, the platform retains 20% across the board. That's £4,800 gone before expenses, taxes, or time are factored in. If PayPal is used for withdrawals, add another 2–3% in currency conversion fees. And if any clients pay late or cancel mid-project, the revenue picture becomes even more unstable.

These aren't exceptional edge cases—they are the norm for platform-based freelancers. Fiverr, another popular gig marketplace, takes a flat 20% on all transactions, with funds released 14 days after client approval. Processing is fast, but predictability ends there. The service fee is extracted before the freelancer even sees the funds, which distorts financial visibility. If you invoice £100, you receive £80—not because of taxes or expenses, but because the platform's cut is built in. Yet many freelancers still refer to "earning £100" per gig, mentally inflating income without adjusting for net realities.

Outside of marketplaces, the pattern persists in a subtler form. Freelancers who invoice clients directly through Stripe or PayPal typically face a processing fee of 2.9% + 30p per transaction. On a £2,000 invoice, this amounts to £59—manageable if you charge premium rates, but significant if margins are tight or payment is split across instalments. Some clients insist on bank transfers, which can involve wire fees or international charges. Others request payments through procurement platforms like SAP Ariba or Coupa, which introduce bureaucratic drag and administrative complexity, often requiring time-consuming vendor registration and multi-step approvals—labour for which the freelancer is rarely compensated.

Even when fees are low, *time delays act as hidden costs.* A common scenario involves net-30 payment terms, meaning the client has 30 days from receipt of the invoice to pay. This delay—standard in large firms—can stretch into net-45 or net-60 depending on internal workflows or invoice processing cycles. In the meantime, the freelancer may be paying for tools, software, or subcontractors out of pocket. The cost here is not just the absence of funds, but the *cost of cashflow instability.* When payment arrives late, savings must be dipped into or other client work overbooked to compensate, creating knock-on effects across your workflow.

The consulting world offers its own variant. A freelance strategist might agree to a £10,000 engagement over two months, only to find that payment is contingent on departmental sign-off, legal review, or budget disbursement cycles. If the contract specifies payment upon project completion, the entire sum is effectively *held hostage* until every deliverable is signed off. This creates pressure to deliver more quickly, accept scope creep, or reduce quality just to release funds. What appears to be a lucrative project becomes, in operational terms, a cashflow gamble.

Some freelancers try to offset this by charging deposits or milestone-based payments. This can improve liquidity, but it often depends on client sophistication. Individual clients or small businesses may baulk at upfront charges or staggered billing, assuming that freelancers work like salaried employees—paid only after tasks are complete. Without clear education or contractual safeguards, freelancers end up subsidising their clients' operational inefficiencies.

There is also the matter of administrative drag. Every payment—regardless of platform—requires tracking, confirming, reconciling, and often reminding. A late payment requires follow-up. A rejected invoice must be reissued. A payment made in two parts across different dates must be reconciled. None of this time is billable, yet it can amount to several hours per month—hours that siphon energy and cognitive bandwidth from client-facing work. This is the invisible labour of freelance finance: the effort to get paid for work already done.

Then there are chargebacks and disputes. While rare, they are disproportionately damaging when they occur. A client who disputes a charge on PayPal or Stripe can initiate a hold on funds, forcing the freelancer to produce documentation and evidence of delivery. These disputes can drag on for weeks, during which time the funds are unavailable. Worse, platforms often default in favour of the buyer unless airtight contracts and deliverables are on file. The freelancer, once again, shoulders the risk without institutional recourse.

What emerges from all of this is a deeper insight: *payment is not just a transaction—it is a process ecosystem.* And that ecosystem has structural inefficiencies that freelancers must plan around. Pricing must absorb not just direct costs and taxes, but the *cost of getting paid.* This means factoring platform commissions into your minimum viable rate. It means understanding that not all revenue is equal—£500 from a direct bank transfer with net-7 terms is categorically more valuable than £500 from a platform with 20% fees and net-30 release cycles. Smart freelancers price accordingly.

The solution is not to avoid all intermediaries—some platforms offer reach, credibility, and client access that freelancers could not generate alone. Nor is the answer to demonise clients with slow payment cycles—many operate within the limits of complex corporate systems. The key is *awareness.* Knowing where your money is going, how long it takes to arrive, and what it costs to secure is the foundation of healthy financial planning.

This awareness allows you to make strategic trade-offs. You may accept higher fees from a slower-paying client if the project fits your portfolio. You might lower your platform reliance over time as you build a referral base. You may renegotiate payment terms or offer discounts for early settlement. You might invest in invoice tracking software or automate your follow-up sequences to reduce admin overhead. Each of these moves becomes intelligible only once you see the full picture—not just of what you earn, but of *how you earn it.*

At its core, freelancing demands that you treat every aspect of your business as a design challenge. The cost of getting paid is not a glitch in the system—it *is* the system. And once you understand its shape, you can build around it, buffer against its risks, and price your work not for vanity, but for viability. The result is not just higher income, but cleaner boundaries, fewer surprises, and a freelance practice that runs with the kind of clarity your clients already expect from you. The infrastructure of money matters just as much as the work that earns it. Those who grasp that difference move not only faster, but further—with fewer cracks underfoot.

From Projects to Patterns

Freelance income often arrives in bursts: a project lands, the invoice is issued, funds arrive—sometimes immediately, often weeks later. The experience is episodic, unpredictable, and deceptively disjointed. Each project feels like a self-contained event, with little connection to what came before or what's coming next. This perception, though intuitive, is financially dangerous. It encourages reactive behaviours—overspending in flush periods, panic in lean months—and it obscures one of the most powerful truths of freelance finance: *your income has a pattern, even if it doesn't have a schedule.*

Freelancers frequently describe their earnings as "random" or "all over the place." But randomness is rarely the actual issue. The deeper problem is *a lack of pattern recognition.* Freelancers track invoices, not cycles. They respond to each project as a one-off instead of identifying recurring client behaviours, seasonal industry rhythms, or their own bandwidth and marketing ebbs. What seems like chaos is often an unobserved cadence.

The path to financial stability begins by shifting your lens from *projects* to *patterns*. This means no longer evaluating your income in isolation—month by month, invoice by invoice—but instead zooming out to observe trends across quarters, years, and sectors. It means understanding that while individual projects may vary wildly, *your business has a seasonality*. The trick is to uncover it, map it, and plan around it—not in spite of its irregularity, but because of it.

A practical example illustrates the point. Consider a freelance illustrator who books several commissions in the run-up to Christmas—greeting cards, book covers, advertising assets. December is frantically busy. January, by contrast, is silent. The lull feels like a personal failure, but it is structural: clients aren't briefing new creative work at the start of the year. That gap isn't random—it's cyclical. The same illustrator may find steady work resurging around March, as spring marketing campaigns roll out. By documenting this pattern over time, they can begin to anticipate the feast-famine curve. Instead of being caught off guard, they can design for it: saving excess from Q4, blocking out rest time in Q1, and initiating marketing campaigns in February.

This shift transforms financial behaviour. When you know your income is seasonal, you stop making decisions based on this month's revenue. You stop panicking during slow periods or misallocating windfalls. Instead, you build a cashflow model that reflects your *actual income rhythm*, not the one you wish you had.

This rhythm is not the same for everyone. A freelance software developer working in B2B may have their biggest months in Q2 and Q4, aligning with corporate budgeting cycles. A freelance wedding photographer will likely see intense earnings in summer, followed by slower winters and early springs. A copywriter working with startups might see spikes around launch events or investor cycles. What matters is not the specific shape of your pattern—it's the *act of recognising that a shape exists*. You don't need perfect regularity. You need predictable *tendencies*.

To make this actionable, freelancers should track income at a monthly and quarterly level across multiple years. Spreadsheets, simple charts, or accounting dashboards can reveal recurring themes: Which months tend to be highest? Which ones lowest? How much variance occurs within client types, industries, or platforms? What's the average payment lag from invoice to deposit? Over time, these observations yield strategic insight. You begin to distinguish between outliers and norms. A sudden drop in February might not be a crisis—it might just be February.

The psychological benefit is profound. Uncertainty is stressful. But *uncertainty about things that are actually predictable* is exhausting. Once you recognise that your income is seasonal, not chaotic, you can reduce volatility fatigue and design systems that accommodate reality rather than fight it. You build savings buffers during high-earning months, not just as a safety net, but as a structural requirement. You avoid overcommitting in your high-output seasons and use quiet periods for rest, marketing, or professional development—not guilt-driven overwork.

Patterns also offer leverage. When you understand your most lucrative months or client segments, you can optimise around them. You might raise rates in your high-demand season, or create packages to encourage clients to book ahead of their usual timing. You might test new offerings in your low season to diversify income, rather than scrambling for last-minute work. You may even align personal life decisions—holidays, moves, sabbaticals—with periods of intentional pause, rather than hoping the calendar cooperates.

Some freelancers resist this kind of tracking, believing their work is too varied to reveal a trend. But variance and pattern are not opposites. Even businesses with diverse project types and clients show seasonal behaviours once enough data is captured. The pattern may be based on *you*—your marketing cycles, energy levels, or availability—rather than external forces. But the outcome is the same: if you look long enough, a rhythm emerges.

This mindset shift is particularly powerful for freelancers who oscillate between scarcity and abundance without knowing why. Many assume that more marketing, more hours, or more hustle will flatten the curve. But without recognising the pattern beneath the noise, they build systems on false assumptions. They hire too soon in a good month, then slash costs in a bad one. They avoid investing in tools or training because income feels unreliable, even when long-term trends show consistency. They underprice during low season, damaging their brand, then overwork during peak demand, damaging their health.

The irony is that many salaried workers already understand seasonality—they just experience it passively. Teachers expect slower summers. Retail workers prepare for Q4 madness. Corporate teams align projects around fiscal quarters. The structure is embedded in the job. Freelancers, by contrast, must *create their own awareness*—not because they are less professional, but because no system exists to do it for them.

Treating income like a season means building a freelance practice that reflects reality. It means planning expenses, pricing strategies, and savings goals not around idealised monthly income, but around *rolling averages* that account for fluctuation. It means being honest about what your business is likely to earn in Q1 versus Q3, and building your expectations accordingly. And most importantly, it means creating stability not by chasing predictability where it doesn't exist, but by *anticipating volatility where it does.*

This is not a compromise—it is a form of mastery. Freelancers who understand their financial patterns are not at the mercy of cashflow surprises. They are not seduced by artificial growth in strong months or paralysed by quiet ones. They move with clarity, grounded in data, and empowered by design. Their income may not be a stream, but it *is* a cycle. And cycles, once recognised, can be prepared for, adapted to, and ultimately leveraged—not feared.

Mapping income across time is not a technical exercise. It is a philosophical one. It requires you to stop treating each project as an isolated win and start treating your business as a living system—responsive, seasonal, and subject to forces both within and beyond your control. Once you make this shift, your freelance income stops being a source of surprise and becomes a source of strategy. You stop surviving your career and start shaping it. And from there, everything changes.

Chapter 3
Budgeting in a World Without Paydays

Traditional budgeting assumes a regular cadence of income. It presumes pay arrives like clockwork—weekly, bi-weekly, or monthly—and that expenses can be neatly apportioned to match. The whole system rests on predictability: steady paycheques, foreseeable outgoings, incremental saving. Freelancers, by contrast, operate in a financial climate that actively defies these assumptions. Payments are irregular, sometimes delayed, and earnings fluctuate from month to month. Trying to force a conventional budget onto this reality is not merely frustrating—it cultivates anxiety, inconsistency, and a false sense of control. The answer is not more discipline in spreadsheets but an approach designed for irregularity, one that starts by recognising you do not live in a world of paydays.

This chapter confronts an uncomfortable truth: for most freelancers, traditional budgets are obsolete before they are complete. A salaried worker can reasonably project income twelve months ahead; a freelancer may glimpse one or two months, and even then with uncertainty. Yet expenses remain rigid—rent is due, groceries cannot wait, bills insist on their schedules. The mismatch between fluid income and fixed obligations is the heart of the freelance budgeting challenge.

The instinct is often to try harder: create more detailed categories, track every possible expense, refine the budget to the last penny. But precision here can be a trap. If your model assumes £3,500 will arrive by the 10th and it lands on the 28th, your meticulously crafted plan collapses. The problem is not skill or effort—it is using the wrong instrument entirely.

Enter the anti-budget: a system not defined by rigid categories or artificial precision, but by adaptive structure. It is designed for volatility. Income is treated as a wave, not a line. Instead of splitting expenses into a dozen micro-categories—entertainment, transport, dining out—the focus is on purpose-driven buckets. These are few but essential: essentials, buffers, taxes, business reinvestment, and discretionary spending. When money arrives, it is allocated across buckets proportionally, according to operational need rather than calendar expectation.

Central to this method is the concept of the Minimum Viable Month: the absolute floor necessary to operate safely, both personally and professionally, for a single month. It encompasses non-negotiables: rent, utilities, groceries, insurance, debt servicing, and core business tools. This number is not aspirational; it is foundational. Once known, everything above it becomes strategic: taxes, savings, reinvestment, discretionary pay. Without this clarity, freelancers are effectively flying blind—unable to gauge whether current earnings can sustain future obligations or how many lean months they can weather.

With this foundation, cashflow management becomes far more deliberate. Income spikes are no longer invitations to splurge—they are opportunities to build reserves. Low-income periods are anticipated, not panicked over. By diverting a portion of revenue into an income buffer, freelancers can simulate a stable payroll, "paying" themselves consistently regardless of month-to-month fluctuations. The effect is not only financial stability but psychological steadiness: reduced decision fatigue, fewer panic-driven choices, and the mental bandwidth to plan strategically.

Smoothing income, however, demands a shift in temporal perspective. Monthly budgeting, convenient as it is, assumes regularity that freelancers rarely enjoy. Thinking in quarters rather than months aligns more closely with freelance cycles—project ramp-ups, client payments, and delivery schedules—and with quarterly tax obligations. A 90-day horizon allows you to see the rhythm of work: when you are prospecting, producing, collecting. It encourages decisions based on momentum and strategy rather than immediate balances.

This approach liberates decision-making. Expenses can be timed against project completion rather than bank balances. Pipeline health can be assessed over months, not weeks. Investments in growth—tools, training, subcontractors—are made from surplus, not speculation. Most importantly, it removes the quiet shame freelancers feel for "failing" at conventional budgeting. The issue is not moral; it is design. Systems built for salaried lives cannot measure the wind, yet we have been trying to apply them to unpredictable income.

This chapter is not about budgeting harder; it is about budgeting smarter. It offers tools built for the freelance reality, creating visibility, stability, and clarity even when income fluctuates dramatically. Budgeting as a freelancer is not about predicting the future; it is about constructing a system that functions when the future is uncertain. Knowing your Minimum Viable Month, routing income into buffers, adopting a quarterly mindset—these steps transform chaos into manageable structure.

The aim is not to impose order on volatility but to create a framework that accommodates it without surrendering control. It honours the rhythm of freelance work while guiding you toward stability, autonomy, and financial fluency. In a world without predictable paydays, success is defined not by a single project's earnings, but by the systems you put in place when income finally arrives. This chapter begins the work of showing you how.

The Anti-Budget Budget

The traditional monthly budget—meticulously constructed, spreadsheet-bound, and rigidly categorical—is a relic of salaried thinking. It assumes predictability: that income arrives on schedule, expenses can be divided into fixed buckets, and the balance between the two is mostly stable. It works because it is built for environments with steady cashflow, automatic deductions, and employer-mediated benefits. For freelancers, however, this model collapses under the weight of real-world irregularity. Income doesn't arrive on a timetable. Expenses vary with project cycles. A windfall in March may be followed by radio silence in April. The result is a persistent mismatch between budgeting expectations and the lived reality of independent work. What's needed is not a minor tweak to conventional tools, but an entirely different operating model—one that abandons the illusion of precision in favour of adaptive structure. This is the logic behind the anti-budget.

The anti-budget doesn't start with line items like "dining out" or "transport." It starts with purpose. It accepts that if income fluctuates, then allocations must flex too. Rather than constructing fragile monthly plans that implode with every late payment or cancelled project, it divides income into *broad functional buckets* that serve the long-term health of both the business and the individual. These aren't arbitrary categories. They are deliberately chosen to reflect the foundational needs of a self-employed financial life: essentials, savings buffers, taxes, operational reinvestment, and discretionary spending.

The first and most important bucket is *essentials*. This includes everything you need to keep your personal and professional life running—housing, food, utilities, insurance, minimum debt payments, core subscriptions. This bucket defines your financial baseline. Knowing the monthly cost of your essentials gives you a minimum viable income target. It's the floor that allows you to survive uncertainty without spiralling into panic. Once this figure is clear, you stop measuring success by the size of a single project and start measuring it by how consistently your income covers this critical threshold.

The second bucket is *savings buffers*—what cushions you from volatility. This includes an emergency fund, an income smoothing account, and any set-asides for large irregular expenses (annual software fees, professional licences, travel). This bucket doesn't need to be fully funded all at once. Its purpose is to grow slowly, as income permits, until it provides a runway long enough to handle dry spells or unexpected costs without resorting to credit cards or financial triage. For freelancers, this buffer is not optional—it is structural. Without it, every dip in income becomes a crisis. With it, you gain not just financial resilience, but the psychological space to make better decisions.

Then comes the *tax bucket*. For many freelancers, tax season is not an administrative milestone—it's a source of dread. This is almost always due to a lack of ongoing allocation. When tax is treated as a year-end surprise rather than a built-in component of every payment received, the result is either scrambling or debt. The anti-budget corrects this by treating tax as a non-negotiable percentage of each payment—separate, automatic, and sacred. Whether you set aside 20%, 25%, or 35% will depend on your location, earnings level, and deductions. The point is not to guess perfectly—it is to be consistently prepared.

Another vital bucket is *business reinvestment*. This includes courses, equipment, marketing, subscriptions, contractors, or anything that enhances your capacity to earn in the future. Many freelancers conflate business costs with personal expenses, or they delay strategic investments out of fear. By maintaining a distinct reinvestment bucket, you give yourself permission to grow without compromising essentials or savings. You stop treating growth as a luxury and start managing it as a disciplined input into your earning engine.

Finally, there is the *discretionary bucket*—the money you can spend without guilt, overanalysis, or second-guessing. This includes travel, entertainment, hobbies, and spontaneous pleasures. In traditional budgeting, discretionary spending is often the first to be over-controlled and the first to implode. The anti-budget recognises that freedom and flexibility are not enemies of financial stability—they are part of its purpose. Budgeting isn't about self-denial. It's about protecting freedom over the long term. A healthy discretionary bucket allows you to enjoy success when it comes, without compromising the systems that keep you grounded when it doesn't.

Crucially, the anti-budget doesn't operate on a strict monthly cycle. It adapts to income timing, project cadence, and personal circumstance. When you get paid, you allocate proportionally—regardless of when or how often that payment arrives. If you earn £4,000 one month and £1,500 the next, the system flexes, but the structure remains. Essentials are prioritised first. Tax is set aside before temptation strikes. Buffers are topped up in good months and drawn from in lean ones. Reinvestment is paused when necessary, accelerated when possible. Discretionary spending expands and contracts accordingly. The system works not because it is perfect, but because it is *responsive*.

This responsiveness is not a cop-out. It is an intentional design. The anti-budget is not about relinquishing discipline. It is about *applying discipline where it matters most*—not in obsessively categorising coffee purchases, but in ensuring you are structurally solvent, buffered against shocks, and aligned with your long-term goals. It focuses your energy on financial architecture, not micro-management.

For example, imagine a freelance editor who receives three large payments in August, totalling £9,000. A traditional budget would attempt to allocate this across specific line items for groceries, gas, subscriptions, and so on—most of which fluctuate month to month. But the anti-budget zooms out: £3,000 goes to cover essentials for September and October. £1,800 to tax. £2,000 to buffer savings. £800 to business development. £1,400 to discretionary. No granular tracking is required. No assumptions about timing are made. The system responds to the shape of the income, not to the structure of the calendar.

Over time, this approach builds consistency—not by flattening your income, but by *smoothing your financial experience of that income*. You begin to make decisions based on your total financial picture, not the anxiety or exuberance of a single invoice. You stop overcompensating in lean months and overspending in strong ones. You move from fragile budgeting to durable cashflow management.

The deeper shift is philosophical. Traditional budgeting often assumes that the purpose of money is control. The anti-budget assumes that the purpose of money is capacity. Its goal is not to restrict, but to enable. It is designed for a life where income varies, work is creative, and risk is embedded. It does not punish volatility. It manages it. And in doing so, it returns power to the freelancer—not by eliminating uncertainty, but by making it navigable.

Ultimately, the anti-budget replaces perfection with clarity, rigidity with resilience, and anxiety with awareness. It reflects the reality of independent work: that what matters is not how much you earn in a given moment, but what systems you have in place when you do. In a world without steady paydays, this kind of budgeting is not just pragmatic. It is essential. It gives you the stability of structure without the tyranny of overplanning. And that, in the unpredictable terrain of freelancing, is the closest thing to financial fluency you can build.

The Minimum Viable Month

Financial stability for freelancers begins not with revenue goals, investment strategies, or elaborate spreadsheets, but with one deceptively simple figure: the minimum viable month. This number—often overlooked, rarely calculated with precision—defines the absolute minimum amount of money you need to keep your personal and professional life operational for a single month. It includes the hard obligations that don't care whether a client paid on time: rent or mortgage, food, insurance, utilities, essential debt payments, and the baseline costs of running your business. Knowing this number is not just helpful—it is essential. It represents your financial floor. And until you know it, every decision you make is built on guesswork.

In salaried employment, the minimum viable month is often irrelevant. Paycheques arrive like clockwork, and surplus can be tucked away or spent depending on mood, habit, or ambition. But in freelance life, income does not respect the calendar. Some months bring a flood, others a trickle. Clients delay. Projects stall. Payments land out of sync with expenses. This volatility means that without a clear sense of your financial baseline, you're likely to overextend in high months and panic in low ones. Worse, you may not even recognise how close you are to a shortfall until the overdraft warning pings or the rent is due and unpayable.

The purpose of the minimum viable month is not to restrict ambition but to provide clarity. It is the number that tells you how much cashflow you need to avoid slipping into financial instability. It allows you to plan your income smoothing strategy, size your emergency fund accurately, and understand exactly how many months of buffer you have at any given time. In short, it replaces financial anxiety with actionable data.

Begin with housing. This is typically the largest recurring expense and the least flexible. Whether you rent or own, the cost is fixed and non-negotiable in the short term. Add essential utilities: electricity, heating, water, and internet. These are required not only for comfort but for basic business continuity. Then factor in groceries—not aspirational organic shopping but realistic, functional food costs. Next, account for non-discretionary debt payments: credit cards, student loans, or car repayments where minimum monthly payments are due regardless of income fluctuations.

Now move to insurance: health, renters, professional liability, or other policies that form your personal and business safety net. In many countries, freelancers must purchase these independently, and they are often among the first items skipped when cash is tight—at exactly the moment they are most needed. Then add essential business costs: software subscriptions, hosting fees, banking charges, mobile phone contracts, and any service that directly enables your ability to earn. This is not a full profit-and-loss review—it is a filtered assessment of what must be paid *even when you're between projects*.

What emerges from this calculation is your minimum viable month. For some, it may be £1,800. For others, £3,500 or more. The figure will vary based on geography, household composition, debt levels, and professional context. The point is not what the number *is*—it is that the number is *known*. Once you have it, you can use it to frame almost every major financial decision. If you know that £2,200 per month keeps the lights on and food on the table, then a £4,500 project is not just income—it's two months of breathing room. A quarter with £15,000 in revenue becomes more than a success metric; it becomes the foundation for a six-month buffer.

This kind of clarity transforms your relationship with your finances. It helps you answer vital questions quickly and intelligently. *How many months of living expenses do I currently have in reserves? How many clients would I need to cover the next three months if no new leads arrived? How many lean months can I absorb before debt becomes necessary?* These are not theoretical questions—they are survival-level considerations for freelancers. And the answers depend entirely on knowing your baseline.

The minimum viable month also improves your pricing logic. It adds gravity to your project quotes. When a potential client pushes back on a fee, you're no longer defending a number in the abstract—you're evaluating it against your actual cost of staying afloat. If a project only covers half of your minimum viable month and requires your full time, it is not just underpaid—it is unsustainable. This doesn't mean you must reject every low-budget opportunity, especially in early career stages, but it does mean you engage those opportunities with your eyes open and your trade-offs explicit.

Moreover, this clarity grants you the power to communicate financial needs within your household or to collaborators. When your income is irregular, it can be difficult to explain why a £5,000 month doesn't necessarily feel secure. But if everyone understands that your monthly floor is £3,200, the need for buffers, strategic pacing, and deliberate savings becomes self-evident. Transparency around this number helps replace guilt or shame with mutual understanding and forward planning.

It's worth noting that the minimum viable month is not a static figure. It will shift as your life and business evolve. Rent may increase. Insurance premiums may change. New tools may become indispensable. Or, conversely, you may downsize, consolidate subscriptions, or restructure debt. The key is to revisit the number quarterly—or whenever there's a significant shift—to ensure that your financial plans reflect your current reality. This is not a one-time calculation. It is a living metric, a health check, and a benchmark.

Some freelancers confuse the minimum viable month with a bare-bones emergency budget. They are related but distinct.

An emergency budget is your austerity plan—the figure you'd need to survive in a crisis, with all discretionary spending stripped and most non-essential services cut. The minimum viable month, by contrast, is your *normal operations baseline*. It's what allows you to live and work sustainably, not just survive. It enables continuity, not stagnation. And for that reason, it should be respected as a non-negotiable metric, not a wishful estimate.

Understanding your minimum viable month also anchors your income smoothing and anti-budget strategies. If you want to create a buffer that covers three months of income volatility, you now know exactly how much that buffer must be. If you receive an unusually large payment, you can calculate how many months of baseline it covers. You begin to manage not just projects or accounts, but *time*. You understand how long your money will last, how soon you need to pursue new work, and when it's safe to rest, invest, or experiment.

Most importantly, this number gives you back control. One of the most disorienting aspects of freelance life is not just the variability of income, but the ambiguity of what's enough. Without a defined baseline, freelancers oscillate between overconfidence and anxiety, spending freely one week and second-guessing essentials the next. The minimum viable month stabilises this pendulum. It says: *this is the line*. When you cross it, you're covered. When you don't, adjustments are needed—not as a failure, but as a signal.

No financial system for freelancers can be effective without this foundational number. It is the point around which all other planning orbits. It enables prioritisation, protects against chaos, and clarifies the cost of saying yes—or no—to any opportunity. It replaces vague hope with structured awareness. And in a working life shaped by uncertainty, there are few tools more powerful than knowing, precisely and without sentiment, what it takes to keep going. Not thriving, not scaling—just *continuing*. From that platform, everything else becomes possible.

Smoothing the Spikes

Freelance income doesn't arrive like a steady heartbeat. It arrives in pulses—unpredictable, irregular, and often asynchronous with the needs of life. A month of intense delivery might produce a temporary cash surge, while a lull in projects can mean weeks without a single invoice clearing. Yet essential expenses—rent, food, utilities, insurance—continue regardless of your billing cycle. This dislocation between earnings and obligations is not a flaw in freelancing; it is a defining feature. The critical financial skill is not simply earning more, but managing *when* money arrives relative to *when* it is needed. This is the logic behind income smoothing—and at its core lies a deceptively powerful mechanism: the income buffer.

An income buffer is not a savings account in the abstract. It is a tactical reserve, deliberately constructed to offset volatility. It allows you to draw a consistent personal "salary" even when professional income is lumpy. Unlike an emergency fund, which is designed to protect against external shocks, an income buffer is a tool for structural cashflow management. It bridges the gap between unpredictable earnings and predictable living. It transforms feast-and-famine cycles into sustainable cadence. And it does this not by fixing volatility—which is impossible—but by absorbing it.

Building such a buffer begins with a mindset shift: from reactive to proactive finance. Instead of spending what arrives, you begin *holding* part of each inflow until patterns stabilise. This requires not only restraint, but visibility—specifically, knowing your minimum viable month. That figure—the absolute monthly amount required to meet your personal and business essentials—serves as the target baseline. If your essentials require £2,500 and you earn £4,000 in a strong month, the instinct may be to upgrade lifestyle or defer planning. But the smarter move is to divert at least £1,000 of that surplus into your income buffer. This is not saving for saving's sake. It is reserving for rhythm.

Over time, these allocations accumulate into a fund that allows you to smooth your financial experience, even if your income remains spiky. For instance, suppose you've built a buffer equal to two months of essentials. In a slow month, you can "pay" yourself from that reserve, maintaining stability without reaching for credit or cutting essentials. When the next strong month arrives, the buffer is replenished. Income volatility doesn't vanish—it becomes manageable. Instead of living at the mercy of each project, you begin to run your freelance life like a business: planned, paced, and buffered.

A key element of success here is structural separation. Your income buffer must live in a dedicated account, inaccessible to casual spending. This is not psychological theatre—it is a practical safeguard. Funds that mingle with daily-use money are vulnerable to impulse. A separate buffer account enforces intention: you are not "saving money" in general, you are preserving your ability to *pay yourself* consistently. That distinction matters. It reframes the buffer not as an emergency stash, but as an operating mechanism.

The amount to aim for will vary. A one-month buffer offers immediate relief; a two- to three-month buffer provides resilience; beyond that, you begin to approach true financial agility. But even a partial buffer is powerful. Many freelancers assume that unless they can save several thousand pounds, smoothing is out of reach. This is untrue. Even a few hundred pounds can stabilise a week, cover a late payment, or avoid a credit card charge. The goal is not perfection; it is *progressive insulation*.

Crucially, this system doesn't just serve your bank balance—it serves your psychology. Income volatility creates cognitive volatility: stress, decision fatigue, irrational scarcity behaviours. A buffer disrupts that spiral. It gives you space to evaluate opportunities without desperation. It enables you to reject low-paying work without financial panic. It allows you to schedule rest or invest in long-term growth without undermining your basic needs. In other words, a buffer isn't just money—it's *leverage.*

Case studies illustrate this power clearly. A freelance web developer in Manchester builds her buffer over six months, setting aside 20% of each invoice. During a two-month gap in client work, she continues to "pay" herself £2,800 monthly. Her expenses are covered, her mental state remains steady, and she uses the time to redesign her portfolio. Contrast that with a freelance copywriter in Bristol who treats high-income months as windfalls. When work dries up, he scrambles, underprices projects, and takes on clients he would otherwise decline—ultimately compounding stress and reducing quality. The difference is not talent. It's planning.

That said, smoothing is not passive. Buffers must be maintained. Strong months invite temptation. But the most effective freelancers treat income allocation like business discipline, not personal impulse. They automate transfers to buffer accounts, set percentage-based allocations, and adjust quarterly based on income trends. Some even pay themselves on a delay—holding income for two weeks before releasing it into personal accounts. These aren't rituals of deprivation. They are *systems of self-stability.*

Importantly, smoothing works best when paired with quarterly thinking. Freelancers who plan in 90-day cycles are better positioned to allocate intelligently. They see the peaks and troughs, identify surplus ahead of time, and pace their outflows accordingly. If a retainer ends in June, they begin planning in April. If tax payments loom in January, they anticipate in October. Buffers make this planning possible. Without them, every shift becomes an emergency.

The beauty of income smoothing is that it does not require extraordinary discipline, financial education, or income level. It requires awareness, structure, and consistency. It replaces the fragile optimism of hoping things work out with the durable confidence that you've planned for when they don't. It respects the reality of freelance life without being dominated by it. It enables freedom by enforcing structure. And in doing so, it changes the freelancer's posture—from reactive survivor to strategic operator.

Freelancers often ask what stability looks like in a world without paydays. This is the answer. Not guaranteed income, but *guaranteed adaptability*. Not steady earnings, but *steady cashflow*. Not a fantasy of predictability, but a system that makes volatility livable. That system begins with the buffer. Build it small. Build it consistently. Protect it fiercely. And use it not as a shield from uncertainty, but as a lever for control. The spikes won't stop coming—but with the right architecture, they won't knock you off balance.

Monthly vs. Quarterly Thinking

Freelancers are often told to budget like salaried employees—track monthly income, allocate to categories, and measure success by what's left over at the end of each 30-day cycle. This guidance, while well-intentioned, is structurally flawed. It reflects a worldview built for predictable income, regular paydays, and employer-mediated stability. Freelance income, by contrast, is staggered, project-based, and delay-prone. One month might produce three invoices and a windfall; the next, nothing but inbox silence and overdue payments. The mismatch between financial models and freelance reality is not a minor irritation—it's a source of chronic confusion and cashflow mismanagement. For freelancers, the month is too short a lens. The quarter—90 days—is where visibility begins.

Monthly planning invites overreaction. A slow April feels like failure, even if March and May are strong. A spike in June prompts overspending, even if July is dormant. By confining analysis to arbitrary calendar endpoints, monthly thinking distorts perception. It encourages decisions based on temporary cash positions rather than broader trends. It overemphasises recent outcomes and obscures the structural dynamics of freelance income: project cycles, payment delays, seasonal rhythms, and tax requirements. The month is too volatile to serve as a reliable planning unit.

Quarterly thinking offers a different architecture. A 90-day view captures the natural cadence of most freelance businesses. It allows for planning that reflects the *flow* of work rather than the *frequency* of pay. Projects are scoped, delivered, and invoiced across weeks or months, not within tidy four-week brackets. Clients may approve work in January, pay in February, and initiate the next round in March. A monthly view slices this story into misleading fragments; a quarterly view preserves its integrity. It allows freelancers to treat their income as a system, not a series of disconnected events.

The logic extends beyond perception. Quarterly planning aligns with *cashflow lag*. Most freelancers experience a delay between effort and income. Work completed in week one is invoiced in week three and paid in week six. In a monthly model, this sequence creates gaps that appear problematic. In a quarterly model, it is expected. You begin to see that the money arriving today was earned last month, and that this month's effort will fund the next. This temporal awareness transforms how you relate to income. It reduces the emotional whiplash of slow weeks and high-output months. It introduces a rhythm.

It also aligns with *quarterly tax cycles*. In many countries, freelancers are required to pay estimated taxes four times a year. Monthly systems rarely accommodate this naturally. They treat taxes as an afterthought, a future problem to be solved with future income. Quarterly systems, by contrast, build tax planning into their architecture. Freelancers can review earnings and expenses every 90 days, calculate their estimated obligations, and set aside funds accordingly. This reduces surprises, penalties, and last-minute scrambles. It integrates compliance into cadence.

Moreover, quarterly thinking supports *strategic review*. Every 90 days, you can step back and assess key metrics: how much you earned, how many hours you worked, which clients were profitable, which drained you, and where time was lost. You can audit your pricing, evaluate your buffers, and decide whether your systems are keeping pace with your goals. This periodic reflection introduces a natural feedback loop—frequent enough to allow course correction, but spaced enough to permit real data to accumulate. Monthly reviews are often too noisy; yearly reviews are too late. The quarter strikes a practical balance.

This approach also shifts how freelancers interpret risk. A quiet month becomes data, not drama. A lean February, when viewed in isolation, may seem catastrophic. But if Q1 as a whole meets your revenue baseline, the panic subsides. You see the full arc, not the moment. This enables calmer decisions—about marketing, investing, resting, or raising rates. It encourages thinking in *systems*, not symptoms. You move from reacting to *this month's dip* to planning for *this quarter's outcome*.

Consider a freelance UX consultant who tracks income monthly. In January, she earns £7,000; February, £2,000; March, £4,000. The February dip unsettles her, prompting frantic outreach and discounting. But in quarterly terms, she earned £13,000—an average of £4,333 per month, more than her minimum viable threshold. The "problem" was not revenue, but *timing*. Had she planned quarterly, she would have known February was covered by January's surplus and March's pipeline. Her behaviour—and stress—would have been completely different.

Quarterly planning also supports more coherent *client management*. Many freelancers work on multi-month engagements: product builds, rebrands, long-form content strategies. These projects involve staggered milestones, shifting scopes, and evolving timelines. Monthly views often obscure the true status of work in progress. But when you plan in quarters, you align more closely with how projects actually unfold. You can forecast capacity, manage delivery timelines, and space client acquisition efforts more sustainably. You stop stuffing new work into full months or panicking during lulls—you begin to pace for endurance, not speed.

This model also sharpens focus. When you think in quarters, you can set *strategic themes*—a product launch, a rebranding effort, an outreach campaign—without derailing your finances. You give yourself room to prioritise without the immediate pressure of monetisation. You know you have 90 days to execute and evaluate. This fosters depth, not just activity. It supports deliberate, meaningful progress. And it inoculates against the freelancer's greatest enemy: chronic short-termism masquerading as hustle.

Of course, monthly tools still have their place. Day-to-day expense tracking, calendar scheduling, and cashflow monitoring remain useful. But these are *operational tools*, not strategic frameworks. They help manage mechanics, not direction. Monthly habits serve quarterly thinking—not the reverse. When the two are confused, planning becomes reactive. When the hierarchy is respected, planning becomes dynamic.

Some may argue that quarterly thinking feels too big, too abstract, or too ambitious for those just starting out. But the opposite is true. It is especially powerful for freelancers in the early stages, where volatility is highest and patterns are still emerging. It allows for experimentation without existential dread. It enables new freelancers to observe trends without overreacting to every fluctuation. It provides enough runway to learn and adapt, without the false urgency of monthly panic.

The ultimate value of quarterly thinking lies in its psychological shift. It grants freelancers the permission—and the framework—to step off the treadmill of constant reaction. It replaces the illusion of control through hyper-monitoring with actual control through structured awareness. It acknowledges that volatility is part of the freelance terrain, but that *volatility is not unpredictability* if you zoom out far enough. The month is noise. The quarter is signal.

When you plan in 90-day blocks, you make better decisions—not because you predict the future with perfect accuracy, but because you understand the contours of your working life with greater honesty. You know that not every week must be productive, that not every month must be profitable, and that success is not built in 30-day windows. It is built in quarters—through clarity, consistency, and a deliberate refusal to be ruled by the randomness of individual days. From that vantage point, freelance finance becomes not a guessing game, but a strategic craft. And that makes all the difference.

Chapter 4
Separate Your Money, Save Your Sanity

Most freelancers aren't undone by a lack of talent or diligence—they falter under the quiet, cumulative chaos of poor financial architecture. Not the kind of spectacular mismanagement that lands in the headlines, but the subtle, everyday decisions that entangle business and personal finances into a confusing knot. A common manifestation? The single-account trap. Everything—client payments, tax set-asides, rent, subscriptions, groceries, coffee runs—is lumped together. On the surface, it seems simple: money in, money out. In reality, clarity is the first casualty.

This "one-account mistake" is surprisingly pervasive. Skilled professionals—writers, designers, consultants, developers—often default to a single current account. It feels efficient, minimal, bureaucratically lean. But simplicity here comes at a cost. When personal and business transactions mingle, it's impossible to see what your work truly costs or earns. Tax deductions are lost, spending surges in flush months, and when the dreaded tax season arrives, you are left combing through a year of mingled entries, attempting to separate necessity from indulgence.

Freelancing demands more than habits; it demands infrastructure. Without it, even disciplined behaviours buckle under decision fatigue. By separating funds, you do more than tidy accounts—you reduce the cognitive load of managing your livelihood. Questions that once gnawed at you—How much do I owe in tax? Can I afford this software? Should I save or spend?—are answered by design, before the money even lands.

This chapter introduces the freelance finance stack: a layered, compartmentalised structure mirroring a healthy business. Its principle is deceptively simple: assign every pound a job, and a place to do it. Rather than pooling everything together, distribute funds across four core accounts: an income holding account, a tax savings account, an operating expenses account, and a personal spending account. Each serves a distinct function, clarifying what is available to spend, owed to the government, invested in your business, or reserved for future allocation.

The income holding account is your central receiving station. All client payments arrive here first, untouched. It is a buffer—a pause between earning and spending. Instead of reacting impulsively, you respond with intention, routing funds deliberately. This small step introduces a behavioural shift that shields the system from impulse.

From there, funds flow into the tax savings account. Untouchable, sacrosanct, predictable. A fixed percentage of every payment is set aside for taxes, removing guesswork and anxiety. Automation is key; once integrated into your process, tax season stops feeling like an ambush.

Next, the operating expenses account: the working capital of your business. This is where software, subcontractors, training, subscriptions, and other tools are paid. It's also where you draw a salary. By separating this from personal spending, you gain clarity on your operational costs and see, unvarnished, what it truly costs to run your practice.

Decisions—hiring, reinvestment, purchasing—are now grounded in fact rather than illusion.

Finally, the personal spending account: rent, groceries, transport, lifestyle. You fund it like a salary, establishing a rhythm that separates making money from accessing money. This distinction is profound. It stabilises your life, prevents feast-and-famine overspending, and reinforces the psychological boundary between personal and business finances.

The strength of this stack is not merely structural but behavioural. Automation of fund routing—weekly, biweekly, monthly—reduces friction, eliminates repetitive decision-making, and replaces anxiety with calm, rules-based movement. Purchases are no longer reactive, taxes are not last-minute scrambles. Decisions are preemptively accounted for.

Structure alone is insufficient; visibility is equally essential. Many freelancers monitor balances but fail to visualise flows. Without seeing bottlenecks, leakages, or client dependencies, control is illusory. Diagramming your system—whether on paper, whiteboard, spreadsheet, or app—is diagnostic. It exposes the architecture of your finances in real time, granting both insight and authority.

The payoff is not purely functional; it is cognitive. Financial chaos produces mental noise. When money is tangled, thinking suffers. Worry increases, difficult conversations are deferred, procrastination escalates, and short-term choices undermine long-term objectives. Separation is not about perfection—it is about peace of mind. It frees mental bandwidth for the work that matters: delivering value, cultivating relationships, and developing your craft.

This chapter is your blueprint. It guides the transition from reactive to intentional, scattered to structured, anxious to composed. It dismantles the illusion that simplicity means a single account, replacing it with a model built for the complexity of self-employment. Freelancing requires you to be your own CFO. Earning is just one side of the equation—managing is equally critical. And it all begins with separation: not as an option, but as a principle. A principle that saves sanity, future-proofs your work, and anchors your finances in a system that truly functions.

The One Bank Account Mistake

For many freelancers, the first major financial decision happens almost by accident: which bank account to use. Often, without much thought, they choose the account they already have—the same one they've used since university, with direct debits for Spotify, gym memberships, rent, groceries, and the occasional impulse buy. Into this account they funnel client payments. Out of it flows everything else. Income and outgoings swirl together in a fog of digital activity that feels manageable—until it isn't. What begins as a gesture of simplicity gradually becomes a persistent obstacle to financial clarity, tax compliance, business growth, and peace of mind. The one-account setup, though convenient, is a foundational structural error—and a costly one.

At the heart of the problem is this: *when everything is in one place, you can't see what anything really means*. You receive £3,000 from a client and feel flush, unaware that £1,200 of that money must eventually go to taxes, £600 will be consumed by operating costs, and £300 is earmarked for next month's rent. Without separation, these distinctions blur. The illusion of liquidity encourages overspending, and the absence of boundaries leads to a perpetual cycle of reactive decisions. You're not managing a business—you're surviving on momentum.

Tax is one of the first casualties. In a mixed-account environment, it's easy to underestimate your obligations. Because the money sits in the same space as your weekly shop and your Netflix subscription, it feels like it's yours. By the time quarterly or year-end filings are due, what should have been set aside is long gone—absorbed into everyday life. Freelancers in this position often resort to short-term borrowing, partial payments, or procrastination. None of these outcomes stem from malice or incompetence; they stem from design. *A system that obscures what belongs to the business, what belongs to the government, and what belongs to you personally will always result in poor decision-making—no matter how diligent you are.*

Equally problematic is the erosion of deductible tracking. When business expenses are tangled with personal ones, the administrative burden of separating them retroactively becomes intolerable. You miss legitimate write-offs—not because they didn't happen, but because you can't locate or justify them. You forget which subscriptions are professional and which are personal. You don't remember whether that lunch with a client was work-related or not. You abandon your own records and leave money on the table. And when the tax office asks for clarity, you have little to offer.

More subtly, the one-account mistake undermines your ability to *understand* your business. Without separation, you have no accurate picture of profitability. You can't distinguish between months where you earned a high income and spent heavily on production, and those where you worked lean and generated a strong margin. Every transaction is flattened into the same feed. You're left reacting to balance totals rather than managing income and expenditure. The numbers tell you how much is in the account, but not what's happening underneath.

This blindness corrodes savings discipline. When income and expenses are combined in one pot, you rely on willpower to save. You tell yourself you'll move money "later," after this expense or that invoice. But later never arrives. The account, designed for flow not function, offers no signal of when to pause, allocate, or withhold. And because there's no mechanism for separating surplus from obligation, everything feels temporary. You save reactively—if at all—and spend based on what you *see*, not what you *should* preserve.

It's worth examining why so many freelancers fall into this trap. The answer is partially cultural and partially behavioural. We are conditioned by traditional employment, where money arrives pre-filtered. Taxes are withheld, pensions are automated, and spending money arrives pre-packaged. This gives the illusion of simplicity. Freelancers, in trying to recreate that simplicity, mistake minimalism for efficiency. They assume that fewer accounts equal fewer problems. But in freelancing, *clarity requires compartmentalisation*. The complexity of your financial responsibilities cannot be reduced to a single ledger without severe trade-offs.

There is also the matter of emotional inertia. Changing banking setups feels tedious, bureaucratic, and overwhelming. Opening new accounts, creating transfer schedules, updating payment information—it all carries the weight of admin. But it is admin that pays dividends. Freelancers who overcome the inertia and separate their financial flows experience an almost immediate cognitive lift. They report lower anxiety, clearer decision-making, and a greater sense of control. They stop operating in panic mode and start thinking like professionals.

Consider a graphic designer based in Edinburgh. For years, she ran her freelance business through her personal current account. Each month was a juggling act. When her income was high, she overspent; when it dipped, she panicked. She regularly missed VAT filing deadlines and underpaid her taxes. Eventually, after a difficult audit, she restructured her finances: one account for income collection, another for taxes, one for business expenses, and a final one for personal use. The impact was immediate. She began routing income into categories the moment it landed. Her tax payments were pre-funded. Her business expenses were transparent. And she could finally answer the question, "Can I afford this?" with confidence—not guesswork.

This shift is not about sophistication. It is about *structure*. And structure is not a luxury—it is a requirement. You don't need to be earning six figures or running a team to benefit from separating your finances. In fact, the earlier you build the system, the easier it is to scale. The infrastructure you put in place when you're earning £2,000 a month is the same one that will serve you at £10,000. But if you wait until you're "busy enough" or "earning enough," the habits become harder to change. Complexity increases. Friction grows. And so do the consequences of mismanagement.

One objection often raised is that managing multiple accounts feels like overkill. But digital banking has made this easier than ever. Most banks now allow multiple fee-free accounts, instant transfers, and category labelling. You can create virtual envelopes, schedule automations, and monitor flows with minimal friction. The problem is rarely technological—it is conceptual. We've been taught that our finances are personal, not professional. But as a freelancer, *your money is both*. You are not just the worker—you are the financial operator. And operators require dashboards, not guesswork.

Ultimately, the one-account mistake is not just a bookkeeping oversight. It is a signal of unexamined assumptions about money, control, and identity. It reflects a reluctance to see freelancing as a *business*, with structure, systems, and protocols. But once you do, the path forward becomes obvious. You don't need complexity—you need clarity. You don't need more money—you need better flow. And that begins with the simple, profound act of separating what belongs to your business from what belongs to your life.

The clarity that follows is not abstract—it is visceral. It is the difference between scanning your banking app with anxiety and scanning it with understanding. Between reacting to your balance and acting on your plan. Between being constantly surprised and being consistently prepared. The cost of mixing your finances is not just tax trouble or missed savings. It's the erosion of your confidence. The solution is simple. Separate the flows, and you reclaim control—not only over your money, but over your mental bandwidth and your capacity to lead your freelance practice with intention.

The Freelance Finance Stack

There is a fundamental difference between being self-employed and running a business, and that difference is structure. The freelancer who treats income as a flood of money to be managed instinctively—received, spent, saved, or ignored—is operating without infrastructure. And when structure is absent, strategy becomes impossible. You can't optimise what you can't see. You can't plan around what you haven't defined. The freelancer who intends to grow, stabilise, and take control of their money must act like a financial operator, not a passive recipient of irregular income. At the core of this shift lies a deceptively powerful tool: the freelance finance stack.

The finance stack is not a metaphor. It is a literal system—a four-account architecture designed to create clarity, discipline, and cashflow consistency in the context of volatile income. It is the financial equivalent of compartmentalised functionality in engineering: each account has a singular purpose, each purpose supports operational stability, and together they produce coherence where chaos previously ruled. This is not about complication for its own sake. It is about removing ambiguity from the most crucial financial decisions a freelancer makes—how to allocate income, prepare for tax, fund their business, and pay themselves consistently. It is, in short, the difference between surviving as a freelancer and *operating as a business*.

At the top of the stack sits the **income holding account**. This is where all client payments arrive, and where *nothing else* happens. No bills are paid from this account. No spending occurs. Its purpose is containment and staging. Think of it as an airlock. Money comes in, is observed, logged, and held until it is distributed intentionally. This brief pause—the moment between receiving and allocating—breaks the instinctive chain between earning and spending. It forces reflection, introduces discipline, and prevents the common freelancer mistake of making decisions based on temporary abundance. When income lands directly into a personal spending account, it invites immediate action. When it enters an income holding account, it invites *deliberate allocation*.

From there, the first and most crucial transfer goes to the **tax savings account**. Freelancers operate without automatic withholding, which means tax responsibility is fully self-managed. Treating tax as a future problem is the fastest route to financial stress. The tax savings account prevents this by carving off a fixed percentage—typically 25% to 35% depending on jurisdiction, deductions, and income level—*every time income arrives*. This isn't a mental note. It's a structural feature. The money is moved, sequestered, and left untouched until quarterly payments or year-end obligations are due. No "catching up," no borrowing from other funds, no last-minute panic. Freelancers who run their tax obligations through this account system report a dramatic reduction in anxiety—not because taxes become less burdensome, but because they are no longer treated as unpredictable.

The next allocation flows into the **operating expenses account**. This is your business's working capital. Software subscriptions, contractors, domain renewals, equipment purchases, professional development, advertising—*anything required to keep the business running and earning* comes from this account. Crucially, this separation forces you to see the cost of doing business in real terms. If your email platform, web hosting, and client acquisition tools total £750 per month, that figure is no longer buried within your personal spending—it stands alone, visible and non-negotiable. This changes how you view pricing, growth, and reinvestment. It also helps you prioritise wisely. When expenses are no longer abstract, decisions become sharper. Is that new online course an indulgence or a necessary upgrade? Your operating account will tell you.

What remains flows into your **personal spending account**—your freelancer "paycheque." This is what funds your rent, groceries, travel, and personal savings. It is not the same as profit. It is *what you get paid*. The key here is regularity. Even if client income is erratic, your personal spending account should be topped up on a consistent rhythm—weekly, biweekly, or monthly. This creates stability. You are no longer reacting to your client payment schedule; you are managing your household finances like someone with a salary. You can budget, plan, and save with confidence because the amount you live on is consistent. And because the account is insulated from the income inflow, you cannot spend what hasn't been transferred. You protect yourself from your own optimism.

These four accounts—income holding, tax savings, operating expenses, and personal spending—form the basic stack. They replace impulse with process. They impose clarity on complexity. And they reduce the need for constant financial decision-making. When set up properly, this system begins to *run itself*. You stop asking, "Can I afford this?" and start checking the relevant account. You stop wondering if you've set enough aside for taxes and start trusting the structure. You stop blurring the line between personal and business spending and start acting with precision.

It's important to note that this stack is not about how much money you have—*it's about how you manage the money you do have*. A freelancer earning £1,500 a month can benefit from this system as much as one earning £15,000. The structure scales. The percentages may shift, the flow rates may vary, but the logic holds. The earlier you build the system, the fewer habits you need to unlearn later.

The psychological impact of this separation cannot be overstated. Freelancers often live with low-grade financial stress—not from actual shortfalls, but from lack of visibility. They don't know what's available, what's reserved, what's safe to spend, or what belongs to the business. The finance stack replaces this fog with dashboards. It turns instinct into insight. And in doing so, it enables the one quality that is essential for long-term sustainability: *financial confidence*.

Examples abound. A freelance strategist in Leeds sets up the four-account model after years of running everything through one account. She begins routing 30% of every invoice to tax, 20% to business expenses, and pays herself a stable £2,200 per month. Six months in, she's no richer in absolute terms—but her financial anxiety has dropped to near zero. She can answer client questions without worrying whether she can afford next month's rent. She books a holiday knowing her operating costs are covered. She takes on fewer clients, but does better work—because her mind is no longer divided.

The stack also makes seasonal planning easier. With consistent income routing, you can look ahead to high-tax quarters or leaner project periods and adjust early. You see not just what you have, but what's *coming*. You stop navigating your freelance finances by rear-view mirror. Instead, you use a system that mirrors the professional architecture of successful businesses—because your freelance career *is* a business, and it deserves systems that reflect its complexity.

Some freelancers hesitate to adopt this setup, fearing it will feel cumbersome. But modern banking has made this frictionless. Digital banks allow instant transfers, automated rules, and multiple fee-free accounts. Some even provide visual tools to track buckets and flows. Implementation requires a few hours of effort. The payoff is measured in *years* of clarity.

The freelance finance stack is not a clever hack or financial gimmick. It is a durable operating system. It reflects a deeper truth: that structure, not income, is what determines financial resilience. That confidence is not a function of earnings, but of knowing *exactly* where your money is and what it's doing. And that the difference between a struggling freelancer and a thriving one is rarely about talent—it is about systems. When you build the right stack, you build a career that doesn't just survive volatility—it operates through it, with clarity, discipline, and control.

Money Routing as a Habit

Consistency is the antidote to chaos in a freelance financial life, but consistency does not emerge from willpower alone. It must be engineered. Freelancers face not only variable income but also variable decision-making. Each time a payment arrives, they are forced to re-evaluate: How much do I keep? What's owed to tax? Can I afford to reinvest? Should I pay myself more this month? These questions, repeated frequently and without system, create an invisible burden—*decision fatigue*. And over time, decision fatigue degrades the quality of financial choices, not because of recklessness, but because of sheer cognitive depletion. The solution is not more effort. It is design. It is creating a money routing habit so seamless, it becomes automatic—removing the need to decide from scratch every time.

The practice of money routing is deceptively simple: on every payday, your incoming funds are distributed to designated accounts according to predefined percentages. These routes match the financial architecture outlined in the freelance finance stack—income holding account, tax savings account, operating expenses account, and personal spending account. But while the structure provides the *where*, the habit of routing ensures the *how and when*. It is the operational layer that activates the system.

Automated money routing does not merely remove tasks; it installs discipline. It replaces sporadic planning with predictable flow. It ensures that your business is funded, your taxes are covered, and your personal life is stabilised without requiring heroic effort or perfect timing. For freelancers navigating delayed payments, seasonal fluctuations, and sporadic windfalls, this discipline is not optional—it is essential. Without it, every financial decision becomes a negotiation. With it, your freelance practice begins to resemble a well-run enterprise.

To understand why this matters, consider a freelancer who receives £6,000 from three different clients in a single week. Without a routing system, that lump sum sits in their main account, indistinct and misleading. It creates the illusion of abundance. There's no immediate visual cue to signal what portion of that money is reserved for tax, which part is necessary for upcoming business expenses, or how much they can safely draw for personal use. They are likely to under-save, overspend, or defer decision-making until the money begins to evaporate. Worse, each new payment restarts the cycle. Financial management becomes reactive, exhausting, and prone to inconsistency.

Now contrast that with a freelancer who receives the same £6,000 but has a pre-programmed routing habit. On receipt, 30% (£1,800) is automatically transferred to the tax account, 20% (£1,200) to the operating expenses account, and 50% (£3,000) is held for personal pay, with a scheduled monthly transfer of £2,000 to their personal account, preserving the rest for future smoothing. The process takes minutes. There is no mental arithmetic, no subjective rationalising, no delay. Every pound has a job, and every job has a destination. The freelancer is not only better prepared—they are psychologically steadier. *The system absorbs the complexity, not the freelancer's brain.*

It's worth noting that automation here does not mean inflexibility. In fact, it creates *freedom within structure*. You can modify routing percentages quarterly, based on income trends, tax policy changes, or shifts in business investment. You can establish a buffer for months where income is delayed. You can even pause or adjust certain flows when transitioning between high and low seasons. What matters is not rigidity, but intentionality. You are building a default, not a prison. And the default saves you from drift.

The most effective way to install this habit is to time it with client payment arrivals. Every time money lands in your income holding account, the system activates: either manually through a 10-minute routine or automatically through banking rules and scheduled transfers. Many digital banks and fintech tools now support programmable transfers, making it possible to "set and forget" key components. Some freelancers choose to batch payments weekly or biweekly, allowing for a smoother rhythm and fewer disruptions. The optimal cadence depends on volume and variability, but the core principle remains: *routing must be regular, rule-based, and unambiguous*.

Beyond mechanical efficiency, money routing offers behavioural benefits. When you separate allocation from spending, you create psychological friction against impulse. The simple act of seeing £3,000 in your holding account, rather than your personal account, introduces pause. You begin to internalise the fact that what you earn is not the same as what you *keep*. This behavioural cue, repeated over months, builds financial maturity. You stop living at the edge of your cashflow and start managing above it.

Case studies underscore the effect. A freelance marketing consultant in Birmingham, after years of cashflow anxiety, implements a routing system with 25% tax, 15% operations, and a capped monthly draw of £2,400. Within a year, he builds a three-month buffer, avoids late VAT penalties, and finally feels comfortable raising rates. A UX designer in Brighton routes income weekly, automating her tax and operations transfers every Friday. The habit becomes second nature. She calls it "finance Friday," blocking 15 minutes in her calendar to check balances, confirm transfers, and audit her routes. What once felt like a chore now feels like a rhythm—a ritual that sustains her business, not distracts from it.

Crucially, the act of money routing reframes your role. You stop behaving like an employee waiting for predictable paydays and start acting like the financial operator of your enterprise. You become the CFO, not just the creative. And as a CFO, you don't merely earn—you allocate, buffer, plan, and stabilise. This mindset shift is foundational. Financial power doesn't come from hustle; it comes from *habitual design*.

None of this requires elaborate spreadsheets or complex software. You can start with a notebook and a weekly calendar reminder. You can evolve into automation when you're ready. The point is consistency, not sophistication. The freelancer who moves £150 methodically every Friday is doing more to stabilise their business than one who earns £5,000 in a burst and spends three weeks deciding what to do with it.

Money routing is not a hack. It is *infrastructure disguised as habit*. It is the moment when freelancers stop reacting to income and start governing it. It is where clarity replaces improvisation, where stress is swapped for system, and where the invisible labour of financial decision-making is finally offloaded to structure. For the modern freelancer, this is not just a helpful tool—it is a strategic necessity. And the sooner it is installed, the sooner the real work of building, growing, and sustaining a viable creative business can begin.

Visualising Your System

Freelancers often speak of their finances in terms of balance: "I'm doing okay," "It's tight this month," "I had a good quarter." But these vague assessments typically emerge from emotional temperature checks rather than concrete financial awareness. The truth is that most self-employed professionals operate without any visual map of how their money moves. They track income through client invoices, expenses through a stack of receipts or a disjointed spreadsheet, and savings through occasional glances at their banking app. What they lack is a *system-wide view*—a visual representation of how money enters, moves through, and exits their financial ecosystem. Without this map, blind spots form. Bottlenecks are missed. Leaks persist. And planning becomes a series of hopeful guesses. The remedy is deceptively simple: *draw your system.*

Visualising your money system is not about producing a beautiful graphic. It is about *building a mental and literal model* of your financial architecture. It's how you step outside the monthly noise to see the full mechanics of how you manage, allocate, and protect your income. It allows you to spot inefficiencies that don't show up in your account balances—like cashflow clogs, mismatched timing between income and bills, or expenses that exceed your operational margin. And it gives you the diagnostic precision of a CFO, not just the survival instincts of a freelancer.

At its core, a visual money map answers four questions: Where does money come in? Where does it go first? How is it distributed? And how do I access it? Each of these layers reveals potential risks and design flaws when left implicit. Consider a freelancer who receives £4,000 in client work across three projects. That money lands in their current account, where it mingles with personal spending, grocery purchases, and a pending tax payment. Without separation or structure, it's nearly impossible to answer even basic questions like, "How much of this is profit?" or "Can I afford to upgrade my software next month?"

Now imagine that same freelancer sketches a simple flowchart. At the top, income sources: clients A, B, and C. Then, a central holding account. From there, visual lines split into three or four purpose-built accounts: tax savings (30%), operating expenses (20%), personal pay (50%), and perhaps a long-term savings buffer (optional). Suddenly, the map *shows* what the numbers alone could not: where friction arises, where overdraw risks lurk, and whether the system is balanced or overloaded. This view is more than informative—it is transformative. *You cannot optimise what you cannot see.*

The process of visualising also uncovers *dependencies*. For example, if 80% of your freelance income consistently comes from one client, the risk concentration becomes stark on the page—even if it feels manageable in practice. Or if your operational expenses account runs dry before your monthly software subscriptions hit, the visual trail will reveal the mismatch in timing that causes recurring shortfalls. Seeing your financial flows spatially reveals not only amounts, but *sequences*—the order in which money moves, and the delays, dead ends, or unnecessary loops that silently undermine your stability.

There is also behavioural power in visibility. Abstract systems fade from memory; visual ones stay salient. When freelancers build and reference a money map—even if hand-drawn or low-tech—it creates a psychological cue for accountability. They are less likely to ignore tax set-asides or delay income routing when they see the system as a living structure. The act of drawing is not decorative. It is *functional cognition*. In behavioural terms, it converts complexity into comprehension. You stop treating your finances as a foggy dashboard and start operating from a blueprint.

Modern tools can support this effort, but they are not required. Some freelancers create clean diagrams in Notion, Miro, or Figma. Others use whiteboards or sticky notes. A surprisingly effective method is pen and paper—especially when revised monthly. What matters is *not* the aesthetic, but the logic. The goal is a visual representation that tracks your unique flow: what's coming in, what's being withheld, what's being used to run your business, and what's available for personal life. Annotate percentages. Mark recurring dates. Highlight transfers. Add notes where you spot bottlenecks.

For example, a designer in Manchester builds a visual flow with her three client accounts at the top, feeding into her holding account. Below that, she maps transfers: 35% to tax, 20% to operations, 5% to an emergency buffer, and the remainder to personal pay. Then she annotates typical outflows: software, contractor fees, student loan repayments, rent. The act of mapping reveals something she hadn't seen before—her buffer is growing slower than expected because she pays herself before setting it aside. She adjusts the sequence. Instead of waiting until the end of the month, she routes her income buffer *first*, then pays herself what remains. The change is subtle. The impact is profound.

This system also aids communication. For freelancers who work with partners, accountants, or even virtual assistants, a visual map becomes a shared reference. It allows others to understand your financial priorities and constraints without trawling through spreadsheets. It creates alignment. It reduces misunderstandings. And when circumstances change—a new client, an expense spike, a tax shift—the map can be updated in minutes, ensuring everyone stays on the same page.

More strategically, a visual system supports *scenario planning*. You can draft alternate versions: What happens if I raise my rates? What if I lose a client? What if I take on a recurring retainer? By adjusting flows and allocations on your map, you simulate the financial implications of choices before making them. This elevates your decision-making from reactive to proactive. You begin managing your business like a strategist, not just a service provider. You stop chasing clarity in the rear-view mirror and start driving with foresight.

Importantly, visualising your system isn't a one-time task. Like any map, it must reflect changing terrain. Your income streams will shift. Your expenses will evolve. Your priorities will mature. Revisiting your system quarterly, or at key inflection points—new client wins, large purchases, tax recalculations—keeps your understanding sharp. Over time, this ritual becomes as essential as invoicing or budgeting. It becomes the meeting you have *with yourself* to assess your financial architecture and refine its design.

For freelancers juggling creativity with commercial reality, this practice is liberating. It externalises what would otherwise remain a swirl of assumptions, memories, and approximations. It gives shape to what matters most: the movement, timing, and structure of your financial life. It doesn't require perfection, but it does demand attention. And in return, it offers something rare in self-employment—*financial visibility that you can act on, trust in, and grow from.*

Chapter 5
Taxes Are Not Optional

Taxes occupy a peculiar space in the freelance mindset—omnipresent yet often ignored, understood more in theory than in practice. They lurk in the background as work gets done, clients pay, and projects conclude, quietly accumulating. For many self-employed professionals, tax planning feels like a distant, abstract threat, something to defer or hope resolves itself. Yet it rarely does. Avoidance carries a cost that goes beyond money: cognitive strain, emotional tension, and operational friction all mount, eroding confidence and clouding decision-making.

The impulse to sidestep taxes is hardly a character flaw. It is, in fact, a rational response to an inherently taxing system. Unlike salaried employees whose deductions are automatic, freelancers must calculate, report, and remit taxes themselves—often juggling multiple income streams, currencies, and jurisdictions. Anticipating obligations months in advance, tracking deductions without guidance, and navigating forms designed for institutional proficiency is a formidable cognitive load. It is little wonder taxes become a blind spot—tolerated until they impose real consequences.

At the root lies a structural mismatch: freelance tax responsibility is built for compliance, not comprehension. Government systems assume steady paycheques, uniform benefits, and automatic withholding. Freelancers operate in the opposite reality: sporadic income, diverse clients, and unpredictable timing. They must engineer withholding mechanisms, maintain audit trails, and build buffers—all without institutional scaffolding. The freelancer effectively becomes their own tax authority, often before fully recognising their enterprise as a business.

This mismatch triggers predictable behavioural patterns. Psychologically, taxes engage loss aversion, temporal discounting, and learned helplessness. Parting with money feels painful; future obligations seem abstract and remote; the complexity of the system encourages avoidance. Together, these tendencies spiral, creating a scenario where the freelancer earns more while simultaneously falling behind on obligations. Busyness masks risk, but a clock is always ticking.

The consequences extend beyond psychology. Operationally, failing to manage taxes distorts understanding of real earnings. Freelancers overestimate disposable income, underprice services, and make spending decisions based on gross revenue rather than post-tax reality. Deferred tax obligations creep into every financial choice, often unnoticed until the cost becomes unavoidable.

Countering this requires both structural and psychological shifts. First, taxes must be reframed—not as a threat, but as a recurring allocation of income. Like rent or software subscriptions, they are a standing cost of business. Set aside a portion of each invoice as it arrives. Precision is secondary to consistency. Habit matters more than exact percentages; a rule-of-thumb approach—say 25–35%, depending on circumstances—is far superior to improvisation.

Second, adopt quarterly thinking. Many jurisdictions require estimated tax payments every three months. While this surprises newcomers, it aligns with income cycles, promotes cashflow realism, and creates structured points of reflection. Quarterly payments are not inconveniences—they are tools, offering periodic clarity, a checkpoint to review income, adjust buffers, and manage volatility.

Third, track deductible expenses diligently. Home office costs, software, travel, equipment, professional development, and insurance can reduce taxable income, but only if recorded. Deductions are not loopholes; they reflect the real cost of running a business. Simple systems—one dedicated card, weekly 15-minute receipt reviews, a spreadsheet or app—are sufficient. The goal is functional visibility, not forensic accounting.

Underlying all this is a mindset shift: taxes are not punishment, but a signal of value creation. Avoidance destabilises; engagement stabilises. Successful freelancers, whether operating consultancies, digital agencies, or intellectual property ventures, manage taxes actively. Outsourcing execution is common; abdicating responsibility is not. Mastery begins with ownership.

This chapter does not offer a technical manual. It reframes tax avoidance emotionally, and supplies practical, non-jargon strategies. It outlines allocation models, decodes quarterly payments, demystifies deductions, and positions clarity as cheaper than avoidance. A durable freelance business cannot outsource its tax relationship entirely. Hiring experts is possible, but mindset, planning, and discipline begin with the freelancer.

When taxes are integrated from the outset, confidence grows, margins sharpen, and decision-making shifts from reaction to intention. Taxes are unavoidable. But so is the professional identity you are building. Treating tax as part of the business—rather than a hurdle—represents one of the most high-leverage moves a freelancer can make. It begins, as all powerful changes do, with perspective: clarity leads, systems follow.

Why Taxes Feel So Overwhelming

The tax obligations of freelancers do not rise and fall according to the intensity of the work they perform. They accumulate quietly, consistently, and impersonally—indifferent to how inspired or busy the professional feels. And yet for so many in the self-employed world, taxes are the single most persistently deferred aspect of their financial life. They know they should be setting money aside. They've heard stories of painful back-tax bills and penalties. And still, invoices are sent, money arrives, expenses are paid—and tax planning remains suspended in a haze of uncertainty and avoidance. The question is not whether freelancers understand the importance of taxes. It is why they find the task so psychologically and behaviourally difficult to engage with in the first place.

Unlike salaried employees, who experience taxation through passive deduction—where national insurance contributions, pension payments, and income taxes are siphoned from their pay before it even reaches them—freelancers are confronted with the full, untaxed volume of their earnings upfront. This apparent windfall is misleading. It presents a figure that feels like ownership when it is, in truth, only partial entitlement. The psychological impact of this is significant. Behavioural economists have long noted the phenomenon of *mental accounting*—our tendency to treat money differently depending on its perceived source, label, or timing. Freelancers are prone to treat incoming revenue as "theirs," even when a substantial portion belongs to the state. Without institutional withholding, the responsibility to subtract future obligations rests entirely with the individual's foresight and discipline—an invisible cognitive tax on top of the actual financial one.

But the challenge goes deeper than poor maths or disorganisation. At its root, the aversion to tax planning stems from a potent mix of behavioural tendencies that reinforce one another in subtle, persistent ways.

Start with *loss aversion*. Studies in behavioural science consistently show that humans experience the pain of loss more intensely than the pleasure of gain—often by a factor of two. For freelancers, setting aside money for taxes doesn't feel like prudent budgeting; it feels like taking money *away* from themselves. There's no immediate reward. The sacrifice feels real, while the benefit—avoiding penalties months later—is abstract and emotionally distant. With every invoice paid, the temptation is to delay the subtraction "just until things stabilise," even when history shows that the moment of stability never quite arrives.

Then there is *temporal discounting*, our tendency to undervalue future outcomes relative to present ones. A freelancer might intend to save for tax "after I pay off this bill" or "when I get through this client project," treating the tax obligation as something that can wait—despite knowing, rationally, that waiting compounds the difficulty. The tax deadline feels distant, intangible, and unthreatening compared to more immediate pressures: rent, equipment upgrades, marketing, or just the relief of finally being paid. The future is discounted. The present wins.

This delay often breeds a third response: *denial by complexity*. Tax systems are notoriously opaque. Terminology varies across jurisdictions. Filing requirements shift depending on income thresholds, industry category, and even local tax laws. Freelancers face forms that ask questions they don't understand, calculations based on fluctuating variables, and inconsistent advice across accounting software, online forums, and peers. When faced with that kind of ambiguity, avoidance becomes not only tempting but cognitively efficient. If a task is too hard to define, it is pushed down the priority list—even when the stakes are high.

At this point, *learned helplessness* can emerge. The term, originating in psychological experiments, describes a state in which repeated exposure to difficult or incomprehensible situations leads individuals to disengage entirely. Many freelancers report feeling that they are "bad with money" or "not the kind of person who can figure out taxes." They internalise failure as identity. Instead of seeking better systems or clearer guidance, they resign themselves to being overwhelmed, hoping each year that their tax bill won't be too bad and treating every payment to the tax authority as a kind of inevitable punishment rather than a manageable cost of doing business.

There is also a socio-cultural element to this pattern. Freelancing is often sold—especially in digital and creative economies—as a lifestyle of freedom. The imagery is one of laptops by the beach, late-morning starts, and projects that align with personal values. Tax compliance sits awkwardly within that narrative. It feels bureaucratic, antithetical to autonomy, and laden with drudgery. This cultural mismatch breeds a kind of soft rebellion: freelancers do not actively defy the tax system, but they delay engaging with it as a way of preserving the illusion of creative sovereignty. They do not want to feel like a cog in someone else's machine. Yet in the process, they overlook the fact that *true autonomy includes fiscal self-leadership*.

These forces—loss aversion, temporal discounting, complexity-induced denial, and identity-based avoidance—do not operate in isolation. They reinforce each other. A single late payment turns into a habit of under-saving. A confusing government website creates the belief that taxes are inherently unknowable. A single painful experience with a large year-end bill becomes proof that tax planning is futile or best avoided. And perhaps most dangerously, the absence of immediate negative feedback allows the avoidance to persist. Unlike bounced cheques or client complaints, tax penalties are often delayed. That delay gives the illusion that everything is fine—until it very much isn't.

It is worth noting that this psychological burden is compounded by the *structure* of self-employment. Freelancers do not only need to estimate their income taxes; they often need to track and report VAT or sales tax, account for business expenses, plan for national insurance contributions, and meet quarterly payment deadlines. There are no payroll departments, no automatic alerts, no built-in compliance systems. Each layer of responsibility adds friction. Each decision introduces uncertainty. And without a coherent framework, even the most conscientious freelancer can become paralysed.

Yet the solution is not to become a tax expert. It is to *reduce friction*. To treat tax planning not as a project to be tackled once a year, but as a behaviour embedded in every financial action. The first shift is mental: to stop seeing tax withholding as a loss and begin treating it as a reallocation. It is not your money disappearing. It is your business acknowledging its obligations. That mental shift alone creates space for more rational planning.

Next comes structural alignment. Every payment received should trigger a pre-set action: a percentage allocated to a separate tax account, untouched until needed. This allocation should be based on real historical data—your average annual tax rate, adjusted for deductions—not on wishful estimates. The smoother and more automatic this process becomes, the less it demands attention, and the more reliably it protects your business from shocks.

Finally, freelancers must normalise periodic review. Taxes should not be addressed once a year in a haze of panic. They should be reviewed quarterly, at minimum—ideally as part of a broader financial rhythm that includes income audits, expense reviews, and buffer checks. Even five minutes a week, spent confirming that allocations are on track, is a more effective safeguard than two days of frantic document gathering in January.

When seen clearly, the feeling of being overwhelmed by taxes is not a failure of intelligence or work ethic. It is the predictable outcome of a system that places a high administrative burden on individuals without giving them the tools, training, or psychological framing to succeed. But it can be reversed. Through behavioural design, structural clarity, and a reframed understanding of tax as a tool for sustainability rather than punishment, freelancers can reclaim not just financial control, but mental space.

Mastery over taxes doesn't mean enjoying them. It means making them part of the architecture of a functional freelance business—predictable, accounted for, and never again left to chance. When that shift happens, a remarkable transformation occurs: anxiety becomes clarity, avoidance becomes rhythm, and taxes lose their emotional charge. What remains is simply a system—one you run, not one that runs you.

How Much to Set Aside—Really

Ask ten freelancers how much they set aside for taxes, and you're likely to get ten different answers—some guess, others hope, a few simply shrug. Behind this variance is not just a lack of information, but a lack of system. Unlike salaried employees, who have their tax obligations automatically deducted and calculated by employers, the self-employed must reverse-engineer their obligations from irregular income, imperfect projections, and a patchwork of shifting guidance. The result is a chronic pattern of under-saving, over-guessing, and miscalculation that turns a predictable obligation into an annual crisis.

What freelancers need is not a perfect answer, but a consistent rule—one grounded in sound logic, adaptable to context, and easy to apply. The question is not what the tax code requires down to the decimal point. It is what percentage of gross income a self-employed person should withhold immediately to stay ahead of tax obligations across a typical fiscal year. *Precision is the enemy of consistency when the goal is habit formation.* In this context, a clear, country-agnostic baseline is more helpful than endless case-by-case specificity.

The starting point is understanding what the withheld tax actually needs to cover. At minimum, it includes income tax. In most countries, this is progressive, meaning it increases with income. For freelancers, there's also often a second layer: self-employment tax, covering pension contributions, social security equivalents, or national insurance. In some cases, there may also be regional levies, VAT, or goods and services tax obligations. The relevant percentage, therefore, must account for *more than just basic income tax rates.* It needs to reflect the full stack of obligations the freelancer is expected to pay out-of-pocket, without employer mediation.

A reasonable, default rule of thumb for freelancers earning a modest to mid-level income across developed economies is to set aside **30% of gross income**. This figure is not arbitrary. It approximates the combined effect of a 20–25% income tax rate (after personal allowances and deductions) plus 5–10% in national insurance or self-employment levies. It errs on the side of caution without being punitive. It accommodates minor fluctuations in income while providing a reliable baseline that most freelancers can implement without needing to consult a tax calculator every week.

For higher earners—especially those consistently earning into the top tax brackets in their country—the figure should rise proportionately. In the UK, for example, freelancers earning above the basic rate threshold face a 40% income tax plus 2% National Insurance, which brings the total tax burden closer to

42%. In such cases, setting aside **40–45%** of gross income is prudent. In the United States, self-employment tax alone accounts for approximately 15.3%, with federal income tax layered on top. Again, the 30–35% range becomes the realistic floor, not the ceiling.

For freelancers with volatile income—whose earnings spike dramatically in one quarter and fall in the next—percentage-based saving is the only method that scales with reality. If a freelancer earns £3,000 in one month and £9,000 the next, withholding 30% each time ensures that their tax buffer grows proportionately with their actual obligations. Trying to set aside a flat amount (e.g., "£500 a month") fails as soon as income deviates from the average. Percentages move with the business. They align saving with earnings in real time.

Some resist this approach because 30% feels like a large cut. But that perception is a function of flawed mental accounting. If a freelancer earns £5,000, sets aside £1,500, and uses the remaining £3,500 for expenses and salary, they are not "losing" money. They are pre-allocating what already belongs elsewhere. The 30% was never truly theirs. It was held temporarily, pending remittance to the government. Refusing to accept that is what leads to year-end panic and tax debt. *Clarity does not reduce your wealth—it reveals what part of it is usable.*

There are, of course, nuanced variations depending on jurisdiction. In countries with generous allowances and low self-employment levies—such as certain Nordic or Eastern European nations—the effective tax burden on modest freelance income may be closer to 20–25%. In such cases, setting aside a conservative 25% might suffice. In countries where VAT registration is mandatory above certain income thresholds, the tax set-aside should also include *collected VAT that must be paid later*—even though it isn't technically income. This is another reason why freelancers must distinguish between cash flow and taxable profit. What you collect is not what you keep.

The percentage rule becomes more accurate when applied to *net profit*, not gross revenue. But here lies a problem: most freelancers don't track business expenses with enough rigour to calculate net profit in real time. They know how much came in, but not exactly how much went out. In this context, calculating tax set-aside from *gross income* is safer. It simplifies the decision and builds a financial buffer. Later, at filing time, any over-saving can be redirected—towards emergency funds, retirement accounts, or investment. *Over-saving is recoverable. Under-saving is costly.*

To operationalise this habit, the most effective freelancers automate it. As soon as a client payment lands, 30% is moved—immediately and non-negotiably—into a separate, dedicated tax account. This account should not be connected to their daily spending card. It should be psychologically and practically separated. This physical separation reinforces cognitive discipline: the money is not seen, not touched, not part of the spending equation. It is ring-fenced for obligation. It removes willpower from the system.

It is also worth building periodic adjustments into the rhythm. Every quarter—or with each major income milestone—the freelancer should review their actual earnings against tax thresholds and confirm whether the 30% rate is still appropriate. This process does not need to be technical. Even a five-minute check against local income tax bands can reveal whether an increase in set-aside percentage is needed. If income has grown substantially, raising the withholding rate from 30% to 35% mid-year can prevent shortfalls and absorb unexpected tax liabilities without drama.

For freelancers working across borders, additional complexity arises. Currency fluctuations, multiple tax residencies, and bilateral tax treaties can blur the true picture. In these cases, the 30% rule becomes a *baseline*, not a ceiling. With foreign-source income, tax may be owed both locally and abroad—especially in countries without clear exemptions or residency rules. In such cases, freelancers should consult an accountant experienced in international taxation *but still apply percentage-based withholding* as a default. It's better to have too much set aside than too little in a system where the rules are ambiguous and enforcement is strict.

For newer freelancers, there's also a risk of over-committing. Someone earning £1,200 in their first month may feel that withholding 30% leaves them unable to cover essentials. In these early stages, the freelancer must balance survival with compliance. The key is *proportionality with awareness*: even if 30% isn't feasible in month one, setting aside 10–15% is still vastly better than zero. The goal is to build the habit before the stakes increase. As income stabilises, the percentage can scale. What matters is that the system is established early, so discipline grows alongside revenue.

Ultimately, the question of how much to set aside is not just technical. It is philosophical. It asks whether the freelancer sees themselves as the steward of their finances or the passenger. Withholding 30% is not just about avoiding penalties. It is about affirming a mindset of proactive leadership. It is a quiet act of financial maturity—one that says, "I acknowledge what is mine and what is not. I plan accordingly. I build resilience, not react to crisis."

And that's the true value of this rule—not its arithmetic accuracy, but its behavioural power. It turns tax from a once-a-year stressor into a monthly ritual of stewardship. It replaces doubt with discipline. It reduces surprise. And it gives the freelancer what every business owner needs: the clarity to make decisions based not on guesses, but on what's already accounted for.

Set aside 30%. Adjust as needed. Make it automatic. Treat it as non-negotiable. And when the tax bill comes due, you'll have something rare in the freelance world—peace of mind backed by preparation.

Quarterly Taxes and How to Survive Them

For many freelancers, tax season doesn't come once a year—it arrives four times. While salaried workers are generally required to file a single annual return, self-employed professionals in most jurisdictions are legally obliged to submit *estimated* tax payments at regular intervals throughout the year. These are not optional gestures of good citizenship; they are mandated components of the tax system. And yet, few freelancers fully understand their purpose, fewer still follow them consistently, and almost none treat them with the strategic discipline they deserve. Quarterly taxes, when mishandled, become the source of penalties, stress, and surprise. But when approached with clarity, structure, and foresight, they become just another part of running a well-managed independent business.

The rationale behind quarterly estimated taxes is straightforward. Governments want a steady flow of revenue, not one large annual payout. Salaried employees provide this through employer withholding; taxes are deducted at source and remitted throughout the year. But freelancers and other self-employed individuals earn untaxed income—fees, project payments, consulting retainers, online sales—none of which has tax removed at the point of origin. If left unchecked, this could mean a single lump-sum tax payment due at the end of the fiscal year, placing pressure on both government cash flows and individual ability to pay. To mitigate this, tax authorities in the UK, US, Canada, Australia, and many other nations require self-employed individuals to *approximate* their annual tax liability and pay a portion of it every quarter.

These estimated payments are not based on wishful thinking or personal preference. They are grounded in prior-year earnings or projected current-year income, depending on the taxpayer's circumstances. In the UK, for example, HMRC does not formally operate a quarterly estimated tax payment system for income tax, but freelancers must pay two *payments on account*—each worth 50% of the previous year's bill—in January and July. In the United States, the IRS mandates quarterly estimated payments in April, June, September, and January for freelancers who expect to owe more than $1,000 in tax for the year. The exact mechanics vary by jurisdiction, but the logic is consistent: governments expect ongoing, in-year tax contributions from those not covered by payroll systems.

The difficulty for freelancers lies not in the principle, but in the execution. Estimating income across a twelve-month period in a volatile, irregular business is inherently difficult. Many self-employed professionals experience income that spikes in one quarter and crashes in the next. Projects are delayed, invoices paid late, contracts fall through, or unexpectedly large gigs arrive with little warning. Against this backdrop, projecting annual income in January—or even July—feels speculative at best, irresponsible at worst.

This discomfort with forecasting leads many freelancers to avoid estimated payments altogether, hoping they can sort it all out at year's end. The consequences are both financial and psychological. Governments often impose penalties and interest for underpayment or lateness. More insidiously, avoiding quarterly payments creates a false sense of financial health. Freelancers spend money that should have been withheld, gradually digging a hole that becomes inescapable by December. Tax planning becomes tax damage control.

The solution is to reverse the logic: instead of estimating the total tax due and dividing it into four equal parts, freelancers should *withhold a fixed percentage from each payment as it arrives*, transferring it into a separate tax savings account. This buffer then becomes the source from which quarterly payments are drawn. This approach has three major benefits. First, it aligns with income as earned, not as predicted. Second, it smooths psychological volatility—no one enjoys finding out they owe £4,000 in a single month. Third, it separates the *decision* to save from the *act* of paying—removing friction at the moment of payment because the money is already ring-fenced.

Determining the right percentage to withhold depends on jurisdiction and income level, as discussed earlier. In most cases, 25–35% of gross income is a reasonable range. The key is consistency. The habit of withholding matters more than the precision of the estimate. Errors can be corrected; habits, once built, become resilient.

Quarterly taxes, then, become a matter of timing. Instead of treating April, July, and so on as calendar surprises, they should be scheduled into the freelancer's financial system—marked clearly on both fiscal and personal calendars, planned for in advance, and executed with the same regularity as paying rent or sending invoices. Some freelancers use calendar alerts, automated banking transfers, or even standing orders to ensure these dates are never missed. Others appoint a recurring "money day" at the start of each quarter to review their income, calculate upcoming obligations, and prepare filings. The point is not the method, but the *rhythm*. Freelancers must turn tax payment into a quarterly ritual—unemotional, unambiguous, and automatic.

Technology can assist, but only when paired with awareness. Accounting software such as Xero, FreeAgent, QuickBooks, or Wave can estimate quarterly obligations, generate reminders, and track running liabilities. But software cannot replace discipline. A system is only as useful as the behaviour it supports. Some freelancers find it helpful to maintain a simple spreadsheet, listing each client payment, the amount withheld, and the balance of the tax savings account. This visual map builds confidence that when the tax bill arrives—whether in July or January—it will be matched by an equally solid reserve.

It's also important to acknowledge the emotional aspect of quarterly taxes. They feel punitive, not just because they're frequent, but because they often occur during leaner parts of the year. January and July—two common estimated tax deadlines—fall immediately after or during periods of high personal expenditure: the holidays, summer holidays, family obligations. Without a tax buffer, these payments feel like attacks on joy. But when the buffer is in place, the experience transforms. Taxes become a line item, not a crisis.

To fully survive—and eventually thrive—under a quarterly tax system, freelancers must shift from reactive to anticipatory thinking. This shift is both tactical and philosophical. It involves recognising that the government is not imposing an arbitrary demand four times a year; it is simply asking the freelancer to keep pace with their actual earnings. The real challenge is not the quarterly schedule, but the freelancer's willingness to build a financial infrastructure that accounts for it.

This infrastructure includes:

- A separate tax savings account (mandatory, not optional)

- Automated or habitual withholding from every client payment

- A master calendar with quarterly due dates clearly marked

- A buffer policy that ensures the tax account is never fully drained

- A quarterly review ritual, aligned with broader business planning

By embedding these components into the freelance workflow, quarterly tax payments cease to be exceptional. They become mundane. That mundanity is the goal. For freelancers, financial anxiety is rarely driven by size of expense alone—it's driven by surprise. Removing the surprise removes most of the suffering.

Finally, it helps to zoom out. Quarterly taxes are not merely a compliance burden; they are a sign of a business that is operating with maturity. Paying taxes means you are earning. It means you have obligations because you are part of a functioning professional system. While many dread tax payments, the most successful freelancers learn to view them with quiet pride. They signal participation in a larger economy. They mark the transition from hobbyist to professional. They are not just a cost—they are a consequence of growth.

Mastering quarterly taxes doesn't require perfection. It requires predictability. It requires systematisation. And above all, it requires a mindset that sees taxation not as an affliction, but as a managerial function—something the modern freelancer does not avoid, but executes, with clarity and control.

Track to Deduct

A surprising number of freelancers overpay their taxes each year—not because they earn too much, but because they track too little. In a landscape where margins are already tight, overlooking legitimate business deductions is not just an accounting oversight—it is a structural leak in the financial foundation of self-employment. The reason isn't laziness or negligence; it is that the traditional systems designed for tax compliance assume stable employment, employer-managed reporting, and passive participation. Freelancers exist outside that structure. They must design and manage their own systems of accountability, which includes not just earning money but knowing precisely how it was spent—and what portion of that spending can be reclaimed through deduction.

Every pound not deducted is a pound taxed as profit. It's that stark. Yet the mental fog surrounding tax deductions persists, particularly among creative professionals and gig workers who conflate personal and business finances or dismiss small expenses as unworthy of attention. Over time, these missed opportunities compound into serious financial inefficiency. A £20 software subscription left unclaimed each month is £240 in annual expenses that could have reduced taxable income. Add a forgotten co-working membership, a phone plan used for client calls, that hardware upgrade you paid out of pocket—and suddenly thousands of pounds or dollars have passed silently through your accounts without performing their most basic fiscal function: reducing your tax liability.

Understanding deductions begins with reframing them. They are not loopholes, tricks, or ways to 'game the system.' They are foundational to tax law, recognising that business activity requires investment. The freelancer is, by definition, a business entity—even if it is a one-person operation. If money is spent wholly and exclusively for the purpose of producing income, most jurisdictions allow it to be deducted from that income before taxes are applied. This is not generosity; it is structural fairness.

So what are freelancers actually allowed to deduct? The specific rules vary slightly across countries, but there is remarkable overlap in the core categories. And yet, time and again, these common expenses go untracked, unfiled, or misunderstood.

The Home Office Mirage

Perhaps the most commonly misunderstood deduction is the home office. In the age of remote work, more freelancers are working from kitchens, bedrooms, and spare corners than ever before. Yet many fail to claim even the most basic portion of their housing expenses. The reason is typically psychological: "It's not a real office," or "It's just part of my home." But tax authorities don't require glamour—they require *consistency*. If there is a defined area in your home used regularly and exclusively for work, you may be able to deduct a portion of your rent or mortgage interest, utilities, council tax, and maintenance. In the UK, a simplified flat-rate method exists for those who work from home regularly. In the US, there are specific square-footage formulas. These rules differ, but the principle is stable: if your home facilitates your income, part of it can reduce your tax bill.

Software, Subscriptions, and Cloud Services

The digital infrastructure that supports freelance work is almost always deductible. This includes project management tools (Asana, Trello), time trackers (Toggl, Harvest), invoicing software (QuickBooks, FreeAgent), cloud storage (Dropbox, Google Drive), and design tools (Adobe Creative Cloud, Canva Pro). Even the cost of domain registration, hosting fees, and website builders like Squarespace or Wix can qualify. These recurring costs are often small individually, which makes them easy to overlook. But when aggregated, they form a sizable annual expense—and more importantly, they reflect the true cost of operating a modern freelance business.

Mobile and Internet Use

If your mobile phone or internet connection is used partly for business, then that proportion of the bill is usually deductible. Few freelancers use their phone exclusively for work, so a reasonable percentage—based on actual call logs, data use, or business hours—is appropriate. Internet use can be similarly apportioned. What matters is that the claim is defensible. Freelancers often default to zero, fearing scrutiny. But claiming *nothing* when *something* is legitimate is not prudence—it is financial self-sabotage.

Professional Development and Education

Courses, workshops, books, and certifications related directly to your field may be deductible. This includes online masterclasses, technical training, or even industry publications if they directly enhance your income-producing ability. A graphic designer subscribing to *Creative Review* or a copywriter enrolling in a course on persuasive writing is making a professional investment. What disqualifies a deduction is its personal enrichment value. A meditation retreat may help with stress, but unless you're a mindfulness coach, it's unlikely to qualify.

Travel and Meals—With Boundaries

Client meetings, industry conferences, or travel related to work are generally deductible. However, personal travel, even when loosely justified by business benefits, is not. Meals with clients may be partially deductible, depending on your country's rules, but daily lunches at your desk are not. This is where freelancers must apply both logic and documentation. If you travel to a conference, keep the itinerary. If you meet a client over lunch, note the purpose. Without records, legitimate deductions are easily lost.

Health Insurance and Retirement Contributions

In some jurisdictions, self-employed individuals can deduct health insurance premiums or contributions to retirement accounts. In the US, this includes SEPs and solo 401(k)s. In the UK, pension contributions receive tax relief. These are powerful deductions that not only reduce tax liability but simultaneously improve financial security. They are often missed because they are viewed as 'personal' expenses. But when structured correctly, they are strategic, tax-advantaged business decisions.

So how does one *actually* track all of this? The answer is not found in complexity but in continuity. A simple, repeatable method—however imperfect—is better than a sophisticated system that is abandoned in three weeks. There are three levels of tracking systems, each suited to different temperaments:

1. **Manual logging**: Maintain a dedicated spreadsheet (e.g., Excel or Google Sheets) where each business expense is entered weekly or monthly. Categorise by type: software, utilities, travel, etc. Keep digital or physical receipts in corresponding folders.
2. **Semi-automated tracking**: Use apps like QuickBooks Self-Employed, Wave, or FreeAgent that link to your business bank account and categorise expenses as they appear. You still need to review and approve these categories, but the grunt work is handled.
3. **Fully delegated**: Work with a bookkeeper or accountant who manages expense classification, reconciliation, and audit-readiness. This option is ideal for those with higher incomes or less time. But even here, *you* must supply clear records and receipts.

Whatever method is chosen, the foundational habit is identical: *store evidence at the point of purchase.* Email receipts, scanned invoices, card notifications—these must be forwarded, saved, or flagged in the moment. Delay is the enemy of documentation. The goal is not perfection but audit-readiness: could you explain each deduction with supporting material if asked?

It's also essential to create separation between personal and business accounts. When all expenses pass through a single current account or credit card, the line between deductible and non-deductible becomes irretrievably blurred. A dedicated business account, even for sole traders, improves clarity, facilitates reporting, and reduces the mental load of combing through ambiguous transactions.

What's at stake here is not merely the size of your tax bill. It is the *accuracy* with which you understand your business's financial reality. Deductions reflect not only what you spent, but how you invested in your own professional capacity. By tracking them, you're not only reducing your tax burden—you're sharpening your visibility into what your freelance business truly costs to run, and what it takes to sustain it over time.

Ultimately, deductions are not gifts from the tax code. They are acknowledgements—of labour, investment, risk, and cost. To claim them properly is not only legal and logical, but an act of self-respect. The disciplined freelancer tracks to deduct not out of fear, but out of ownership. They know where their money goes. And they make it count twice: once when spent, again when claimed.

Chapter 6
The Paycheck You Have to Build

Ask a salaried employee when their next paycheque is due, and you will likely get a precise answer—day, hour, perhaps even amount. Pose the same question to a freelancer, and you encounter a mix of hope, estimation, and vague projection. This is not a trivial difference. It highlights the inherent instability of the freelance financial ecosystem: income arrives unpredictably, decisions are often reactive, and self-worth becomes entwined with the shifting tides of a bank balance. Unlike employees, freelancers do not receive a salary; they must construct one deliberately, methodically, and with intention.

This chapter centres on that construction. It begins with a deceptively simple proposition: you can—and should—pay yourself a regular salary, even if your income is irregular. This is more than organisational convenience; it is a psychological and financial discipline that underpins stability. In a world defined by fluctuating invoices, unpredictable client timelines, and market uncertainty, crafting your own paycheque asserts control while laying the groundwork for long-term sustainability. The question shifts from "Did I earn enough this week?" to "How can I smooth what I earn into something dependable?"

The principle is not new. Small business owners have long distinguished between revenue and personal compensation. Yet many freelancers, particularly early in their careers, fail to draw this line. Income flows in, bills are paid, spending continues, and whatever remains is treated as de facto earnings. This blurs professional and personal boundaries, conflating sustainable income with short-term survival.

Without a fixed framework, volatility dictates lifestyle, savings stall, and every financial choice becomes a reaction to the latest payment—or the lack thereof.

Breaking this cycle requires a mindset shift: think like the CFO of your own operation. The starting principle is age-old: pay yourself first. In freelancing, this requires nuance. It means deliberately setting aside a consistent monthly amount as your salary, regardless of whether revenue is robust or meagre. It decouples personal cash flow from the chaotic rhythm of client payments. Instead of reacting emotionally to feast-or-famine cycles, you create a buffer from which to draw—a mechanism that keeps both the business and you, as the employee, stable.

Establishing this "freelancer salary" is not guesswork. It is data-driven and safety-oriented. The aim is not to match a conventional wage or replicate a full-time benefits package. It is to define a sum that is reliably fundable, grounded in historical income and conservative assumptions. Many freelancers stumble here, overestimating in abundant months and underestimating in lean ones. Anchoring your salary in the lower average of your past six to twelve months' net income produces a resilient baseline.

At first, consistency matters more than size. Receiving the same amount each month—even if modest—enables meaningful budgeting, disciplined saving, and mental clarity. It reduces decision fatigue, the cognitive drain of frequent financial choices. Rather than asking, "Can I afford this?" you ask, "Does this fit within my salary?" Chaos gives way to boundaries.

This chapter also confronts a common fear: what if income is insufficient to fund a salary each month? The answer lies in the income buffer, covered previously, and rules for adjusting the salary temporarily. It may take months of restraint and over-earning to establish a reserve, but once it exists, it becomes the engine of your financial rhythm. Your salary no longer fluctuates with every invoice; it becomes a steady draw from a protected account, replenished in good months, safeguarded in lean ones.

The framework extends to strategic raises. In employment, raises arise from external recognition. In freelancing, they emerge through evidence-based recalibration. When income grows, recurring clients multiply, or rates increase sustainably over multiple quarters, your salary can rise accordingly. Raises are acknowledgements of trends, not reactions to short-term windfalls.

A crucial distinction remains: revenue is not salary. A £5,000 invoice does not translate into £5,000 in pay. Taxes, business expenses, buffers, and professional development must be accounted for. Paying yourself too much too soon undermines savings, reinvestment, and resilience. The chapter outlines a structured, repeatable method for determining a sustainable draw—one informed by reality, not aspiration.

The benefits are substantial. Freelancers adopting a salary model report lower anxiety, clearer decision-making, and more control over spending and saving. It diminishes the emotional rollercoaster of windfalls and droughts. Finance becomes infrastructure, separating identity from income: you are not your revenue; you are a professional earning consistently and responsibly.

In the chapters ahead, you will learn to calculate a baseline salary, manage an income buffer, and transition from reactive withdrawals to disciplined monthly transfers. Guidance covers lean months, timing raises, and forecasting adjustments across seasonal or project-driven income fluctuations.

By the end, you will no longer be waiting for a paycheque—you will be crafting one intentionally, intelligently, and systematically. Freelance life may lack an employer, but it need not lack a salary. You can create a steady, strategic income that honours both your ambition and your financial health. That is the paycheque you build.

Pay Yourself First—Literally

It is one of the most misapplied principles in the world of personal finance: *pay yourself first.* For traditional employees, the idea often refers to setting aside a portion of their fixed salary for savings before expenses claim it. But for freelancers, the concept demands a more radical interpretation. It is not merely about savings—it is about *invention.* Freelancers do not just need to save before they spend; they must construct a stable, deliberate salary from an unstable stream of income. To *pay yourself first* as a freelancer is not just a financial act—it is a declaration of autonomy, a mechanism of psychological resilience, and a method of managing complexity in an income model built for chaos.

The logic is straightforward: if no one is issuing you a paycheque, you must issue one to yourself. But few freelancers do. In practice, most treat each client payment as personal income—available to use, spend, or panic over. The result is a volatile financial experience defined by feast-or-famine behaviour, impulsive spending in strong months, and mounting anxiety during the inevitable lean stretches. This is not due to irresponsibility; it is the predictable outcome of operating without a defined system. When income is erratic, so too is one's ability to plan. When planning erodes, so does financial confidence. And over time, this lack of structure becomes not just a budgeting issue but an existential stressor—eroding motivation, limiting growth, and undermining the very independence freelancing was meant to offer.

The antidote begins with a question: *What would it look like if you paid yourself a monthly salary—consistently, on purpose, and irrespective of client fluctuations?* Not as an aspiration, but as a function of design. This is not a hypothetical exercise. Thousands of self-employed professionals have already implemented this approach with transformative results. It stabilises decision-making, improves savings behaviour, and dramatically reduces the mental burden of financial uncertainty. But to implement it well requires more than simply choosing a number and transferring it to your personal account. It requires strategy, discipline, and a redefinition of how you relate to the money you earn.

The first distinction is between *business income* and *personal income*. This seems obvious but is routinely blurred. Just because you were paid £3,500 for a consulting project does not mean you have £3,500 to spend. Taxes, overhead, software licences, and unpaid admin hours must be accounted for. Without a clear firewall between what your freelance business earns and what you—the individual—take home, you risk overspending, under-saving, and misjudging the health of your enterprise. Paying yourself first—literally—means establishing a regular transfer from your business account to your personal one. That transfer is your salary. Not the invoice total. Not the leftovers. A fixed, pre-defined amount that reflects sustainable income based on historical averages, not monthly emotion.

Many freelancers push back against this model, arguing that their income is too inconsistent to allow for a fixed salary. But that's precisely the point. A fixed salary is not a reflection of consistency—it is the *tool* that creates it. You smooth out the peaks and troughs by holding revenue in an income buffer and drawing from it at regular intervals. This transforms erratic cash flow into predictable personal cash flow. And predictability is what allows for structure—housing decisions, loan repayments, retirement contributions—all of which hinge on consistent outgoings, not variable invoices.

Building this system requires two key components: (1) a calculated baseline salary and (2) a reliable income buffer. The baseline is the monthly amount you can pay yourself *without depleting reserves*, drawn from a rolling average of your net income after taxes and expenses. It must be conservative enough to survive lean periods but sufficient enough to sustain your living costs. Most freelancers find that calculating this figure across a six- or twelve-month period reveals more stability than they expect—especially when low and high months are averaged out.

The buffer is what enables this drawdown model. It is the holding zone for incoming client payments—a separate account where money lands before being routed to tax, expenses, and ultimately, your salary. When the buffer is healthy, you pay yourself with confidence. When it dips, you scale back or pause the salary to preserve capital. But the key is that these decisions are based on a defined system, not reactive guesswork. You are no longer at the mercy of a late payment or a slow quarter. You have a financial runway, and you know precisely how long it will last.

Consider a graphic designer who earns between £2,000 and £6,000 per month across various clients. Rather than treating high months as windfalls and low months as crises, she builds a three-month buffer and sets her personal salary at £2,500 per month—reflecting her average earnings minus taxes and fixed business costs. Each month, regardless of earnings, she transfers £2,500 from her buffer to her personal account. When her income exceeds that threshold, the surplus remains in the buffer. When income dips below it, the buffer bridges the gap. She no longer rides the rollercoaster. She owns the controls.

This model does more than create financial stability—it reinforces professional identity. You are not a desperate contractor chasing the next invoice; you are a business owner who has built a predictable compensation model from unpredictable inputs. That psychological shift is profound. It allows for planning. It opens up the space to say no to misaligned projects. It encourages investment in training, rest, and marketing—all of which are critical to long-term success but impossible when you're living from payment to payment.

Yet none of this works without discipline. The temptation to "borrow" from the buffer for a discretionary purchase or inflate your salary after a big month is ever-present. That's why automating your transfers—weekly, biweekly, or monthly—is so critical. You do not want to rely on willpower each time a client payment hits your account. You want a standing instruction that protects you from your own optimism or fear. The automation is not just a time-saver; it is a behavioural safeguard. It ensures you act like a CFO, not a gambler.

Critically, your salary is not set in stone. It should evolve with your business—but always with restraint. A general rule is to consider a raise only after three consecutive months of higher-than-average income, and even then, increase modestly—by 10 to 15 per cent—while continuing to build the buffer. Raises should follow proof of trend, not a lucky quarter. Likewise, if your business contracts or if the buffer shrinks significantly, scale back your salary rather than running it on hope. This agility—paired with the foundational system—turns the salary model into a living framework, one that adapts without collapsing.

To freelance without a salary is to freelance without a structure. It is to reinvent the wheel with every invoice, to live reactively rather than strategically. The beauty of paying yourself first—literally—is that it brings order to uncertainty. It does not require you to guess the future. It requires you to design around the present. To look at what is known—your past earnings, your essential costs, your volatility patterns—and build a salary that respects reality without being ruled by it.

The result is not only a more stable financial life but a more sustainable creative one. You reclaim cognitive bandwidth. You regain confidence. You stop asking if this month's income will be "enough," and you start focusing on higher-order goals: improving your craft, serving better clients, designing better work-life boundaries. Because when you know you'll get paid—on time, by yourself—everything else starts to feel just a little more possible.

Why Monthly Transfers Beat Daily Panic

The psychological terrain of freelance work is not just shaped by what is earned but by *when* it is earned—and more precisely, when that income is allocated for actual use. Without a payroll department to impose structure, many freelancers fall into a dangerous trap: *reactive money handling*. They wait for income to hit their account, and then, often within hours or days, begin distributing it impulsively to bills, purchases, debts, or savings. The cycle repeats with every payment, and what appears to be an agile, real-time system quickly devolves into a pattern of chronic short-termism. Stress spikes, decision quality deteriorates, and long-term planning becomes not just difficult—but emotionally impossible.

This phenomenon is not a failure of willpower or education. It is a behavioural consequence of liquidity appearing and disappearing too rapidly. When every client payment feels like an urgent decision point, cognitive fatigue sets in. This is why *monthly transfers*—regular, structured, and deliberate—represent not merely a budgeting preference but a form of *psychological design*. They shift the financial experience from one of *chaotic immediacy* to one of *predictable cadence*.

Behavioural economists have long studied how humans cope with uncertainty. One of the most consistent findings is that *volatility in input leads to volatility in behaviour*. When income appears in unpredictable bursts, the brain perceives it as a scarce and unreliable resource. This triggers loss aversion, present bias, and short-term decision-making—all of which are documented cognitive distortions that make people more likely to overspend, undersave, or defer planning entirely. In salaried environments, this volatility is managed by the employer. But for freelancers, the burden shifts inward—and without intervention, the emotional toll can be severe.

Monthly transfers are not just about smoothing finances; they're about *smoothing cognition*. When income is routed into a holding account and transferred in predictable blocks—say, on the first of each month—the individual no longer experiences each client payment as a stressor. The question is no longer "Can I afford this today?" but rather, "What is my salary this month?" This framing activates a different part of the brain. It replaces reactive spending with scheduled planning. It installs a rhythm where before there was only noise.

The mechanics are simple but powerful. Instead of spending from every payment as it arrives, freelancers direct all revenue into an income buffer or holding account. From there, they create a scheduled transfer—ideally automated—into their personal spending account once per month. That transfer is their *personal salary*. The amount is not dictated by the most recent invoice, but by a calculated average of sustainable, historical income. The system absorbs the spikes and bridges the dips. And the freelancer regains mental control.

The value of this structure becomes especially clear in months of surplus. Without a defined transfer plan, freelancers experiencing a revenue spike often feel momentarily flush—leading to inflated discretionary spending, new software purchases, or upgraded gear that may not be essential. But when income is held and released in consistent increments, surplus becomes *buffer*, not temptation. It remains available for future planning rather than future regret. This shift is subtle, but powerful. It transforms the freelancer from a reactive actor into a steward of capital.

To understand the impact of batching income transfers, consider the contrast between a freelancer who receives ten payments in a month and transfers funds ad hoc, versus one who transfers a fixed salary on the first of the month. The first is engaging in ten micro-decisions—each one an opportunity for panic, error, or indulgence. The second makes *one* decision, pre-defined and automated. Over the course of a year, that difference multiplies into hundreds of avoided stress moments, improved financial clarity, and far more accurate forecasting.

Real-world examples validate this. A UK-based copywriter who transitioned from daily to monthly transfers reported a 40% reduction in discretionary spending within three months—without feeling deprived. Why? Because her mental relationship with money shifted from "what's in my account today" to "what's in my plan this month." Meanwhile, a freelance developer in Berlin built a three-month income buffer and paid himself a flat salary each month for a full year—even when his business income fluctuated between €3,000 and €9,000. The result was not just financial calm, but the ability to say no to low-margin work and focus on long-term client growth.

The benefits are not merely emotional or anecdotal. They are grounded in the core principles of behavioural design. When a system reduces the number of decisions required, it reduces cognitive load. When a financial plan is based on patterns rather than panic, it becomes scalable. And when money becomes predictable, so too does everything that depends on it—rent, savings, insurance, planning, rest.

Critically, this model also protects freelancers from the illusion of income. Too often, the arrival of a large payment creates a distorted sense of wealth. Without fixed salary transfers, it's easy to believe one is earning more than they truly are. But when monthly income is standardised, those illusions vanish. The reality of average monthly earnings becomes clear—and that clarity is what enables better pricing decisions, sustainable spending habits, and accurate business forecasting.

Some freelancers resist monthly transfers because they fear they may not "have enough" to make the next one. But this fear is best answered not by abandoning the model, but by tightening its feedback loop. Rather than waiting until funds run dry, freelancers can use rolling three-month income averages to recalibrate their salary level. This builds agility into the system while maintaining structure. It allows the salary to flex without becoming erratic. It honours the realities of the freelance economy without surrendering to them.

It is worth noting, too, that monthly transfers are not just a psychological benefit for the freelancer—but also for their household. Partners, spouses, dependents—all benefit from knowing what is coming in, when, and how much. It facilitates shared planning. It removes unpredictability from family conversations. It creates alignment, not anxiety.

Ultimately, monthly transfers are a form of financial storytelling. They tell your brain—and your household—that your business income is not just a chaotic series of events, but a resource to be managed with care and foresight. They impose rhythm on irregularity, turning what feels like turbulence into something navigable. They reduce reactivity, protect against scarcity-driven decisions, and foster the very stability freelancers so often trade away when leaving traditional employment.

This system does not require perfection. It requires intent. It requires a mindset that says: *I do not need to spend everything I earn the moment I earn it.* I can build a buffer. I can batch my income. I can create a structure that protects my mental bandwidth, even when clients and cash flow are unpredictable.

To freelance is to accept uncertainty. But to thrive as a freelancer requires more than tolerance for volatility. It requires *designing* against it. Monthly transfers are one of the simplest, most effective tools in that design. They are not a luxury for high earners. They are a necessity for anyone serious about turning their freelance income into a sust

The Safety-First Salary Formula

Ask a freelancer how much they earn, and you'll often get a number that reflects ambition more than accuracy. Revenue tallies may impress on paper, but the real story of financial sustainability unfolds far beneath the surface. Unlike salaried employees, freelancers must convert irregular earnings into stable living income. But this transformation—from erratic income to reliable cash flow—rarely happens by accident. It requires a method. It requires discipline. And it requires a mindset shift: treating oneself not merely as a creative or technician, but as a responsible financial steward of one's enterprise.

The freelance economy doesn't come with payslips—but it still demands a payroll.

At the heart of this necessity lies the Safety-First Salary Formula: a structured approach to determining a freelancer's sustainable monthly draw. It acknowledges the volatility of project-based earnings and designs a strategy that protects against the twin threats of income drought and lifestyle creep. This is not a budgeting trick or a shortcut for frugality—it is the scaffolding for long-term viability.

Freelancers, particularly those early in their independent careers, often fall into the trap of "payment mirroring"—spending in proportion to what comes in. A flush month invites lifestyle upgrades; a dry one brings austerity. Over time, this psychological rollercoaster erodes not just financial security but mental resilience. The solution is to decouple spending from earning through a self-imposed salary: a fixed, predictable amount transferred from the business side of one's finances into personal use, regardless of how much was earned that week.

The first step toward a reliable freelance paycheck is understanding historical income trends. Most freelancers underestimate how instructive their past 12–18 months of earnings can be. By averaging net income over this period—after subtracting business costs and tax reserves—a foundational baseline begins to emerge. However, the raw average is only the beginning. What matters more is the *range* between best and worst months. The Safety-First approach focuses not on the average income but on the *lower bound of predictability*. In other words, it builds your salary around your financial minimum viable reality—not your aspirational peak.

This is where the buffer ratio enters. Just as companies keep working capital to weather shocks, freelancers must maintain an income buffer—typically three to six months of personal salary—before formalising their paycheck system. Without this safety net, a fixed salary can turn into a liability rather than a safeguard. The buffer should reside in a designated holding account and serve one purpose only: to fund your salary during low-income months without scrambling or resorting to debt.

Once the buffer is in place, the formula simplifies. Let's say you calculate that, after taxes and business expenses, your net annual income over the last 18 months has averaged £45,000. If your income volatility swings are modest and your buffer equals at least three months of projected salary, you might safely set your salary at £3,000 per month—totalling £36,000 annually, leaving additional room for reinvestment or savings.

This strategy not only absorbs volatility but creates consistency, which unlocks the true power of personal financial planning: the ability to forecast, save, invest, and rest without checking your bank app every morning.

It also improves psychological clarity. There is a profound difference between *feeling like you got paid* and *actually getting paid*. Many freelancers conflate invoice payments with personal income, leading to premature lifestyle upgrades or lax expense monitoring. A defined, automated transfer—say, on the first of each month—establishes financial boundaries. It introduces rhythm. And it ensures that your business serves your life, not the other way around.

The brilliance of this formula lies in its adaptability. In strong earning periods, excess revenue continues to build the buffer. Once your reserves exceed the six-month mark, you gain two valuable forms of freedom: *temporal* (the ability to take breaks without panic) and *strategic* (the ability to reinvest or increase your draw). This is when you revisit your salary—not because the market is booming, but because your internal metrics justify the raise. Financial maturity is not about reacting to revenue spikes with spending; it's about aligning your salary with patterns, not peaks.

Of course, no formula is immune to disruption. Unexpected expenses, market shifts, client losses—all of these require periodic recalibration. The Safety-First Salary Formula is not a static solution; it's a dynamic framework. Its value lies in how it evolves with your business, not in how strictly it enforces a number. As you grow, your data grows with you, and your salary should track that growth cautiously—not impulsively.

It's worth noting that some freelancers find the idea of paying themselves a salary oddly restrictive. Isn't freelancing supposed to be about freedom? Shouldn't they enjoy the perks of high-earning months without imposing bureaucratic rituals on themselves? But this objection misunderstands the role of constraint. Self-imposed structure is not the enemy of freedom—it is its precondition. Only by stabilising your financial ground can you experiment, innovate, and take the creative risks that make freelancing worthwhile in the first place.

In broader economic terms, freelancers who use salary systems are less susceptible to consumer debt, less prone to burnout, and better equipped to invest in retirement planning and long-term asset building. In other words, the freelance economy needs more CFOs—not more free spirits who leave their financial fate to luck and late payments. And the Safety-First Salary Formula is one of the most effective tools for cultivating that mindset shift.

This approach also reframes the relationship between identity and income. When you treat your creative labour as a business with a structured salary, you begin to detach personal worth from monthly fluctuations. Your value becomes consistent, even if your workload isn't. And in a field where self-doubt and comparison are constant temptations, this emotional stability is worth more than any invoice.

To implement this system, you do not need complex tools or financial expertise. A spreadsheet, a clear income buffer, and the discipline to make regular transfers can go a long way. Over time, those transfers will come to represent something more than just money. They will represent control. Continuity. And perhaps most importantly, peace of mind.

In a world where volatility has become the norm, building your own paycheck isn't just a strategy—it's a form of self-respect. It tells the world, and more importantly yourself, that you are not just surviving the freelance life. You are designing it.

When to Give Yourself a Raise

For freelancers, the idea of a raise rarely arrives with fanfare. There is no formal review cycle, no HR department calculating your market worth, no email from management announcing a bump in pay. The freedom of self-employment means you answer to no one—but it also means that financial advancement doesn't happen unless you actively author it. The freelancer's raise is not awarded. It is engineered. And knowing *when* to increase your own salary is one of the most consequential decisions you'll make in building a financially resilient freelance career.

At the core of this challenge lies a paradox. Freelancers are more likely than salaried workers to experience short-term spikes in revenue. But they are also more likely to *mistrust* those spikes. One good month could be a fluke. Three could be luck. So we hesitate. We hoard. We defer better pay for ourselves, even as our workloads expand and our businesses mature. But indefinite caution carries its own risks—chief among them burnout, stagnation, and resentment. There must be a framework for recognising legitimate growth, and converting it into tangible personal benefit.

The disciplined freelancer does not give themselves a raise because they feel flush—they do it because the numbers justify it.

The first and most robust benchmark is buffer health. Before any salary increase is considered, a freelancer should have at least three to six months of personal salary stored in their income buffer—set aside explicitly to smooth volatility. This is your financial shock absorber. If you're already drawing a regular monthly salary and your buffer continues to grow steadily over a six- to nine-month period—despite regular withdrawals—that's a strong signal that your business is generating not just peak revenue but *surplus consistency*. In other words, your average earnings are no longer volatile outliers; they've become the new normal.

A second benchmark is capacity. If you're operating at near or full workload—consistently booking out your available hours, declining new clients, or subcontracting work you don't have time to handle—that's a sign your services are in demand and potentially underpriced. In traditional businesses, this would trigger a capacity-based price review. For freelancers, it should trigger two parallel questions: *Can I increase my rates?* and *Can I afford to increase my salary without compromising buffer health or business reinvestment?* If the answer to both is yes, a raise may be overdue.

Seasonality also plays a pivotal role. One strong quarter does not warrant a raise. But if a year's worth of cash flow data shows that high-earning periods recur predictably—and your expenses remain steady—then you're operating with *seasonal reliability*, not volatility. A freelance graphic designer who earns 70% of her income from Q2 and Q4 campaigns may not need a monthly income increase, but she may be in a position to raise her annualised draw, smoothing distributions across the year. A raise, in this case, doesn't require changing the *timing* of income—it requires recalibrating the *share* that becomes personal salary.

Client base evolution is another critical factor. When your average project size increases, or your clients shift from one-offs to retainers, you gain not just more revenue but more predictability. Retainer agreements, in particular, are a stabilising force in freelance finance. They justify confidence in longer-term planning—and therefore in higher fixed personal income. This is the moment to review your salary—not based on aspiration, but based on structural change.

That said, any raise should be conservative at first. An effective rule of thumb: increase your salary by no more than 10–15% at a time, and re-evaluate after 90 days. This trial period functions like a test environment. It gives your system space to adjust—buffer flow, expense coverage, mental stress—without locking you into a financially risky pattern. If your buffer holds steady or continues to grow after the raise, and your projects continue to flow, you've validated the increase. If not, you can scale back without dramatic upheaval. This is not failure—it's responsive calibration.

Freelancers must also recognise the difference between a raise and a windfall. A windfall—a large contract, a viral product, a sudden spike in demand—can dramatically inflate a month or quarter's earnings. But unless those revenues are part of a repeatable pattern, they do not justify a salary raise. They justify strategic allocation: perhaps a top-up to the income buffer, a business investment, a debt repayment, or a retirement contribution. Treating windfalls like stable income is one of the fastest paths to burnout and budgetary chaos.

There is also a behavioural case for timely raises. Underpaying yourself for extended periods corrodes your internal sense of worth. It blurs the line between financial prudence and self-neglect. You start to associate freelancing not with opportunity but with self-denial. A well-earned raise—deliberate, supported by data, and sustainable—restores a healthy feedback loop. It tells you that your effort leads to reward, not just survival. And this psychological clarity is a foundational asset in sustaining a long-term independent career.

Of course, a raise does not always mean transferring more money to your personal account. It might mean formalising benefits—such as contributing to a private pension, setting aside funds for a sabbatical, or building toward a major life goal like home ownership. In many countries, tax efficiency improves when certain "raises" are directed toward savings vehicles rather than cash income. A thoughtful freelancer knows the difference between earning more and *keeping* more—and makes strategic decisions accordingly.

Some will ask: how often should I revisit my salary? There is no universal cadence, but a biannual review is a strong starting point. Every six months, revisit your buffer, analyse your average monthly revenue and expenses, note any changes in client profile or pricing, and assess your personal financial needs. This review is not a time to fantasise. It is a time to measure. If your systems are stable and your reserves growing, then a modest increase is not just justified—it's responsible.

It's also important to decouple your salary from lifestyle inflation. A raise should not immediately translate into bigger spending. It should first reflect increased *security*—a stronger buffer, a clearer savings rate, better infrastructure for your freelance practice. Only when those foundations are sound should you consider upgrading discretionary spending. This distinction—between *lifestyle improvement* and *lifestyle inflation*—is one of the marks of a mature freelancer.

Ultimately, giving yourself a raise is not about indulgence. It is about alignment. It's the moment where your systems catch up with your ambition, where your financial operations recognise your business evolution. And it is a reminder that, unlike traditional employment, no one is coming to do this for you. You are your own finance department. You are your own advocate. And when your metrics support it, you are also your own best boss.

The raise you give yourself is not a reward for past effort. It is a vote of confidence in your future stability. It says: I know my numbers. I trust my systems. And I believe that the way I've built this business deserves to pay me—not just sporadically, but sustainably. That belief, backed by rigour, is not just empowering. It's how freelancers build lives—not just projects—on their own terms.

Chapter 7
Building a Freelance Emergency Fund

The mythology surrounding freelancing often glorifies freedom while glossing over fragility. On the surface, independence feels powerful—you choose clients, set rates, and shape your own schedule. Yet beneath that autonomy lies a less-discussed reality: freelancers operate under a persistent financial precarity that traditional employees rarely experience. There is no redundancy pay. No employer-backed sick leave. No statutory safety net. And, crucially, no guaranteed payday. When a client delays, disappears, cancels, or collapses, the consequences land squarely on the freelancer's shoulders.

For this reason, the conventional advice—three months' savings for emergencies—doesn't translate neatly. That guideline presumes consistent income and standardised reemployment timelines. Freelancers navigate a far more volatile terrain: sudden revenue droughts, delayed invoices, shifting project cycles, sectoral seasonality, or health setbacks with no paid fallback. In this world, cash flow doesn't merely slow—it halts. The cliff is nearer, the landing steeper.

Within this context, an emergency fund becomes not a discretionary luxury but a structural necessity. And its significance extends beyond mere size; it concerns design, philosophy, and deployment. It is not a static repository for rare catastrophes, but a dynamic system that anticipates the defining feature of freelance life: irregularity. A well-crafted emergency fund acts not only as a safety net, but as an enabler of continuity, dignity, and strategic decision-making. It ensures that when disruption strikes—whether personal or professional—the response is execution, not panic.

This chapter challenges the illusion that discipline alone can manage freelance volatility. Will self-restraint bring in delayed payments faster? Will it counteract a client disappearing overnight? No. What freelancers need is a liquidity model tailored to their reality—not borrowed from conventional payroll logic, nor inherited from traditional budgeting, but engineered around the cadence of actual cash flow.

We begin by questioning the standard three-month formula. For a freelancer, it is often a mirage. It implies a neat return to earning capacity once ninety days elapse. Reality is messier: the runway to recover lost contracts or replace vanished clients can stretch six months or longer—particularly when leads dry up, referrals pause, or entire sectors contract. Freelancers relying on agency work, platform gigs, or consulting often face whiplash income: sudden gaps, no warning, no severance. What they require is not only a longer cushion but a differently contoured form of financial insulation.

Enter the tiered framework. First, the bare-bones emergency fund: enough to cover essential non-negotiables—rent, groceries, medications, insurance, and minimum debt obligations. This is the immediate crisis buffer, preventing a single bad month from cascading into debt. Next, the buffer fund: a mid-tier reserve to smooth medium-term volatility, manage unexpected business costs—software renewals, tech repairs, legal fees—and support professional continuity. Finally, the opportunity fund: a higher-order reserve designed not merely for survival, but for leverage—to pivot business models, take a sabbatical, or fund creative projects without financial strain. These distinctions are functional, not semantic, forming pillars of a resilient freelance finance system.

But the question is not only size—it is placement. Where these funds reside affects accessibility, security, and returns. High-yield savings accounts provide liquidity and safety but may erode during inflation. Money market funds or cash-equivalents offer a compromise: liquid yet slightly more productive. Allocating reserves to long-term investments, equities, or mutual funds might increase returns but exposes capital to market volatility when it may be urgently needed. This chapter equips freelancers with strategic thinking to align fund type with tiered purpose—not merely chasing the highest yield.

Equally important is mindset. Many approach emergency savings with guilt, treating withdrawals as moral failures. This perspective is corrosive. The emergency fund exists to function—to smooth stress, preserve agency, and provide breathing room when unexpected events occur. Using the fund is not a sign of weakness but proof of preparation.

A healthy emergency reserve also reshapes risk tolerance. It allows you to decline misaligned projects, replace clients strategically rather than frantically, and price services with integrity instead of fear. In effect, it transforms you from a reactive agent into a proactive architect of your business. Without this foundation, every delayed invoice, negotiation, or personal curveball threatens to pull you back into scarcity thinking, where strategic decisions rarely flourish.

Finally, the chapter explores practical structures and automation to make emergency funding actionable. Percentage-based allocations from every payment, automated transfers to tiered accounts, and quarterly reviews of fund adequacy reduce emotional friction. The challenge is not merely to build a fund once, but to maintain a system that sustains itself, even when attention drifts.

This chapter does not teach you how to endure a disaster—it teaches you to remain intact when freelance life inevitably throws curveballs. True financial health is measured not in abundance, but in resilience during contraction. Freelancers who internalise this principle—treating safety not as luxury but as operating standard—do more than survive: they endure, adapt, and return stronger. Not through chance, but through structure.

An emergency fund is not about fearing the worst. It is about preparing for reality. Long-term freelance success does not belong to those who avoid trouble, but to those who build enough runway to outlast it.

Why Freelancers Need More Cushion

The most dangerous financial advice a freelancer can follow is the kind designed for someone with a steady job. Chief among these is the oft-repeated rule of thumb: keep an emergency fund of three months' worth of living expenses. It sounds prudent. Conservative, even. But what is rarely acknowledged is that this figure emerged from a salaried worldview—a world where income is predictable, job loss is a statistical anomaly, and sick leave is paid. For freelancers, these assumptions do not hold. *Stability is not the default; it is the exception*. And applying traditional financial safety benchmarks to a non-traditional income model is not just inadequate—it is negligent.

Freelancers do not just contend with income volatility. They contend with *payment volatility*. This is a critical distinction. A salaried employee knows not only how much they will earn, but when they will earn it. A freelancer may land a £10,000 contract, only to find themselves chasing the invoice 90 days later while rent, insurance, and daily life proceed on schedule. In the absence of a robust financial cushion, the intervening period becomes a time of escalating stress, reactive borrowing, and missed obligations. The client's delay becomes the freelancer's crisis.

This is not rare. It is structural. Surveys of freelancers across sectors consistently reveal a high incidence of late payments—particularly in creative, consulting, and contract development fields. In some cases, clients operate on net-60 or net-90 payment terms *by design*. In others, the delay is more insidious: corporate bureaucracy, finance department backlogs, or simply disregard. The freelancer, lacking legal muscle or HR advocacy, absorbs the uncertainty. In this context, a three-month fund is not a cushion. It is a timer—counting down to collapse if cash doesn't arrive in time.

Then there is the issue of *dry spells*. Freelancers do not always lose income gradually. Often, they lose it all at once. A major contract ends. A retainer is cancelled. A platform changes its algorithm or terms of service. A personal health issue requires weeks or months off work. Unlike traditional employees who often receive severance or transition support, the freelancer receives nothing—except silence. They must rebuild their client base or business model from scratch, during a period when stress is high and confidence low. These are not hypothetical risks. They are documented patterns in freelance careers.

And yet, too many freelancers continue to plan their emergency reserves as if they are short-term bridges between gigs, rather than buffers against structural uncertainty. This is where the traditional three-month rule shows its most dangerous flaw: it assumes that recovery from loss is linear. That income will return swiftly and predictably. But freelance recovery curves are rarely smooth. Replacing a lost anchor client may take six months. Rebuilding trust after a burnout may take longer. And crucially, most freelancers do not go from zero to fully booked overnight. They *ramp*. Which means their emergency savings must cover not just the absence of income, but the *gradient of rebuilding*.

Moreover, freelancers face health and income risks simultaneously. A salaried worker who becomes ill receives sick pay. A freelancer receives silence—and possibly an apologetic email from a client finding a backup provider. Consider a freelance designer who breaks their dominant wrist, or a consultant hospitalised with pneumonia. Without a health buffer, their illness becomes an income shock. Without an income buffer, the income shock becomes a debt spiral. Freelancers who ignore these interlocking risks do not lack work ethic—they lack *a model of planning grounded in their actual risk profile.*

This is not fear-mongering. It is precision. The solution is not to catastrophise, but to recalibrate. For freelancers, the concept of an emergency fund must be reframed: *not as a static pile of money, but as a system of protection against professional volatility*. The fund should not merely be sufficient to survive—it should be sufficient to buy time, sustain choice, and preserve dignity during disruption.

This reframing begins by discarding the arbitrary three-month standard and replacing it with a custom benchmark. One that considers:

Average invoice delay time in the freelancer's sector

Client concentration risk—how much income depends on a single client

Health coverage gaps—whether sick pay, disability insurance, or public support are available

Recovery time—how long it has historically taken to replace major contracts or rebuild after burnout

For some, this may mean targeting a six-month buffer. For others, nine months. What matters is that the number be *derived from the freelancer's own income pattern and risk exposure*—not borrowed from a payroll paradigm.

Equally important is how the fund is designed. A single monolithic pot can feel inert or psychologically distant. Many freelancers benefit from a *tiered reserve model*. For instance:

A **core cushion**, covering non-negotiables like housing, food, medication, and minimum debt service

A **business continuity buffer**, covering expenses like software, equipment, advertising, and professional fees

An **adaptive runway**, funding the time and costs required to reposition after a disruption—whether through training, marketing, or portfolio rebuilding

Each of these tiers serves a different function. Together, they do more than preserve solvency. They preserve *momentum*. Because what often kills a freelance career is not a single bad month—it's the exhaustion of making survival decisions repeatedly, without time to think, plan, or rebuild.

And yet, many freelancers resist building this kind of cushion, not out of ignorance, but out of emotional conflict. Savings, for many, feel like a tax on creativity. Or worse, a confession of instability. But that belief is a relic of a different era—one where employment was fixed, and volatility meant failure. In freelance life, volatility is *normal*. Anticipating it is not pessimism. It is competence.

The most sustainable freelancers are not the most gifted. They are the ones with the longest runway. They are the ones who do not have to take every job, say yes to every underpriced brief, or panic when a client ghosts them. They are the ones who understand that cashflow volatility is not an aberration, but a system feature—and they build accordingly.

To freelance successfully over the long term, you don't just need talent. You need *slack*. Slack is what lets you think clearly under pressure. Slack is what lets you pivot instead of capitulate. Slack is what separates the freelancers who flame out after a few turbulent years from those who build careers with staying power.

Three months might be enough for someone with predictable income and institutional backing. But for freelancers, *that is not the baseline.* The real baseline is unpredictability. Which means the real solution is a buffer built not for theory, but for lived experience.

Because freelancing is not a gamble. It is a responsibility. And *responsibility without resilience is a fragile promise*—to your clients, your finances, and yourself. The best freelancers honour that promise by doing what traditional systems never taught them to do: build a cushion that reflects who they actually are. Not who the world assumed they'd be.

How Much Is Enough?

Ask a freelancer how much they need in savings, and you'll rarely hear a precise answer. More often, it's an aspirational guess, rounded generously upwards or vaguely downwards—"six months, maybe?"—anchored not to their actual income dynamics but to conventional wisdom borrowed from salaried contexts. The problem is not their ambition. The problem is the question. *"How much is enough?"* implies a singular, static number—something definitive and universal. For freelancers navigating volatility, the better question is: *enough for what?*

No one emergency fund serves all functions. A freelancer's financial resilience is not built around one target number but three distinct layers of preparedness, each tied to a different type of disruption, decision, or opportunity. Understanding these tiers—and assigning them realistic figures based on your income, expenses, and ambitions—is how you build a savings strategy that works in practice, not just theory. It is not about hitting a number once. It is about maintaining the right buffer at the right level for the right risk.

The first layer is the **Bare-Bones Reserve**. This is the non-negotiable floor—the minimum needed to keep your essential life functioning during a temporary income freeze. It assumes no frills, no extras, and no optimism. Just rent or mortgage, food, utilities, insurance, medication, and basic transport. Not every bill makes the cut here. Streaming subscriptions don't. Business upgrades don't. Not even debt payments, unless defaulting would carry irreversible damage. The purpose of this fund is survival, not comfort. Its value lies in clarity. When work dries up or payments stall, *this is the figure you must be able to cover*. Nothing less. Nothing more.

To calculate it, track your last six to twelve months of personal spending and isolate only those expenses that would continue in a financial drought. Then apply a conservative time frame—typically 3 to 6 months, depending on your risk exposure. If your clients pay promptly, you're in a high-demand field, and you carry few dependents, three months may suffice. If you have irregular income, health vulnerabilities, or client concentration risk, aim higher. The right number is not the average—it's the one that *keeps you housed, fed, and stable long enough to find your footing again*.

Next comes the **Stability Buffer**, often mistaken as part of the bare-bones reserve but conceptually distinct. Where the first fund handles emergencies, this second tier is about *cashflow management*. Freelancers do not just face gaps in earnings; they face timing mismatches between income and obligations. A Stability Buffer smooths those spikes. It's what allows you to pay bills on time even when a client delays payment or a project shifts into next month. It's what prevents you from dipping into your core savings every time your revenue hiccups.

This buffer should sit in an account you can access immediately—ideally your income holding or operating account—and be sized to match one to two months of *regular operating expenses*, both personal and professional. It is not a static fund to protect in perpetuity. It is a working fund, replenished in flush months and drawn from during thinner stretches. Its psychological function is significant: it lets you respond to a tight week with calm rather than anxiety. It shifts your posture from reactive to proactive.

The third and most often overlooked layer is the **Opportunity Fund**. This is not about crisis. It is about *choice*. Most freelancers understand the need to protect against loss. Fewer plan for the upside—say, the chance to take a course, invest in better gear, build a prototype, or take a sabbatical to write a book or develop a new service. Opportunity requires availability. And availability requires *pre-funded space*. The irony is that many freelancers dream of independence and self-direction, only to spend years stuck in client-to-client survival mode because every new investment feels too risky.

An Opportunity Fund creates the financial margin to say yes to strategic moves—without disrupting your safety net or scrambling to justify short-term losses. It is the difference between reacting to your calendar and shaping your trajectory. There is no single formula for its size. But a meaningful benchmark is to allocate a percentage of every high-income month—say, 10%—into this fund, up to a cap that represents one to two months of desired strategic downtime or investment. You may not use it every year. But when the right moment arrives, *you'll have the means to act, not just the ambition.*

These three layers—Bare-Bones, Buffer, and Opportunity—work in concert. They are not hierarchical in prestige, but in sequence. You cannot build a meaningful Opportunity Fund if your core savings are fragile or your bills routinely bounce. But nor should you stop at mere survival. The goal is not to white-knuckle your way through lean months. The goal is to build *freedom from volatility-induced distortion*. To create space where your best thinking, clearest judgement, and longest-range decisions can operate unpressured by financial chaos.

This framework also guards against one of the most common freelance traps: the temptation to over-save and under-invest in the business. Without clarity about function, savings can become inert—sitting in a single account, untouched out of fear, even when strategic spending could drive growth. But when each fund is defined and purposeful, decision-making becomes sharper. If you're drawing from your Stability Buffer, you know it's a timing issue, not a structural crisis. If you're dipping into your Opportunity Fund, you can evaluate it as an investment, not a survival cost. *Precision in intent creates precision in action.*

Equally important is that these tiers allow for modular progress. You do not need to "build your emergency fund" all at once. You can build each layer in phases. Start by funding your Bare-Bones Reserve. Once that's in place, shift focus to smoothing volatility with your Buffer. Then, as surplus grows, begin accumulating for Opportunity. This sequence ensures that each pound saved is doing the right job at the right time, rather than sitting idle or mismatched.

Freelancers often internalise the idea that financial safety is a luxury they'll earn *later*, once business is booming or clients are consistent. But the opposite is true. *Safety is what enables sustainability*. It is not the reward for a successful freelance career. It is the infrastructure on which one is built.

The real risk is not lack of talent or work ethic. It is misalignment between income variability and financial preparedness. When you treat your finances as if they belong to a salaried life—relying on a single savings figure to cover all scenarios—you build a house with no foundation. But when you segment your emergency strategy into tiers tied to purpose, timing, and growth, you build not just resilience, but *intelligent resilience.* One that protects you from panic, equips you for pacing, and empowers you to seize the moments that define careers.

"How much is enough?" isn't a number. It's a system. One that adapts to the reality of freelance life, rather than resisting it. One that stops confusing caution with hesitation, or preparedness with pessimism. And one that makes your freedom as durable as it is desirable.

Where to Keep It

Liquidity without erosion. That's the central challenge when deciding where to house a freelance emergency fund. You need access without penalty, stability without stagnation, and a yield that outpaces inflation—without exposing yourself to the whims of markets you can't afford to wait out. The question isn't merely *where to put your money*, but *how to structure it so it serves you across time, volatility, and circumstance.* For salaried workers with predictable income and employer safety nets, a simple savings account often suffices. But for freelancers, whose earnings move in cycles rather than straight lines, the storage vehicle matters as much as the savings itself.

Emergency funds are not investments. They're tools. And like any tool, their utility depends on the context in which they're deployed. The cash you might need *tomorrow* cannot be exposed to risk or delay. The money you *might* need three months from now must be protected against inflation but still instantly available. And any reserve for longer-term contingencies—downtime, new projects, sabbaticals—should work harder without undermining the safety it's meant to guarantee. This nuanced positioning rules out one-size-fits-all solutions. Instead, it demands a tiered approach based on *purpose, timeline, and risk tolerance.*

At the most accessible end of the spectrum is the **traditional high-street savings account**, beloved for its familiarity but largely inadequate in yield. Its key benefit is immediacy. Funds can be transferred or withdrawn without notice, often through the same interface as your main current account. For a subset of your emergency fund—the portion covering the next 30 days—this proximity is useful. It reduces friction, which in urgent situations is worth more than a modest gain in interest. But beyond that short window, the opportunity cost is significant. Most standard savings accounts still offer interest rates well below inflation, eroding purchasing power over time. Worse, they tend to breed complacency. Money sits idle. The saver feels falsely secure.

This is where **high-yield digital banks** and **online savings platforms** enter the picture. These institutions—often operating without physical branches—offer rates two to five times higher than legacy banks, without sacrificing accessibility. Many are regulated under the same financial protections (e.g. the FSCS in the UK), making them no less secure than brick-and-mortar banks. They offer a valuable middle tier: a place for your 1–6 month buffer that *needs to stay liquid*, but shouldn't lose value to inertia. Unlike traditional banks, many also allow automated sub-accounting, letting you mentally or digitally segregate funds into categories like "bare-bones living," "upcoming tax," or "professional development." *Clarity is not just visual—it is behavioural.* Systems that encourage visibility and intention tend to promote better habits.

That said, not all high-yield platforms are equal. Some limit withdrawals. Others require minimum balances. Still others are promotional-rate traps—offering enticing rates for the first three months, then quietly slashing them. The solution is not to avoid them, but to remain actively engaged. Review your rates quarterly. Consider rotating funds if another provider offers significantly better yield without additional risk. *Laziness is the real cost here—not mobility.*

Once your immediate and midterm needs are secured, you can explore options that slightly sacrifice liquidity in exchange for *preservation and modest growth*. These are not investments in the traditional, long-term sense, but *cash equivalents*: assets that maintain stable value while generating yield better than inflation. For example, **premium money market funds**—especially those backed by government bonds or blue-chip instruments—offer better returns than bank deposits, with daily or near-daily redemption. They're ideal for the Opportunity Fund or longer-term contingencies. Crucially, they avoid the principal risk of equities while offering more than nominal yield. Their role is not to outperform the market, but to preserve capital *with dignity*.

More adventurous freelancers sometimes ask whether to put emergency reserves into **short-term bond ETFs**, **dividend-paying stocks**, or even **cryptocurrencies**, arguing that leaving money in cash "feels like wasting it." This reflects a common cognitive distortion: equating idle capital with lost opportunity. The fallacy here is assuming that *all money must perform*. Emergency reserves are not growth assets. They are stability assets. Introducing volatility to their function defeats their purpose. If your money might be needed during a market downturn, then exposure to that same market isn't diversification—it's duplication of risk.

That said, some freelancers do choose to keep a *fraction*—often from the Opportunity Fund—in lower-risk, higher-yield instruments like **short-duration bond ladders**, or **peer-to-peer lending with guaranteed tranches**. These moves can make sense *if* they follow two principles: first, that access to the funds is reasonably prompt (ideally within seven days); and second, that the potential return compensates for the illiquidity and minor risk. If you're earning a marginal 0.5% over your digital bank but sacrificing flexibility, the trade-off likely isn't worth it. But if you're earning 2–3% more on capital you won't touch for six months, it may be a rational allocation.

Psychological distance also matters. The funds you need to access in crisis must feel *available*. If the account is buried in an investment app, tied up in instruments you don't fully understand, or subject to lock-up terms, you're unlikely to act decisively when speed matters. Conversely, if the money is too close—just a tap away from your debit card—it becomes vulnerable to impulse spending or self-justified withdrawals. *Where you store your reserves affects how you think about them.*

An optimal setup, therefore, often involves three components:

1. A **rapid-access savings account** connected to your main current account, holding 1 month of essential living expenses. This is the fast-response fund. It's there for broken laptops, delayed invoices, urgent dental visits.
2. A **high-yield online savings account or regulated money market fund**, holding the next 3–6 months of expenses. This is your buffer zone—stable, visible, and earning. You don't touch it unless you're genuinely in a cashflow gap.
3. An **opportunity reserve**, placed in a slightly higher-yield instrument, earmarked for strategic moves or extended downtime. It's semi-liquid, planned rather than reactionary, and reflects your ambitions more than your fears.

This tiered model gives you both control and efficiency. It ensures that your short-term needs never jeopardise your long-term security. It also builds discipline through structure—each account serving a distinct role, each withdrawal subject to its own rationale. The point isn't to maximise returns at every level. It's to optimise *function across time horizons*.

The freelancer's emergency fund is not a static number. It's a *living ecosystem*—adaptable, intentional, and informed by

not the exception. Planning systems must reflect this. The emergency fund is not a backup plan. *It is the plan.* Until that framing is internalised, its use will continue to feel like an act of surrender.

There's also the myth of financial virtue—the idea that "real professionals" never touch their buffers unless catastrophe strikes. This purist ideal belongs more to austerity psychology than modern financial strategy. Using your fund when client payments stall, projects dry up, or life throws curveballs isn't undisciplined—it's a form of *controlled disbursement.* The key is intentionality. Did you decide to use the fund, or did you slip into it by avoidance? Was it part of a plan, or a reaction to chaos? *Guilt is a symptom of reactive behaviour. Clarity is the antidote.*

The antidote begins with scenario planning. In practice, this means assigning pre-approved conditions under which your fund can be accessed—before you ever need to do so. These aren't rigid rules, but boundary markers. For example: "If income falls below X for more than two weeks, draw 20% from the buffer to cover essentials." Or: "If a medical expense exceeds £500 and isn't covered, initiate a structured drawdown over three months." By pre-authorising categories of need, you remove ambiguity in moments of stress. *Ambiguity fuels shame. Structure grants permission.*

There's also value in *rehearsal.* Simulate a withdrawal even when you don't need one—just to practise the mechanics. See how it feels. Observe your resistance. Doing so decouples the act from crisis and reframes it as ordinary stewardship. Just as fire drills normalise evacuation procedures, financial drills normalise adaptive strategy. The goal is to make the act *unemotional,* not dramatic. The fund exists to be used *calmly, not reluctantly.*

This mindset also prevents a separate but equally damaging phenomenon: hoarding. Some freelancers are so averse to drawing on reserves that they treat their emergency fund like a relic—untouchable, sacred, inert. As a result, they stretch their stress beyond reason, delay payments, juggle credit cards, or neglect opportunities that could restore momentum faster. The paradox is painful: in trying to protect their future, they compromise their present. Worse, they forget that the fund is not just for *survival*, but for *stability*. It exists to buy time, preserve energy, and restore clarity. Spending it is not indulgence. It's stewardship of your capacity to operate.

Consider a real-world example: a freelance designer in London who has built a six-month fund based on bare-bones expenses. A key client suddenly pauses work for a quarter. Rather than deplete emotional bandwidth by scrambling for low-quality replacement gigs or accepting underpriced work, they use their fund to maintain their standard operating rhythm, pitch new high-fit clients, and rebuild pipeline intentionally. The result isn't just financial survival—it's professional integrity. *The fund didn't rescue them from collapse; it preserved the conditions for quality decisions.*

This is precisely why the language around emergency funds must evolve. We talk about them in binary terms: "emergency" or "not," as if the line is objectively obvious. But most financial stress emerges in grey zones—delays, mismatches, plateaus—not dramatic disasters. The fund should serve these conditions too. In fact, it often makes the most impact when deployed *early*, not at breaking point. Using it before a problem spirals is the difference between proactive correction and reactive damage control.

Of course, a fund must also be *replenished*. This is where intention becomes a closed loop. If your drawdown is conscious, then so too must be your replenishment plan. Set a fixed percentage of post-recovery income to flow back into the fund until it's restored. Automate the transfer. Track progress. And most importantly, *celebrate it without penance.*

Rebuilding the fund is not punishment for having used it. It's a renewal of the strategy that protected you.

In this way, emergency fund usage becomes not a one-time event, but a cycle—trigger, response, recovery, recalibration. That cycle is a sign of maturity, not fragility. You are not supposed to live above the threshold of risk at all times. You are supposed to design a system that lets you *dip below the surface without drowning*.

Finally, we must reject the emotional binary of guilt vs. relief and instead cultivate what could be called *confident withdrawal*. That is, the ability to draw from the fund not with hesitation, but with composure. To say: "I saw this coming. I planned for it. I am executing the plan." That mindset is not just financially intelligent—it's psychologically liberating. It turns what might otherwise feel like a defeat into an act of resilience.

Because ultimately, an emergency fund is not about hoarding cash. It's about building the *confidence to pause, redirect, and endure*. And in the unpredictable landscape of freelance work, that confidence is your most valuable asset.

Chapter 8
Long-Term Wealth Without a Pension

Ask a freelancer how they intend to fund their later years, and the answer is often a nervous laugh, a vague gesture toward "investments," or a shrug that conceals unease. Unlike salaried employees, whose retirement scaffolding is frequently automatic—auto-enrolment, employer contributions, tax-deferred vehicles—freelancers exist in a vacuum. No one sets aside money on their behalf. No HR department nudges them with calculators or default rates. And crucially, no social contract assumes they will stop working at sixty-five. In the absence of a formal horizon, the long term fades from view. Not irrelevant, but largely unacknowledged.

This chapter begins by dismantling the illusion that retirement is a static endpoint or a guaranteed outcome. For freelancers, it is neither. It is a slow, deliberate construction: voluntary, uncertain, and profoundly personal. It must be self-initiated, self-funded, and self-managed. That autonomy is empowering, but it carries risk. When planning becomes optional, it is easily deferred. Present bias, aversion to complexity, fear of insufficiency, and a culture celebrating constant motion all conspire against long-term foresight. Layer in the irregular cash flow of freelance work, and the result is a perfect storm for neglect.

The challenge is not merely tactical—it is conceptual. Freelancers are not just without pensions; they are without the mental scaffolding to think in pension terms. This structural blind spot means that even those who excel at short-term financial discipline—saving for taxes, budgeting for lean months, investing in tools—often fail to translate that skill into long-range strategy. They rarely calculate the cost of true freedom from work, and fewer still design a system to buy it.

This is not a question of intelligence. Freelance life is designed for immediacy—projects, invoices, deadlines, client cycles. There is no built-in pathway nudging individuals toward a twenty-year horizon. Retirement, when it enters the mind, appears more as a mirage than a destination. And when discussed, it is often framed through fear, guilt, or shame. This chapter reframes the conversation: long-term wealth-building is not moral obligation or mere risk mitigation—it is freedom-making. A deliberate, quiet act that buys control over time.

The strategy begins with structure. Not ideology, not optimism, but accounts, percentages, and habits. "Start saving" is insufficient guidance for those navigating volatility. Across different jurisdictions, self-employed professionals have access to specific vehicles: Roth IRAs in the United States, SIPPs in the UK, RRSPs in Canada, superannuation in Australia. Each has distinct logic—tax deferral, contribution limits, investment flexibility—and none is inherently impenetrable. Uptake remains low not due to lack of access, but because frictionless entry is rare. Clarity must precede commitment.

Automation is the key. Just as salaried employees have taxes withheld automatically, retirement contributions must escape the tyranny of willpower. Frame it as a recurring transfer to your future self—a standing order. Treat it like rent or insurance. The moment contribution becomes routine, it decouples from emotion. Instead of asking, "Can I afford to save this month?" the question becomes, "What do I need to earn to maintain my contribution?" This shift—from discretionary to embedded—is the hinge of long-term success.

Perhaps the most radical insight is that freelancers do not need to retire to benefit from long-term investing. The traditional retirement model is a relic of industrial-era employment: fixed salaries, physical labour, and an endpoint defined by depletion. Creative or knowledge-based work does not follow that curve. A septuagenarian writer may still love their craft. A consultant might scale back to a handful of projects. A designer could move from execution to advisory. What matters is financial optionality—the freedom to reduce work, pivot, refuse poor clients, or take a sabbatical without catastrophe.

Optionality is funded by assets. Not necessarily millions, but enough in diversified, low-cost investments to underwrite choice: index funds, global ETFs, balanced portfolios—allocated across suitable accounts and left to compound. The returns are slow and often invisible, requiring patience and restraint. Consistency trumps perfection. Starting matters more than optimising.

This chapter also rejects the false dichotomy of wealth versus austerity. Building long-term assets is not about living ascetically; it is about protecting a defined portion of income through systems. Some freelancers adopt profit-first frameworks. Others apply percentage-based allocations—ten per cent to a long-term fund, no exceptions. Others leverage windfalls—exceptional months or bonuses—as contribution spikes. The method varies. The imperative is singular: convert income into capital, monthly, automatically, without waiting for ideal stability.

Because the uncomfortable truth is that stability does not precede saving—it follows it. Without employer pension schemes, freelancers must be both employee and employer in their wealth architecture. They must build systems that reward the future as well as the present. The tools exist, the accounts exist, the markets are ready. What often lacks is conviction—and a human, approachable entry point.

This chapter provides that entry point. Not a rigid blueprint, but a flexible framework: how to navigate pension-like accounts, cultivate long-term investment habits that withstand volatility, and reconceptualise retirement to match modern freelance life. One that prizes choice over chronology, control over certainty, and time over tradition.

There is no pension waiting for you. But there is power in building your own.

The Retirement Problem for Freelancers

Ask a room of freelancers how many have a retirement plan, and the silence that follows will be telling—not because they haven't thought about it, but because they *don't know where to start.* Unlike traditional employees, freelancers operate in a system designed without them in mind. There is no employer making automatic contributions to a pension fund, no matching schemes, no end-of-year reminders from HR, no neatly packaged options presented during onboarding. Retirement, for the self-employed, is not an expectation. It is a private burden carried in isolation, often deferred until it becomes urgent.

This structural absence is compounded by a psychological one. Most freelancers—especially early in their careers—focus on *income survival,* not asset accumulation. Their attention is consumed by finding clients, delivering work, navigating late payments, and managing erratic cash flow. Planning decades ahead in the midst of month-to-month volatility feels unrealistic, even indulgent. *When every month is a negotiation with uncertainty, long-term saving feels like a luxury reserved for someone else.*

This is not a failure of responsibility; it's a failure of design. The modern retirement system was built around industrial-era assumptions: stable employment, predictable income, and age-based exit from the workforce. It was designed for people with bosses, payrolls, and linear careers—not for people whose income fluctuates by 70% across quarters, who receive lump-sum payments with no tax withheld, and who can't even predict what they'll earn next month. Freelancers live in a fundamentally different economic rhythm. Yet they are held to the same expectations as those with employer-funded pensions and automatic deductions. *It's an asymmetric demand: prepare for the future with tools you were never given.*

Even when freelancers do want to prepare, the mental obstacles are formidable. Cognitive biases distort financial planning for everyone, but they hit the self-employed with greater force. Present bias encourages short-term spending over future investing. Complexity aversion pushes people away from tax-advantaged plans that require paperwork or unfamiliar jargon. Loss aversion makes temporary market downturns feel like existential threats, especially when those funds are self-managed. The result is paralysis—*not due to laziness, but because the cost of error feels too high and the rewards too far away.*

This paralysis is made worse by cultural scripts that associate success with constant motion. In many creative and freelance industries, the idea of retirement is not only distant but vaguely incompatible with identity. Artists don't retire, they evolve. Writers don't stop, they publish less. Designers consult. Coders teach. The freelance world is full of people who derive meaning from their work and imagine doing some version of it indefinitely. That mindset can be healthy—*but it should be a choice, not a financial necessity.* Without a retirement structure in place, many will discover too late that "I'll always work" is not a plan but a wish.

There is also a fundamental mismatch between how freelancers earn and how retirement systems expect people to save. Traditional pension logic assumes smooth, incremental income growth—annual raises, regular bonuses, and consistent contributions. Freelance income is lumpy, seasonal, and often sporadic. You might earn £25,000 in one quarter and £4,000 the next. If your retirement strategy is built on a monthly contribution model, these income swings can make it unsustainable. You either miss contributions (which triggers guilt and abandonment), or overcommit in high-income months and regret it later. *The retirement system requires consistency; freelance income resists it.*

What's needed, then, is a mental and structural overhaul. Retirement planning for freelancers must begin with a different premise: that *volatility is the norm*, not the exception. That the future is not a single point (age 65), but a range of possibilities requiring flexibility. That traditional pensions are not the only route to financial security. And that thinking long-term is not an act of denial about the present—but a declaration of agency over what comes next.

The problem is not that freelancers don't care about their futures. It's that their futures have been made unnavigable. If a salaried employee wants to start saving for retirement, the system is built to help them succeed with minimal friction. They check a box during onboarding, and 5% of their salary begins flowing into a pension fund. If a freelancer wants to do the same, they must research available accounts, choose among financial institutions, learn about tax implications, open the account, fund it manually, decide what to invest in, and repeat that process—without any feedback loops, matching incentives, or visible models from their peers. *It's not a fair comparison. The salaried employee is climbing stairs. The freelancer is scaling a wall.*

And yet, the consequences of neglect are far more severe for the freelancer. There is no employer fallback. No redundancy pay. No accrued pension contributions. No one else is going to do the work of compounding. If they don't build it, it won't exist. That is both terrifying and clarifying. *The lack of a safety net is not just a vulnerability—it is an invitation to design your own.*

Designing a retirement system for the freelance life means shifting both strategy and psychology. It means recognising that contributions may need to be seasonal, not monthly. That savings rates must be higher, not lower, to compensate for employer absence. That the goal isn't an age-based exit, but *freedom from financial dependence on your labour*. It means measuring progress not by how much you've saved compared to a peer in corporate finance, but by how much freedom you've purchased relative to your own needs.

It also means replacing shame with strategy. Too many freelancers internalise guilt over not "doing enough" for retirement, as if the system's inaccessibility were their personal failing. But guilt doesn't create consistency—systems do. The real solution isn't motivation; it's automation. What's needed is a process that works even when life doesn't. That process starts with clarity: choosing an account type, setting realistic contribution goals based on your income seasonality, automating transfers when possible, and using windfalls as opportunities to top up long-term holdings. Progress won't be linear, and that's exactly the point. *Freelancer retirement plans must bend with reality, not break against it.*

Ultimately, the problem isn't just about money. It's about permission. Freelancers need to give themselves permission to plan long-term, even in a short-term world. To imagine futures that don't require constant hustle. To define wealth not just as income, but as *unearned time*. And to understand that building towards retirement isn't a rejection of creative life, but a reinforcement of it. Because the freedom to stop working—or to keep working by choice—is the truest form of creative sovereignty.

Retirement for freelancers is not a broken promise. It's an unclaimed possibility. And possibility, unlike pensions, has no expiry date.

Self-Employed Retirement Options

For salaried workers in traditional employment, retirement saving is more or less a background process. Automatic enrolment, matched contributions, predictable payroll deductions—these mechanisms nudge people toward future stability with minimal friction. But for freelancers, none of these structural nudges exist. No employer is matching your pension. No HR department is sending reminders. Retirement saving becomes a decision you must make, remember, structure, and sustain—every single month. That cognitive and logistical burden is precisely why many self-employed professionals delay or neglect long-term planning altogether. The result isn't just underfunded futures; it's also financial anxiety in the present, as the weight of an undefined horizon looms ever larger.

What's often missing isn't money, but *clarity*. Many freelancers assume retirement planning is something that requires wealth or tax advisors or "getting your life together first." In truth, what it requires is a system—a lean, comprehensible, repeatable framework for putting aside money in a way that grows it for later use. The structure matters more than the starting amount. Once the scaffolding is in place, behaviour becomes easier, momentum builds, and the seemingly distant goal of financial independence becomes incrementally real.

At its core, retirement saving for the self-employed revolves around two levers: choosing the right container for your money and developing the habit of feeding it. Most countries offer some form of tax-advantaged account specifically for the self-employed, and while the acronyms vary—IRA, SIPP, RRSP, solo 401(k)—the core principles remain surprisingly consistent. These are not exotic instruments. They are simply designated vehicles that allow earnings to grow either tax-deferred or tax-free, depending on the structure.

Start with the United States. A solo 401(k), also called an individual 401(k), is designed specifically for self-employed individuals with no employees (or just a spouse). It allows for both employee and employer contributions—meaning you, wearing two hats, can contribute more overall. In 2024, you could contribute up to $23,000 as an employee (or $30,500 if over 50), plus up to 25% of net earnings as the employer side, with a total cap of $66,000. Compare this to a traditional or Roth IRA, which limits contributions to just $7,000 annually for most people. The solo 401(k) also allows Roth contributions, meaning you can choose whether to pay taxes now or later.

In the UK, the closest analogue is the SIPP—the Self-Invested Personal Pension. A SIPP offers flexible investment choices and attractive tax relief. For basic-rate taxpayers, the government automatically adds 25% to your contributions (you put in £800, and £1,000 goes into your SIPP). Higher and additional-rate taxpayers can claim even more relief through their self-assessment returns. SIPPs, unlike traditional pensions, give investors control over their funds. You can invest in everything from low-fee index trackers to managed portfolios, and withdrawals can begin from age 55 (rising to 57 in 2028).

In Canada, freelancers have the RRSP (Registered Retirement Savings Plan), which functions similarly to the US traditional IRA. Contributions reduce your taxable income in the current year and grow tax-deferred until withdrawal. As of 2024, contribution room is 18% of your earned income from the previous year, up to a limit of CA$31,560. One distinct advantage is that unused contribution room rolls forward indefinitely—meaning even if you start late, you haven't lost ground entirely.

The trick isn't choosing the perfect account. It's picking *a* tax-advantaged container and using it consistently. Waiting until you've "sorted out" your freelance income is a trap. Your income may never be perfectly predictable—but your commitment to future stability can be. That's what these accounts are for. They give your efforts a compounding tailwind.

What often derails freelancers is the fallacy of the large lump sum. The belief that you must contribute £500 or $1,000 a month or it isn't "worth it" prevents action altogether. But a £100 or $150 monthly contribution over a decade is more powerful than a theoretical £500 you never transfer. Because retirement savings benefit from compounding, time matters more than volume. A five-year delay in starting a retirement plan can require *double* the monthly contribution later to achieve the same end balance.

Automation closes the gap between intention and behaviour. Set up a direct transfer from your income-holding account to your retirement vehicle as part of your money-routing habit. You'll stop treating it as a discretionary expense and start treating it as a non-negotiable part of your overhead—because your future is part of your business's overhead. Framed that way, your pension contributions are not sacrifices; they are strategic investments in the most critical asset you manage: your autonomy.

Choosing what to invest in inside these accounts doesn't have to be complicated. The vast majority of evidence suggests that a diversified, low-fee index fund strategy outperforms most actively managed portfolios over the long run. Vanguard's total market funds, for instance, are widely available, globally diversified, and exceedingly cost-efficient. In the UK, similar exposure can be gained through funds like the Vanguard LifeStrategy series or iShares All-Country ETFs. These aren't just convenient—they're designed to help regular people benefit from long-term market growth without needing to become amateur economists.

You don't need to predict the market. You need to stay in it. And staying in requires *structure*, not willpower.

Finally, it helps to shift how we even think about retirement. For many freelancers, the concept feels alien: "Why would I ever stop working?" But retirement doesn't have to mean ceasing all labour. It means having *the option* not to work for money if you choose not to. It's about reclaiming control of your time, not reaching some arbitrary finish line. What you're building is not just a pension—it's optionality. The freedom to say no to a toxic client, to take a year off to write a book, to decline underpaid work not out of moral superiority but practical solvency. That is the true power of financial independence.

The sooner you see retirement saving not as a distant financial chore but as a design challenge in personal agency, the more engaged—and effective—you'll become. And it starts not with complex spreadsheets or perfect timing, but with one quiet, unsexy, radical act: setting up the transfer.

Automating Long-Term Investing

The most profound financial advantage a freelancer can give themselves isn't a marketing trick, a killer portfolio, or even a high-paying client—it's time. Not the time spent working, but the time given to compounding. Time, when paired with consistency, builds wealth in a way few gigs ever can. Yet many self-employed professionals continue to treat investing like a task for "later," as if retirement planning were a luxury reserved for those with HR departments. It isn't. The ability to *pay your future self on autopilot* is not only available—it's essential.

Most salaried workers are nudged into investing by default. Pensions, matched contributions, and employer-enrolled retirement plans take inertia and turn it into an asset. Freelancers, by contrast, are on their own. They must build from scratch the kind of infrastructure that employers provide automatically. This lack of built-in structure doesn't merely delay retirement planning—it psychologically detaches freelancers from the concept of long-term wealth entirely. Without visible systems or mandated contributions, the future becomes abstract, easy to ignore until it becomes impossible not to.

Automation is the antidote to avoidance. It turns long-term investing from an aspirational goal into a mechanical process—consistent, boring, and quietly transformational. The aim is not to optimise every last basis point or predict market cycles. It's to remove emotion from the equation and let time do its work. Freelancers, who often face income variability, benefit more than most from this discipline—not less.

At the heart of this approach is the simple practice of setting up an automatic transfer from your income-holding account into a long-term investment vehicle. The destination doesn't need to be exotic. Low-cost index funds, globally diversified ETFs, or country-specific retirement wrappers like ISAs (UK), IRAs (US), or RRSPs (Canada) serve the purpose well. What matters most isn't the vehicle. It's the ritual.

Consistency trumps intensity. A freelancer who invests £300 every month for twenty years will typically outperform a peer who delays for ten years and then scrambles to invest £1,000 monthly. The market rewards the early and the steady. It does not reward brilliance postponed.

One of the most psychologically powerful shifts a freelancer can make is to mentally upgrade their investment contribution from "whatever's left over" to "non-negotiable line item." Treat it not as an optional flourish, but as an act of internal payroll. You are both employer and employee. Your future self is on the books now. Set the direct debit and move on.

The argument often raised is one of unpredictability—how can someone automate investing when they don't know what they'll earn next month? The answer lies in proportional design. Rather than fixing a static monthly figure, many freelancers tie their investment transfer to a percentage of income. For example, a rule such as "15% of everything I make gets invested on the 10th of the following month" allows for variance while preserving momentum. This ratio-based system adapts fluidly to feast and famine alike.

Index investing, often dismissed as too plain or passive, is in fact the ideal strategy for the self-employed. It demands no forecasting, no industry knowledge, and no constant rebalancing. It requires only two things: a willingness to buy broad exposure to the global economy, and the patience to hold it through chaos. Unlike active trading, which tempts freelancers to waste valuable working hours chasing short-term gains, index investing liberates attention for the work that pays the bills.

What about risk? Isn't investing risky, especially during volatile markets? Statistically, yes—*over short periods*. But this is precisely why automation matters. By setting regular contributions regardless of market conditions, you engage in what's known as *pound-cost averaging* (or dollar-cost averaging, depending on geography). This strategy cushions the impact of volatility by buying more shares when prices are low and fewer when prices are high. Over time, this flattens the emotional rollercoaster and encourages discipline over drama.

It's also worth emphasising that "long-term" does not always mean "retirement at 65." For freelancers, long-term wealth isn't just about exit plans—it's about *optionality*. An automated investing strategy can fund mini-retirements, career sabbaticals, or resilience during downturns. A solid portfolio gives you time to choose wisely, rather than scramble reactively. Financial independence, even partial, creates intellectual and creative freedom.

Of course, automating investing doesn't mean ignoring it. Periodic reviews—perhaps twice a year—ensure that allocations still match your needs and that fees remain low. But the operational tempo should be deliberate and infrequent. The goal is not to become a financial analyst; the goal is to remove yourself from daily market noise.

Technology makes this easier than ever. Most modern brokerages and robo-advisors offer automation features with minimal setup. You can link your income account, set a transfer schedule, and allocate contributions according to your risk tolerance—all in under an hour. Once done, your system will quietly reinforce your financial future, whether or not you're paying attention.

This is not a luxury manoeuvre. It is a foundational habit. Freelancers often say they crave stability but believe they can't have it until income is consistent. The reality is the inverse: *stability is built through systems, not waiting.* Automating long-term investing is one of the few ways to reclaim the future without surrendering the present.

Every successful freelancer eventually confronts the reality that no one is coming to build their pension for them. But that's not a tragedy. It's an opportunity. In a world without HR departments, becoming your own benefits coordinator is not just savvy—it's mandatory. And the easiest way to begin is not with a spreadsheet or a consultation. It's with a scheduled, recurring transfer. Set it. Forget it. Let time and discipline do the rest.

Beyond Retirement: Building Optionality

The traditional idea of retirement—a fixed age when work ceases and leisure begins—was designed for a world that no longer exists. It was built around lifetime employment, predictable pensions, and an industrial work culture that assumed exhaustion by sixty-five. Freelancers, by contrast, navigate a different landscape entirely. There is no set retirement date. No employer-funded pension. No ceremonial handoff to a gold watch and a golf course. And yet, this is not a loss. It's a release.

For the self-employed, the question isn't "When can I stop working?" It's "How much freedom can I build into my future?" Retirement, in this context, is better understood not as an age, but as a *condition of financial optionality*—the capacity to choose what you do with your time, regardless of whether it earns income. In a world of fluid careers, shifting priorities, and extended lifespans, this reframing isn't merely helpful—it's essential.

Optionality is a more useful framework than retirement because it reflects how freelancers live and work. Many independent professionals don't aspire to stop working altogether. They want to reduce dependence on clients, step away from urgent projects, or explore slower-paced creative endeavours without financial pressure. They want freedom *from* obligation and freedom *to* pursue what matters. Optionality is the architecture of that freedom.

Building optionality begins with recognising that the absence of employer-sponsored retirement doesn't exempt you from long-term planning—it requires you to take full ownership of it. Instead of waiting for someone to offer you a pension, you create one in pieces. You automate investments, track your buffers, and build a portfolio that buys you time, not just returns. Every pound saved today isn't just for "later." It's for *when you want to say no*—to a bad-fit client, an uninspiring gig, or a frenetic schedule.

This shift in thinking reshapes how you measure progress. Rather than fixating on a retirement number or arbitrary date, you begin to assess how many months of autonomy your savings can buy. Can you take a sabbatical? Could you downshift to part-time work? Do you have enough to explore a passion project without stress? These are the milestones of optionality—and they're often achievable long before traditional retirement thresholds.

Yet one of the deepest mental blocks freelancers face is the belief that investing for the future means abandoning the present. The assumption is that every pound set aside is a pound not used for living, learning, or growing today. This binary is false. *Investing in optionality is not deprivation—it's deferral with a purpose.* It's a way of ensuring your future self has the same range of choice that your present self craves. It's not about saying "no" to life now. It's about creating the ability to say "yes" later without compromise.

Importantly, optionality also buffers against risk in a way few insurance policies can. A freelancer with financial reserves can weather illness, burnout, or economic downturns without panic. They can choose rest when their body demands it. They can retrain when markets shift. They can walk away from toxic clients because they are not trapped in a cycle of hand-to-mouth dependency. This is not a luxury; it's a form of resilience.

There's also an ethical dimension to optionality. When you are not desperate, you can act with greater integrity. You can choose clients and causes aligned with your values. You can refuse exploitative arrangements. You can create from a place of fullness, not fear. In a profession where boundaries are often blurred and scarcity is normalised, optionality is a quiet, radical act of self-respect.

Some may argue that this kind of freedom is reserved for the high-earning elite. It isn't. Optionality is not an all-or-nothing proposition. It exists on a continuum. A month's expenses in a separate account is a form of optionality. So is a year's worth of index fund investments. The goal is not to match the pension pots of corporate executives but to create *enough*—enough to buy time, dignity, and creative space.

The tools for building optionality are well-established. Regular contributions to a diversified investment portfolio. Conscious control of expenses. A commitment to retaining a portion of income for your future self, just as you do for tax or business reserves. But what transforms these mechanics into meaning is the intention behind them. You're not hoarding for some far-off fantasy. You're building the freedom to live deliberately.

It's also crucial to note that optionality doesn't mean permanent withdrawal from work. For many freelancers, the idea of "never working again" feels alien or even undesirable. What changes isn't the desire to work—it's the *need* to. When your finances can support you regardless, work becomes elective. You write the book because you want to. You consult because the project excites you. You teach because you believe in the next generation. Optionality restores the agency that necessity erodes.

This reframing is especially urgent given demographic and economic shifts. The old model of retirement at sixty-five, funded by government support and employer pensions, is faltering globally. Life expectancy is rising. Health costs are growing. And the gig economy continues to reshape how work is structured. Freelancers are not outliers—they are a preview of the future. And in that future, building optionality isn't just good practice. It's survival strategy.

But unlike the rigid systems of the past, optionality is adaptable. It can be built slowly, interrupted without collapse, and resumed without shame. It respects the nonlinear lives freelancers often live. Career changes, parental leave, relocations, and reinventions—these are features, not bugs.

Optionality accommodates them. It's the difference between a fixed track and a flexible path.

The cultural narrative around retirement is overdue for replacement. Not because retirement itself is obsolete, but because the assumptions around it no longer serve most people—especially those outside traditional employment. For freelancers, the goal is not to work forever. It's to ensure that *if* you work forever, it's because you choose to—not because you can't afford not to.

Optionality is a form of power. Quiet, steady, unadvertised. It doesn't come from windfalls or shortcuts. It comes from habits, systems, and the refusal to outsource your financial future to circumstance. It doesn't ask you to predict what you'll want at age seventy. It asks you to protect your right to decide.

And that, in the end, may be the most radical freelance benefit of all: the ability to buy not just goods or services, but *time*. Time to think. Time to heal. Time to change. Time to rest. Time to begin again. Optionality is not retirement postponed—it is autonomy accumulated. And it is built, not granted.

Chapter 9
Insurance—The Missing Safety Net

Among the many celebrated freedoms of freelance life—flexible hours, creative control, location independence—there is a conspicuous absence: a safety net. While salaried employees glide through their careers with employer-sponsored health coverage, disability protection, and professional liability policies quietly embedded in benefits packages, freelancers walk a high wire, exposed. The absence of institutional coverage is not a minor inconvenience; for many, it carries existential weight.

Illness or injury is not simply inconvenient—it is financially destabilising. A hospital visit halts revenue, a back injury can cascade into unpaid invoices, missed deadlines, or cancelled retainers. Even a baseless lawsuit can erode savings more rapidly than a downturn in client work. Yet, despite these risks, insurance remains one of the most underutilised tools among the self-employed.

The gap is not merely structural; it is psychological. Freelancers often acknowledge, in theory, that insurance is prudent—but abstract understanding rarely translates into action. Why? Because insurance feels optional until it is essential. It feels expensive until it delivers relief. It feels intangible until tangible consequences arrive. Perhaps most perniciously, purchasing insurance can feel like a wager against oneself—an act of pessimism rather than foresight. That emotional aversion breeds paralysis, leaving exposure unmitigated.

The real peril is not that freelancers face risk—everyone does. It is that they face it largely alone, unbuffered by protections that others take for granted. The moment a designer leaves an agency to work solo, their dental coverage vanishes. A project manager stepping into consulting loses the implicit shield of income protection if illness strikes. A content strategist building a six-figure brand often overlooks professional liability coverage. These omissions are not negligence; they are the natural consequence of a system that fails to instruct freelancers on safeguarding what they create.

What is required is not fear, but architecture: a structured, intentional system of layered protections that grows alongside income and responsibilities. One need not purchase every policy at once, but it is imperative to understand the risks you bear, the coverage options available, and how to prioritise protection sustainably. This is about sequencing rather than perfection. Just as you invest in skills, clients, and operational systems, you must invest in your capacity to withstand the unpredictable.

This chapter reframes insurance as a tool of freedom, not anxiety. When you know your health costs won't bankrupt you, a lawsuit won't undo your livelihood, and a serious illness won't devastate your income, you gain the confidence to take calculated risks—professional, creative, and financial. You can accept a challenging contract without fearing exposure. You can refuse toxic clients without economic panic. You can pause to recover without sliding into debt. The real value of insurance is rarely the payout itself, but the peace of mind it cultivates beforehand.

We will begin by examining the fundamental risks freelancers face—the subtle vulnerabilities that arise not merely from lacking coverage, but from failing to understand it. From there, we will demystify key insurance categories for the self-employed: health, disability, liability, and more. We will explore cognitive and emotional biases that cause capable individuals to postpone essential protection, despite recognising its importance. Finally, we will propose a tiered, actionable model—a "protection stack"—to guide decision-making with clarity, replacing fear and avoidance with informed agency.

This is not a sales pitch for policies. It is a call to reclaim autonomy. Freelancing is already an act of courage: trading security for independence, predictability for potential. Yet autonomy without protection is fragile. Potential without contingency is perilous. Insurance, properly understood, is not dependency—it is infrastructure, enabling independence to thrive under pressure.

Self-employment demands many competencies—creative expertise, negotiation acumen, financial literacy—but above all, it requires self-stewardship. No HR department will intervene. No corporate safety net waits in the wings. You are your own risk manager. With the right mindset and tools, this responsibility can be transformed into resilience—for yourself, for clients who rely on your stability, for the family depending on your income, and for the vision you are building one invoice at a time.

This chapter is an invitation: to pause, assess, and safeguard. To relinquish the illusion of invincibility and replace it with durability. To craft a freelance career not only for achievement, but for endurance. Because the only riskier move than buying insurance is pretending you will never need it.

When You Can't Afford to Get Sick

There is a quiet but dangerous contradiction at the heart of modern freelance life: the very autonomy that makes independent work attractive also makes it exceptionally fragile. For salaried workers, illness is inconvenient; for freelancers, it can be catastrophic. A minor surgery, a sprained wrist, a viral infection lasting two weeks—what would be a paid inconvenience for someone with sick leave becomes a revenue shutdown for the self-employed. There is no HR department to call. No sick pay. No short-term disability coverage unless it has been self-funded. The freelance economy, for all its virtues, remains structurally indifferent to the realities of human health.

This fragility isn't always visible—until it's too late. Freelancers often operate under the illusion of invincibility, partly because the systems around them incentivise denial. Insurance premiums feel like a tax on anxiety. Medical risk feels abstract until it isn't. And productivity culture whispers that downtime is a failure of will. But a single accident, a routine hospital stay, or a bout of burnout severe enough to require rest can dismantle a quarter's worth of earnings in days. The question is not whether one *might* face an income-threatening health event, but whether one has acknowledged the statistical certainty that, over a multi-decade career, it will happen.

The myth of the "lean hustle" lifestyle often ignores this brutal arithmetic. A well-run freelance business cannot merely be defined by its ability to earn. It must also be judged by its ability to *withstand*. Resilience is not measured in optimism but in preparation, and nowhere is this more vital than when illness or injury turns time into a liability rather than a billable asset.

Health insurance, then, is not a luxury. It is income protection, operational continuity, and a form of economic dignity. For freelancers, the temptation is to treat insurance as something optional—useful in theory, deferrable in practice. The premiums can feel unjustified when compared to rent, groceries, or business software. But this perspective fails to account for the asymmetric nature of risk. You might go years without needing cover, but when you do, it is rarely minor. It is rarely cheap. And it is always urgent.

The financial harm of illness compounds quickly. Missed income is only the beginning. Medical bills—especially in systems without universal healthcare—are often opaque, non-negotiable, and misaligned with actual care quality. There are secondary costs too: cancelled client contracts, rushed work that damages reputation, or missed opportunities due to delayed recovery. Without insurance, these costs are paid out of emergency funds, lines of credit, or future ambitions. The effects ripple.

Psychologically, illness also erodes professional confidence. The inability to work provokes guilt, anxiety, and a sense of isolation. Freelancers, by definition, lack institutional insulation. There are no colleagues to delegate to, no built-in continuity plans. When illness strikes, many feel compelled to work through it—not because it's wise or sustainable, but because the alternative is watching both health and income deteriorate in tandem. This is not resilience. It is mismanagement disguised as grit.

This is why viewing insurance purely as a healthcare product is conceptually incomplete. It is better understood as a form of operational infrastructure—an invisible but critical element of business continuity. Health insurance protects your ability to earn. Disability insurance protects your capacity to work over the long term. Liability insurance shields your assets and reputation. Together, they form a financial firewall against interruptions that could otherwise spiral into collapse.

Consider a software consultant who develops carpal tunnel syndrome—a condition that requires weeks of rest and possible surgery. Without insurance, the consultant might delay care, worsening the damage and extending recovery. With it, they can address the problem early, reduce income loss, and maintain continuity through planned downtime. Or think of a freelance photographer who injures their back lifting equipment. Without health coverage, a simple emergency room visit becomes a five-figure debt. These are not extreme scenarios. They are ordinary events with disproportionately severe consequences when insurance is absent.

Yet many freelancers delay purchasing coverage—not because they don't understand the risk, but because the tradeoff feels abstract. Monthly premiums are a tangible outflow. The benefit is probabilistic. This is where behavioural economics offers insight. Loss aversion makes people more sensitive to immediate costs than to potential future losses. Present bias leads us to undervalue future needs in favour of current cash flow. And optimism bias causes us to underestimate the likelihood of adverse events happening to us. Combined, these cognitive distortions make insurance feel wasteful—until it's indispensable.

The solution is not more fear. It is design. A well-structured freelance business bakes risk management into its operations. This includes building insurance premiums into your pricing strategy, viewing them as part of your baseline operating expenses—not discretionary extras. It means comparing policies not just on cost but on payout conditions, exclusions, and support mechanisms. And it means talking to other freelancers, openly, about what has gone wrong—not just what has gone right. Transparency normalises prudence.

For those in countries with public healthcare systems, the calculus is different but not irrelevant. Even in nations with state-sponsored care, freelancers often lack income protection if they're unable to work. They may also require supplemental insurance to access non-emergency services, faster care, or specialist treatment. The point is not that every country has the same gaps—it's that every system has *some*, and freelancers are almost always among the least protected.

The broader imperative is to reframe the narrative entirely. Insurance is not about paranoia. It is about planning. It is not a sign of weakness or pessimism but of professionalism. If your income depends on your ability to show up, think clearly, move your body, or use your hands—then protecting that capacity is not indulgent. It is essential. Health is not separate from your business model. It *is* your business model.

Over the course of a freelance career, you will face illness. You may face injury. These are not moral failings or signs of poor judgement. They are part of being human. The question is not whether these moments will come. It is whether you've structured your business—and your mindset—to absorb them without collapse. Insurance, when properly understood, is not a cost to be minimised but a lever to be managed. It buys time, options, and continuity. And when you cannot afford to get sick, those things are the real currency of freedom.

Health, Disability, and Liability Essentials

For the self-employed, risk does not sit neatly outside the margins of daily work. It seeps into the core business model, silently shaping what a freelancer can or cannot recover from. When salaried employees encounter misfortune—be it illness, injury, or litigation—there is often a backstop: employer-sponsored insurance, paid leave, legal resources. Freelancers operate without such scaffolding. Their protection, if it exists, must be built by design. Without it, the fallout of a single event can be financially existential. *Insurance, then, is not a bureaucratic checkbox. It is operational armour for the self-employed.* And yet, too many approach it reactively—after something has gone wrong.

A well-designed freelance insurance strategy begins with three foundational pillars: health, disability, and liability. Each addresses a distinct category of threat: the cost of care, the loss of earning capacity, and the exposure to legal or contractual damage. Importantly, these aren't just technical products; they are strategic safeguards. Together, they form a triad of resilience that allows freelancers to move through uncertainty without gambling their entire livelihood on hope.

Let us begin with health insurance—the most obvious, and paradoxically, the most commonly deferred. In markets without universal healthcare, going uninsured is not just risky—it is financially reckless. Emergency surgeries, specialist diagnostics, hospital stays—these can cost more than an entire year's income. But even in countries with public systems, freelancers must consider private supplements to cover outpatient treatment, dental, vision, faster access to services, or international care. *The real question is not whether you can afford premiums; it's whether you can afford to self-insure against the most expensive events in modern life.*

Critically, not all health insurance is equal. Some plans appear inexpensive but carry exorbitant deductibles or limited networks. Others deny coverage for common self-employed scenarios—like mental health, physiotherapy, or work-related injuries. A sophisticated approach involves evaluating policies not simply by monthly cost, but by total annual exposure. What will it take to access real treatment? What scenarios are excluded? Can you afford the *gap* between coverage and care?

Then comes disability insurance—the most misunderstood and underutilised policy in the freelance economy. Most freelancers don't believe they need it until the need becomes personal. Disability is not a rare, catastrophic accident. It is also chronic back pain. Tendinitis. Depression. A car accident that limits mobility. A condition that makes creative work slower, less reliable, or impossible. If your income depends on your physical or cognitive capacity—and most freelance income does—then disability coverage is not a luxury. It is wage insurance.

Short-term disability insurance typically covers a few months of lost income after an illness or injury. Long-term disability picks up where the short-term ends, offering protection for years—or even decades. The logic is simple: if you can't perform your work, your revenue disappears, but your expenses do not. *Without income replacement, illness becomes not just a health crisis but a financial collapse.* Yet few freelancers have these policies in place, often because they've never seen a clear, relatable explanation of what disability insurance actually does. That, in itself, is a market failure.

Choosing a disability policy requires precision. Some plans only pay if you cannot do *any* work—not just your current occupation. Others define disability in narrow, technical terms. The most protective plans are "own-occupation" policies, which pay out if you can't perform the job you were doing when you became disabled—even if you could theoretically do something else. This is particularly important for freelancers with specialised skills, like photographers, musicians, or writers. If carpal tunnel makes it impossible to shoot or type, an "own-occupation" policy will compensate. A generic one may not.

The third pillar—liability insurance—often seems remote until it becomes urgent. It is the only product that protects freelancers from the unpredictable (and increasingly frequent) legal exposures of modern business. Did a client claim your work resulted in financial loss? Were you accused of breaching a contract? Did your website get hacked and leak user data? Did you injure someone accidentally on a shoot or at a client site? These aren't hypotheticals. They are common scenarios with real legal consequences. Without cover, you pay for lawyers and settlements out of pocket. *With liability insurance, your business survives the fallout.*

There are two primary forms of liability cover relevant to freelancers: professional indemnity (or errors and omissions) insurance, and public liability insurance. The first covers legal claims arising from your professional work—whether it's a mistake in code, a design that didn't perform as expected, or advice that a client acted on to their detriment. The second covers incidents involving third-party injury or property damage—like tripping over your gear or accidentally damaging a client's equipment on-site.

A sophisticated freelancer doesn't ask, "Is this likely to happen to me?" but rather, "Could I survive if it did?" Legal claims do not always stem from wrongdoing. They often arise from miscommunication, unmet expectations, or opportunistic litigation. *Liability insurance is not an admission of guilt. It is a barrier between your freelance practice and the financial chaos of legal escalation.*

What makes these three categories—health, disability, and liability—essential is not that they are universally required. It's that they protect against qualitatively different types of risk. Health insurance shields your ability to access treatment. Disability insurance protects your income. Liability insurance protects your assets and your reputation. Together, they form a scaffolding that allows you to operate in volatile environments without fear that a single disruption will end your business.

But understanding is not enough. Implementation requires habit. Insurance policies must be reviewed annually. Coverage must evolve as your income, geography, and risk profile change. A part-time freelancer working from home has different exposures than someone running a growing studio with subcontractors. Yet too many treat insurance as a one-time purchase. They buy a policy—often the cheapest one they can find—and forget it exists until it fails them.

The mature approach is iterative. Begin with what's essential, even if minimal. Build up coverage over time as revenue stabilises. Use professional brokers if needed—ideally those who specialise in freelance or small business clients, and who can explain policies in plain language. Reframe insurance not as a burden but as a form of strategic readiness. It is the opposite of paranoia. It is confidence, made durable.

There is no glamour in insurance. No client will ask about it. No portfolio will showcase it. But when things go wrong—and eventually, something always does—it is the invisible infrastructure that keeps you from losing everything else. Freelancers may work independently, but they should not risk independently. *Health, disability, and liability insurance are not bureaucratic extras. They are essential tools in the art of staying in business.*

The Psychology of Insurance Avoidance

The question isn't whether freelancers know they *should* have insurance. Most do. The real question is why they don't act on that knowledge. Why do rational, capable professionals—often meticulous in their craft, organised in their finances, and aware of their vulnerabilities—consistently postpone or altogether avoid acquiring the very tools that could preserve their livelihood in a crisis? The answer lies not in ignorance but in psychology. Understanding why freelancers avoid insurance requires tracing the contours of human cognition: the biases, fears, and narratives that shape financial behaviour beneath the surface of logic.

The most obvious factor is cost aversion—but to call it mere cost sensitivity is to miss the deeper mechanics. Insurance, by design, requires paying now for an event that may never occur. This goes against the grain of how our brains are wired to value immediacy. Behavioural economics has long documented the human tendency toward *hyperbolic discounting*—the preference for smaller, immediate rewards over larger, delayed ones. For a freelancer choosing between a £180 monthly premium and investing the same amount in equipment, training, or marketing, the insurance feels like a forfeited opportunity. The gear delivers utility now. The policy delivers nothing visible until catastrophe strikes. *The brain discounts the future at a punitive rate—making risk management seem wasteful until it's too late.*

Adding to this is the mental discomfort of contemplating disaster. Buying insurance is an exercise in imaginative vulnerability. To do it properly, one must envision illness, accident, litigation—events that threaten identity and independence. This invokes *loss aversion*, a cornerstone of behavioural psychology. Humans feel the pain of potential losses more acutely than the pleasure of equivalent gains. It's easier, then, to avoid the thought altogether. Insurance becomes not just a financial purchase, but a psychological confrontation. Delay is easier than engaging that discomfort.

There is also the potent illusion of control. Freelancers, by necessity, cultivate self-reliance. Their businesses are self-built; their risks, self-managed. That sense of agency can become distorted into overconfidence: a belief that bad things happen to other people—people who are careless, disorganised, or less skilled. This is the *invincibility bias*. It's the voice that says, "I'm healthy. I eat well. I don't need health insurance," or "My clients love me. I'd never get sued." But risk is indifferent to virtue. Good health habits don't prevent a reckless driver from running a red light. A clean legal record doesn't guarantee a frivolous claim won't be filed. The freelancer's mindset—optimistic, self-directed, industrious—is often the very thing that blinds them to the necessity of protective structures.

Trust also plays a role, or rather, its absence. Freelancers often operate at the intersection of institutional scepticism and budget consciousness. Many have been burned by bureaucracies or opaque fine print. They've heard horror stories of denied claims and endless red tape. The result is a default posture of cynicism: why pay into a system that might betray you when you need it most? This is not paranoia—it's a rational response to poorly designed or mis-sold policies. But it also reveals a misunderstanding. *Insurance is not a promise of perfection. It is a probability hedge—a transfer of catastrophic risk to an entity better equipped to absorb it.* To demand certainty from it is to misread its function.

There's also an aesthetic dimension to avoidance. Insurance is dull. It does not spark the imagination or fuel ambition. It does not reward the ego, build a brand, or advance a skillset. It is administrative, often jargon-heavy, and emotionally ungratifying. In a culture that celebrates growth and hustle, insurance feels like inertia. It's the financial equivalent of eating vegetables—not sexy, not exciting, but essential. The freelancer, especially one with limited bandwidth, is more likely to optimise for visibility and progress than for unseen resilience. *But the most successful freelancers over time are not those who avoid misfortune. They are those who remain structurally intact when misfortune arrives.*

Overcoming these psychological blocks is not a matter of more education. Most freelancers don't need to be *taught* what insurance is. They need to be guided through the inner resistance that prevents them from acting. That process begins with reframing. Insurance is not a sunk cost—it is *permission*. It gives you the freedom to say yes to opportunities without fearing the fallout of worst-case scenarios. It allows you to take leave, recover from injury, or defend yourself legally without derailing your career. It transforms random chaos into manageable inconvenience.

The next step is simplification. Complexity breeds procrastination. When the insurance market presents an avalanche of options, acronyms, exclusions, and clauses, the natural human response is avoidance. Providers and brokers who serve freelancers should be evaluated not just on product cost but on clarity. Can they explain a policy without jargon? Do they understand your specific risks as a self-employed person? Freelancers can also leverage community knowledge—asking peers, comparing notes, and building institutional memory where formal systems fail.

Then there's the need to de-couple action from perfection. Many avoid insurance because they fear choosing the wrong policy. But *some cover is almost always better than none.* You can revise and improve over time. Start with the biggest exposures—health and liability—and layer additional policies as income stabilises. Just as with investing, the key is compounding: benefits accrue not just from the policy itself, but from the consistency of coverage over time.

Freelancers must also internalise a paradox: the less often you use insurance, the more valuable it is. If you go years without needing to file a claim, that's not wasted money—it's proof that your resilience has been preserved. The problem isn't the absence of payout. It's the absence of protection when needed. *Insurance is the only product we hope never to use. Its worth lies in the options it protects, not in its day-to-day utility.*

Ultimately, insurance avoidance is not about irresponsibility. It's about fear, friction, and misaligned incentives. The freelance mindset rewards immediacy, agility, and lean decision-making—all of which clash with the slow, anticipatory nature of risk planning. But long-term sustainability in self-employment requires more than talent and grit. It requires structural foresight. Freelancers must build not only income streams but safety nets. Not out of fear, but out of respect—for their time, their work, and their future selves.

To navigate the unpredictable terrain of self-employment, one must accept that freedom without protection is merely exposure. *And exposure, unmanaged, is not entrepreneurship—it is gambling.* Insurance, when properly understood, is not a reluctant expense. It is an operating system for staying in business through the unplanned, the unfair, and the unforeseeable. The psychology of avoidance is real, but it is not destiny. With the right framing, the right advice, and the right sequence, any freelancer can move from procrastination to protection—quietly, decisively, and before they wish they had.

Building Your Protection Stack

Most freelancers do not begin their careers with a perfectly engineered safety net. They start lean—bootstrapping clients, juggling deadlines, and managing their own admin in borrowed time. Insurance, if it appears at all, enters the conversation as a distant afterthought—something for later, something for when you're "more established." But the truth is this: *protection scales better than panic.* What protects your business and livelihood doesn't need to be built all at once, nor does it require excessive spending. What it does require is intention, sequencing, and clarity. That is the essence of the protection stack—a layered, budget-conscious strategy that allows freelancers to build resilience incrementally without overwhelming their finances.

The first layer of any freelancer's insurance strategy must begin where risk is both most likely and most devastating: personal health. Unlike salaried employees with employer-sponsored schemes, freelancers face the full exposure of medical expenses. A single injury or illness can wipe out months of income. It is not the unlikely catastrophe that derails careers—it is the unbudgeted root canal, the torn tendon, the undiagnosed infection. Basic health insurance, even if not fully comprehensive, *buys access*—to doctors, medications, early interventions. That alone shifts the odds in your favour. If a full policy feels unaffordable, some protection is still worth having. Even a high-deductible or outpatient-only plan creates a buffer that separates minor setbacks from cascading debt.

Once health is addressed, the next layer is income protection via disability insurance. This is often misunderstood. People imagine disability insurance as something for freak accidents or rare diseases. But the more statistically likely causes—musculoskeletal disorders, burnout, chronic pain, mental health—are what sideline freelancers most often. Disability insurance replaces income if you're unable to work due to health issues for weeks, months, or longer. Think of it as a freelance sick-leave policy. The irony is that many freelancers purchase software to automate tasks they might do more slowly themselves, but hesitate to insure the *actual machine* generating their income—their bodies and minds. If your livelihood depends on your ability to show up, disability cover is not a luxury—it's a stabiliser.

Layer three is liability—protection against professional errors, contract disputes, data breaches, or accidental harm caused in the course of business. Freelancers who handle client data, give advice, design systems, or publish content are all exposed here. Many assume that only lawyers or medical professionals need malpractice cover, but a web developer who delivers buggy code, a copywriter accused of plagiarism, or a consultant blamed for a project's failure all face similar risks. *Professional indemnity insurance (also called errors and omissions cover)* serves to protect your business from these kinds of client claims. Without it, a single legal notice—regardless of merit—can force you into defensive spending or settlement, even if you did nothing wrong. Legal defence alone is a cost most freelancers cannot casually absorb.

From here, additional coverage can be added based on the nature of your work and life. If you use expensive equipment, consider contents insurance or a separate policy for portable gear. If you rent a coworking space or see clients face-to-face, you may need public liability cover. If you employ subcontractors or virtual assistants, you may be subject to employer liabilities under local law. And if your freelance work feeds a household, life insurance—especially term coverage—should be part of the discussion. *It is not the size of the business that determines the need for insurance—it is the scale of the impact when something goes wrong.*

What makes the protection stack effective is its sequencing. You do not need to purchase all of it at once. Instead, you build it in layers, matching each addition to your risk exposure and income trajectory. Early-stage freelancers with variable earnings can prioritise catastrophic protection and defer lower-priority policies until cash flow strengthens. Think of it as a form of *risk triage*. Ask: What would disrupt your income tomorrow? What would endanger your professional credibility? What would cause a domino effect you couldn't reverse? Then solve for those first.

Budget-conscious freelancers should also understand that cost is not always linear. Some of the most valuable policies—especially term life and basic liability—are remarkably inexpensive if purchased early. Disability coverage becomes more expensive with age or diagnosis. Health premiums tend to rise annually regardless of usage. In other words, *the longer you delay protection, the more it costs to buy in later—sometimes prohibitively so.* Conversely, the sooner you start, the more you lock in affordability and coverage.

The structure of a good protection stack isn't just financial—it's psychological. When freelancers purchase insurance reactively—after an illness, a lawsuit, or a scare—they are already negotiating from a place of fear or urgency. But when you build cover proactively, you shift your mindset from defence to strategy. You operate with a calm that permeates decisions. You pursue larger clients with confidence. You take time off when needed. You engage legal contracts more seriously. And most critically, you stop treating personal catastrophe as a freelance business risk.

To build intelligently, freelancers should work with brokers or advisors who understand self-employed workflows and revenue patterns. Most traditional brokers are trained for salaried employment contexts and may not understand cash flow volatility or platform-based income. Ask specifically whether the policy assumes monthly income, allows lump-sum or irregular earnings, or covers the hybrid workspaces common to freelancers. *The best policies recognise the reality of freelance economics and design coverage that flexes with it.*

It's also worth recognising that the protection stack is cumulative but not static. It should be reviewed annually or after any major professional shift—such as going full-time, expanding into new services, hiring support, or relocating internationally. What made sense in your first year may no longer cover your risk profile in year five. Conversely, some policies may become redundant or overlapped as platforms evolve—for example, if a client platform begins offering limited coverage. The goal is not to spend endlessly on overlapping protection but to *cover the critical gaps that could compromise your independence.*

Culturally, freelancers need to stop viewing insurance as a hedge against fear and start seeing it as an investment in professional credibility. Clients, especially enterprise or regulated organisations, increasingly expect independent contractors to carry liability insurance. Some require it contractually. Having it in place signals professionalism, foresight, and accountability. It positions the freelancer not as a gig worker but as a peer to the businesses they serve.

None of this implies that insurance is a panacea. It does not eliminate uncertainty. It does not replace the need for savings or legal literacy. It does not prevent bad luck. But *it makes bad luck less ruinous.* And in a profession where your health is your office, your output is your asset, and your time is your inventory, this matters more than most realise.

A freelance protection stack is not about planning for disaster. It is about *staying in business* when the unexpected happens—and staying in business, as any seasoned freelancer will tell you, is more important than any short-term gain. It is not glamorous. It will not trend. But it is the kind of quiet infrastructure that separates the amateurs from the professionals, the fragile from the antifragile, and the temporarily successful from the sustainably independent. Build it slowly. Build it wisely. But build it—because when you need it, you won't have time to go shopping.

Chapter 10
Debt, Discipline, and the Dopamine Trap

A steady paycheck cushions many financial missteps. It disguises overspending, masks misallocations, and lends predictability to obligations. Freelance life, however, dismantles that scaffolding. Without consistent deposits, the line between resourcefulness and recklessness becomes perilously thin. Freelancers do more than manage income—they manufacture it, often from erratic sources that spike and stall unpredictably. In this context, debt transforms from a neutral tool into an emotional buffer. It doesn't merely fund purchases; it soothes uncertainty, defers hard choices, and alleviates the tension of feast-and-famine cycles. The challenge lies not just in the money borrowed, but in the rationale behind it and the moment it substitutes for discipline.

Debt is not inherently irresponsible or immoral. In many situations, it is strategic, functional, and even essential, enabling investment in tools, training, infrastructure, and growth. Freelancers, though, inhabit a different terrain than salaried workers. Lacking a reliable floor beneath their financial life, the pressure to cover gaps—anticipated or real—arises frequently. In such a high-pressure environment, credit feels less like a choice and more like a relief valve. Unpaid invoices, looming expenses, necessary client-acquisition tools—all can justify a swipe or a line of credit. Yet desperation-driven debt rarely empowers.

Traditional debt advice seldom maps neatly onto freelance realities. Payment schedules presume stability; budgets assume predictability. Freelancers, navigating uncertainty, cannot rely on those assumptions. Many conventional paydown systems are designed for predictable earnings. Freelancers, however, often cannot forecast next month's revenue. They need systems that flex, scaling with income rather than presuming its steadiness. The danger is not the debt itself, but applying salaried logic to a self-employed context. Rigid repayment schedules without buffers can create more strain than the original loan.

A more nuanced framework is required—one that distinguishes strategic debt from survival debt. Strategic debt carries a purpose, a payoff, and a defined horizon: financing a course that generates revenue, upgrading hardware to increase output, or purchasing a business asset that will repay itself. Survival debt, conversely, is often incurred to maintain appearances, avoid discomfort, or smooth income irregularities without a repayment plan. One builds capacity; the other builds fragility. What matters is not merely the sum borrowed, but the intent behind it—and the mechanism by which it will be repaid.

Discipline, too, demands deeper examination. In financial terms, it is not austerity or self-punishment. It is alignment between resources and values, enacted consistently. Freelancers cannot rely on willpower; it fails. Systems succeed. The goal is to design conditions in which better choices occur automatically. Percentage-based paydown plans, automated account transfers, deliberate spending gaps, and visual progress cues are all behavioural finance tools that embed discipline into infrastructure. Heroic self-control is fleeting; embedded systems endure.

There is also a subtler, psychological dimension—the dopamine feedback loop of irregular income. In a flush month, spending rises impulsively—not from greed, but relief. In lean periods, even small purchases provoke guilt or anxiety. This feast-famine cycle is biochemical. The brain, conditioned by scarcity, over-rewards when resources arrive. Freelancers call this "reward spending" or "catch-up living," but it is essentially the nervous system attempting to regulate a survival threat. The high of expenditure substitutes for the calm of security, leaving a crash—and often a new debt balance—behind.

Breaking this loop requires more than apps or accountability partners; it requires a reconfiguration of emotional architecture. Spending must be decoupled from celebration. Stability, not consumption, becomes the marker of success. Each payment is an opportunity to restore equilibrium—reducing debt, reinforcing buffers, funding future investments. Joy is not eliminated; it is reoriented. Peace is earned, not borrowed.

Cultural norms compound the challenge. In creative and digital industries, borrowing is often normalised: a new laptop, a travel shoot, a bootstrapped brand identity. Social media amplifies this perception, showcasing outcomes without revealing the debt underpinning them. Normalisation is not sustainability. Freelancers must distinguish optics from operations, presentation from solvency.

The first step in mastering freelance debt is honesty. What narratives surround borrowing? Is it a bridge, a crutch, a reward, a shame? Tools are ineffective without self-awareness. This chapter begins not with spreadsheets, but with the architecture of cognition, habit, and emotion. Once freelancers understand why they borrow, every repayment plan gains resilience.

Debt can be instructive. It can signal priorities and teach lessons. But it must never arise from fatigue or frustration. This chapter offers more than technical solutions—it proposes a shift in posture: from reactivity to reflection, from borrowed comfort to designed resilience. The objective is not to vilify borrowing or glorify austerity. It is to help freelancers wield debt as a tool rather than a trap, and to design discipline into their systems rather than rely on fleeting willpower.

Executed well, this transformation restores autonomy, momentum, and energy for the work freelancers do best.

The Lure of Credit When Income Lags

Scarcity sharpens the mind—but not always in ways that serve long-term decision-making. For freelancers, irregular income isn't an inconvenience; it's a defining feature of their professional existence. There are months when invoices flood in, projects land in rapid succession, and bank balances swell. But then come the lulls—when payments delay, leads dry up, or health forces a pause. During these stretches, the psychological tension of "not enough" can be as destabilising as the numerical shortfall itself. It's in that gap—between discomfort and solution—that credit offers its seductive promise: instant relief, a bridge to normalcy, a cushion from uncertainty. But the speed with which it offers help is precisely what makes it dangerous.

Unlike salaried employees, who can map their debts against a predictable future, freelancers must forecast from ambiguity. This distorts their perception of risk. A credit card swipe in a moment of financial strain doesn't feel like overspending—it feels like *survival*. And when future income is always theoretically "just around the corner," every debt decision becomes easier to justify. "I'll pay this back as soon as the client pays." "Next month is usually stronger." "It's just to hold me over." These rationalisations compound, especially when the calendar—and the client—doesn't cooperate. What begins as a short-term measure becomes a recurring pattern. *Credit becomes a habit, not a strategy.*

Yet even awareness of the danger rarely translates into restraint. Why? Because the psychological weight of financial uncertainty is immense. When humans feel a resource is scarce, the brain narrows its focus. Cognitive bandwidth diminishes. Long-term trade-offs lose salience. Research in behavioural economics—particularly the work of Sendhil

Mullainathan and Eldar Shafir—has shown that scarcity itself changes the way people think, inducing tunnel vision that leads to poor decision-making. For freelancers under financial stress, credit doesn't appear as a liability; it appears as *freedom*. The problem is that this freedom is front-loaded. The consequences—interest, stress, reduced flexibility—are all delayed. The immediate benefit overshadows the long-term cost. And so the trap resets, each time reinforced by short-term relief.

What's needed is not just better budgeting or tighter self-control. What's needed is a reframing of debt itself—especially the distinction between *strategic debt* and *survival borrowing*. Strategic debt is used to extend capacity or generate future income. It might fund a new lens for a photographer, professional training for a consultant, or a marketing campaign for a designer launching a product line. Crucially, it is tied to a *deliberate plan*, an expected return, and a repayment mechanism built into cashflow. Strategic debt is optional, considered, and anchored in an income-producing hypothesis. It enhances leverage rather than merely postponing pain.

Survival debt, by contrast, emerges reactively. It's the £300 on a credit card to cover rent when a client ghosts you. It's the short-term loan to pay for groceries while waiting for overdue invoices. It's the growing balance that comes not from one catastrophic event, but from dozens of small acts of necessity. And while it may be emotionally understandable, it is financially corrosive. Survival debt compounds not just financially, but *psychologically*. It erodes confidence, tightens risk tolerance, and increases dependency on future windfalls. Worst of all, it normalises a relationship with money in which shortfalls are outsourced to lenders rather than addressed through structural change.

There is, however, a conceptual tension worth examining: sometimes, the line between strategic and survival debt isn't clear. A laptop breaks. Replacing it is essential to work, but the timing is poor. Is that strategic or survival? A course opens that could lead to higher rates, but only if marketed well and fully completed. Is that investment or impulse? The distinction lies not in the purchase, but in the *planning*. If the debt is accompanied by a realistic forecast, a contingency plan, and an honest appraisal of risk, it leans strategic. If it's accompanied by hope, urgency, and hand-waving—*"I'll figure it out later"*—it leans survival. Clarity comes not from the nature of the item, but from the nature of the decision-making process behind it.

This is where many freelancers get into trouble: they confuse income potential with income reliability. "I've made £5,000 in a month before, so I can carry this £1,500 balance without worry." But past peaks do not guarantee future averages. Freelance income tends to be lumpy, and borrowing decisions made in peak months often become unsustainable in trough periods. The more accurate approach is to assess borrowing capacity not based on the best months, but on *sustained averages minus volatility*. In other words, debt should never be built into a financial plan unless its repayment is feasible under conservative scenarios—not just optimistic ones.

It's also vital to acknowledge that lenders themselves are not neutral actors in this equation. Credit cards, fintech credit products, and even some business banking platforms are engineered to promote borrowing. The interface design, the ease of access, the strategic use of credit limits—they are built to nudge users toward short-term liquidity decisions. This is not conspiracy; it's business. But freelancers must recognise the asymmetry: they bear the full risk of income delay, while lenders earn predictable interest from that volatility. The game is not rigged, but it is stacked.

So how does a freelancer protect against the emotional pull of credit when income lags? One answer lies in *defaults*. If the default during shortfalls is to borrow, that behaviour will repeat. But if the default is to pause discretionary spending, draw from a buffer fund, or activate a predefined emergency protocol, behaviour changes. This requires preparation. A freelancer who anticipates income gaps—and designs for them—will rely less on reactive borrowing. A separate "slow month" fund, a capped spending plan during lean periods, or a percentage-based auto-withholding system can all reduce the psychological urgency that makes credit so appealing.

Another answer lies in *accountability*. Not public shaming or external monitoring, but internal transparency. Freelancers who document their debt decisions—what they borrowed, why, and how they plan to repay—tend to borrow more intentionally. Even a short personal memo attached to a debt decision can interrupt impulsive behaviour. That moment of metacognition—pausing to articulate the logic—often exposes weak assumptions before they calcify into liabilities.

It is also worth cultivating a broader emotional vocabulary around money. Too often, borrowing is entangled with shame, which paradoxically leads to secrecy and repetition. By reframing debt as a neutral tool, one that can be used wisely or poorly, freelancers regain agency. The goal is not to moralise borrowing, but to clarify its consequences. Some debts can expand freedom. Others restrict it. *Knowing the difference requires self-honesty, not just spreadsheets.*

Ultimately, the lure of credit during income lags is a symptom of a deeper problem: the lack of systems that anticipate fluctuation. It's easy to scorn impulsive borrowing when income is steady. But for freelancers operating under uncertainty, *credit is often a stand-in for infrastructure*. The solution, therefore, is not austerity, but architecture. Replace reactive borrowing with responsive planning. Build the capacity to withstand shortfalls without panic. Honour the reality of volatility without surrendering to it. Only then can credit return to its rightful place: a deliberate tool, not a desperate escape hatch.

Healthy Debt vs. Hazardous Debt

Not all debt is destructive. That simple truth, though intellectually obvious, often remains emotionally inaccessible—particularly for freelancers who experience money not in a straight line but as a volatile waveform. Debt, for them, is rarely abstract. It has rhythm and texture: the subtle dread of a credit card balance carried too long, the burst of relief when a client pays just in time, the ethical friction between future obligations and present necessity. But here lies the opportunity: *when understood precisely and used deliberately, debt can be more than survival—it can be leverage*. The difference between healthy debt and hazardous debt is not about the presence of a balance. It's about *what that balance enables*, *how it's planned*, and *what risk it assumes*.

To evaluate whether a debt is productive or precarious, one must start not with the product—loan, credit line, card—but with its purpose. What, exactly, is the borrowed money doing? If the answer is that it funds an asset that will generate future income or increase professional capacity, then the debt leans toward healthy. This might include investing in equipment that expands your service offering, paying for training that opens higher rates, or covering upfront costs to launch a new revenue stream. Here, debt acts as an accelerant—it brings forward a future that would otherwise arrive too slowly. It's tethered to a strategic rationale and a realistic repayment mechanism. *It's borrowed with a reason, not merely a hope.*

By contrast, debt becomes hazardous when it is used to maintain lifestyle, soothe anxiety, or defer structural problems. Using credit to fund consumption—a more comfortable flat, frequent dining out, or gadgets that satisfy a dopamine itch—may feel justified in moments of stress. But it rarely results in financial lift. These purchases do not generate income; they reduce future flexibility. Even small indulgences, when financed through debt, can accumulate into an invisible tax on future freedom. Worse, they embed a mental model in which borrowing is the default response to scarcity. This psychological pattern—normalising lifestyle maintenance through debt—quietly erodes resilience.

The freelancer's unique income pattern complicates the traditional models used to judge good vs. bad debt. Conventional personal finance wisdom often treats debt as a moral hazard—something to avoid unless tied to appreciating assets like property or education. But this framework was built around salaried, W-2 income earners. For freelancers, liquidity gaps are routine. Strategic borrowing is not about hedging against emergencies; it's about enabling continuity. The key, then, is to differentiate *investment debt*—used intentionally, with return assumptions—from *emotional debt,* which emerges from discomfort avoidance.

The distinction sharpens when repayment terms enter the picture. Healthy debt includes a plausible exit ramp. If the borrower can model the income stream that will service the debt, with reasonable margin for delay or underperformance, the debt aligns with sustainability. This is true even if the repayment horizon is long—what matters is *the structure, not the speed.* Hazardous debt, however, is characterised by ambiguity. No clear plan exists for paying it off beyond vague optimism. The interest rate compounds quietly in the background. Payments become reactive rather than proactive. And the debt begins to distort decision-making—limiting risk appetite, narrowing focus, or triggering guilt spirals that sap cognitive bandwidth.

Another dimension is the *emotional signature* of the debt decision. Healthy debt tends to feel strategic. It is approached with clarity, intention, and due diligence. It is accompanied by questions like: What is the expected return? What is the worst-case scenario? What alternatives exist? Hazardous debt, in contrast, tends to feel impulsive or defensive. It comes with a narrative of justification rather than strategy. It's accompanied by rationalisations: "I deserve this." "I can't say no to this opportunity." "Everyone has debt." These phrases often mask deeper emotional discomforts: fear of missing out, professional insecurity, or a desire to match perceived peer lifestyles.

Consider the case of a freelance developer who takes on a £10,000 loan to enrol in a high-end technical certification. The programme lasts six months and, if completed, opens the door to enterprise-level contracts that pay 3–5x her current rate. She's calculated a realistic timeline for completion, estimated how many months it would take to break even at her current workload, and has a fallback plan if the contracts take longer to arrive. This is healthy debt. Now compare that to a freelancer who, after a slow month, puts a holiday and several online shopping sprees on a credit card with 22% interest, planning only to "deal with it later" when a big client comes through. This is hazardous debt—not just financially, but psychologically.

One may argue that "all debt is bad until proven otherwise." But this is an unhelpful oversimplification. *Debt is a tool, and like all tools, it depends on the hand that wields it.* Just as a hammer can build a house or destroy one, credit can construct momentum or collapse it. The freelancer's task is not to eliminate debt from their financial landscape—it is to *interrogate it.* Where is it taking you? Under what assumptions? And who benefits if you're wrong?

An underexamined aspect of healthy debt is *timing*. Even a strong rationale can be undermined by poor sequencing. Taking on a business loan when you're already juggling personal debt creates a compounding risk. Using a credit card to prepay for future work without locking in the contract exposes you to cashflow mismatches. Strategic borrowing only functions when cash timing, capacity, and risk are coordinated. This is where freelancers often stumble—not because they're irresponsible, but because no one has taught them to model volatility. Bank underwriters assume income stability; freelancers must *design for instability*.

One of the most valuable practices for freelancers navigating debt decisions is the creation of a *debt evaluation protocol*. This might be a checklist, a spreadsheet, or even a personal conversation with a financially literate peer. The format is less important than the discipline. What matters is establishing a repeatable process that interrogates each borrowing decision with consistency. Questions to include: Is this debt funding an asset or an experience? Is the expected return financial, reputational, or emotional—and is it measurable? How certain is the timeline of that return? What happens if it doesn't arrive? Can this be deferred or approached another way?

A freelancer who integrates this kind of review into their workflow will borrow less emotionally and more effectively. They'll also build a mental map of their own financial decision-making—where they're strong, where they rationalise, and where they tend to blindspot risk. That awareness is not just financially protective—it's psychologically liberating.

Finally, debt decisions should never be made in isolation. The same loan that is strategic for one freelancer might be disastrous for another. Context matters: income pattern, personal obligations, mental health, risk tolerance, and professional trajectory all shape the health of a given debt. This is why comparisons are dangerous. Just because a peer built a business on credit doesn't mean it's prudent for you. *Your constraints, not someone else's outcomes, should govern your borrowing logic.*

Healthy debt supports growth, improves resilience, and expands optionality. Hazardous debt narrows choices, increases fragility, and distorts behaviour. The line between them is not moral but structural—what you're borrowing for, how you plan to repay, and what it costs you if you're wrong.

The goal is not to eliminate debt, but to design for it wisely, use it intentionally, and never confuse temporary relief with sustainable progress. That clarity, in itself, is a form of financial power.

Paydown Plans for Irregular Income

Most debt advice is written by and for people with regular paycheques. The formulas assume predictability: that income arrives on the same day each month, that it can be neatly split between fixed bills, variable expenses, and extra repayments. This framework crumbles in the face of freelance income. For self-employed workers, cash flow is neither linear nor polite. Payments arrive late, jobs stack up unpredictably, and one month's abundance can be followed by a slow, silent drought. Under these conditions, debt repayment becomes not just a financial challenge but a cognitive one—*how do you make promises to creditors when you can't even predict your next invoice date?*

The traditional "minimum payment + snowball or avalanche" method assumes the borrower has a baseline of income security. But freelancers operate on a fundamentally different timeline. Their budgeting requires flexibility without losing discipline—a system that contracts in lean months without collapsing, and expands in high-income periods without slipping into lifestyle inflation. For this, rigid payment schedules are insufficient. Instead, *a percentage-based repayment approach—anchored in revenue, not calendar—offers a model that adapts to uncertainty without surrendering accountability.*

Consider this: a freelancer commits to repaying 20% of their monthly post-tax income toward debt. If they earn £3,000, £600 is allocated to repayments. If they earn £1,500, they contribute £300. If they earn nothing, the repayment pauses without penalty to their psychological momentum. This approach shifts the frame from obligation to proportion. It respects the realities of freelance volatility while maintaining *intentional traction*. Crucially, it reduces the shame spiral that often accompanies missed fixed payments—a spiral that frequently leads to avoidance, denial, and the long-term consequences of compounding interest.

There's a psychological elegance to percentage-based planning. Humans are disproportionately more willing to act when the cost feels proportional rather than absolute. This is why tipping culture, commission rates, and profit-sharing schemes work: they scale with circumstance. For freelancers, this also introduces a layer of financial *self-awareness*. Every time income is received, they're prompted to ask: "What percentage of this should I allocate to progress?" That question builds a muscle that most traditional debt frameworks bypass entirely—the muscle of *adaptive financial decision-making*.

But a percentage plan alone is not sufficient. Debt needs direction. To build a working system, freelancers must also rank their debts by type, interest rate, and emotional weight. While conventional advice pits the snowball (smallest balance first) against the avalanche (highest interest first), freelancers benefit from a more nuanced lens: *the stress-weighted repayment model*. Here, you assign weight not only based on interest rates but also on how psychologically burdensome each debt feels. Sometimes the debt with the lowest balance or interest creates the most anxiety—because of who it's owed to, what it represents, or how it affects credit access. Paying down that debt first may yield a disproportionate increase in emotional clarity, which in turn fuels broader financial momentum.

A hybrid system emerges: use a set percentage of each payment as your debt pool, then split that pool across your liabilities using a tiered priority model. This model might include:

Tier 1: High-interest consumer debt or emotionally distressing balances

Tier 2: Medium-interest balances that don't generate psychological strain

Tier 3: Low-interest or long-term debt with manageable terms

This approach restores *a sense of agency*, even when income is unpredictable. The freelancer doesn't need to dread a fixed calendar date—they simply respond in proportion to what arrives, with a clear, pre-decided logic.

Technology can aid this system. Tools like percentage-based banking apps (e.g., You Need a Budget, Monzo pots, or budgeting features in Revolut and Starling) allow you to instantly siphon a portion of any incoming payment into a designated "Debt Repayment" pot. This is not just logistical—it's behavioural. Automating the moment of allocation reduces the risk of future rationalisation. If the money is set aside the same day it's received, there's less temptation to reroute it toward lifestyle creep or "just this once" indulgences.

Another lever for progress lies in rethinking the *language* of repayment. The term "minimum payment" is psychologically corrosive. It invites minimalism, not momentum. Freelancers can benefit from reframing payments as *progress investments*—micro-signals to their future selves that despite the chaos of self-employment, they are still moving forward. Even a £50 payment made in a low-income month reinforces the habit of engagement. It preserves the narrative that debt is *being addressed*, rather than accumulating silently.

For those whose income is highly seasonal or project-based—e.g., designers working on large quarterly contracts, or consultants with episodic retainers—a variation of the system can be built around *revenue thresholds*. For example: "Any time

I earn over £4,000 in a month, I'll allocate an extra 10% of the surplus toward debt." This threshold model avoids penalising good months with rigidity, while still converting windfalls into long-term benefit. It transforms debt repayment from a punishment into an act of *strategic harvest.*

Of course, debt is not an island. Its resolution must integrate with broader freelance financial planning: taxes, savings, reinvestment, and personal sustainability. A percentage-based repayment system should *coexist* with other proportional allocations—for example, 20% to taxes, 15% to savings, 5% to a wellness fund. By embedding repayment into the broader money architecture, debt becomes part of a *system*, not an emergency.

What about months when income is too low to make any progress? This is where pre-commitment to "income smoothing reserves" becomes vital. In high months, freelancers can set aside a portion of surplus to cover minimum debt contributions in future dry spells. This internal buffer functions like a self-issued insurance policy—designed not to eliminate volatility, but to ensure that volatility doesn't compromise forward motion.

It's also worth noting that irregular income debt repayment is as much about *expectation management* as it is about numbers. Freelancers must train themselves to accept a truth salaried workers rarely confront: *there will be lean months.* The test is not whether the plan always works perfectly, but whether it continues to function imperfectly without abandonment. A freelancer who makes 8–9 good payments a year is still on track. The enemy is not inconsistency—it is disengagement.

And finally, freelancers must contend with the cultural silence around debt. Because freelance life is so often publicly curated as a narrative of freedom, control, and autonomy, conversations about personal debt can feel taboo. Yet the reality is that many freelancers, especially early in their careers, carry credit card balances, personal loans, and tax arrears. To move forward, they must first normalise that fact—not in the sense of excusing it, but in acknowledging that debt is a tool many have used, imperfectly, to survive the transition from employment to independence.

Debt is not a moral failure; it's a mathematical reality. The freelancer's job is to bring structure to that reality—to build a system that absorbs volatility, respects psychology, and preserves progress. A paydown plan that flexes with income is not just convenient—it is essential. It creates continuity in the midst of unpredictability, and it teaches a financial posture that salaried workers rarely need but freelancers cannot afford to ignore: *resilient discipline.* And in freelance finance, resilience is the real compounding asset.

The Dopamine Cost of Spending

Freelancers do not get paid weekly. They get paid randomly. And when money arrives not as a predictable stream but as sporadic bursts, it affects more than cash flow—it rewires the emotional relationship to spending. Unlike salaried workers who experience stability and pattern, the freelancer's reward cycle is uneven and often erratic. The brain, which evolved to seek regular cues of safety and pleasure, responds to this volatility by intensifying reward-seeking behaviour in moments of perceived abundance. This isn't mere indulgence; it's a neurochemical reality. When income finally lands after a long stretch of scarcity, the dopamine response is amplified—not because of what the money can buy, but because of *what the money represents*: relief, freedom, success, and sometimes revenge against recent deprivation. That emotional spike—fuelled by scarcity's release—drives impulse spending more effectively than any external marketing ever could.

To understand the freelancer's spending patterns, one must begin not with budgets but with biology. Dopamine is not a pleasure molecule per se—it is a molecule of anticipation. It fuels the *pursuit* of reward, not the experience of reward itself. In the freelance cycle, dopamine spikes when an invoice gets paid, not when the money is saved. The anticipation of finally being able to "catch up," treat oneself, or feel in control triggers a psychological high. And like any high, it seeks a behavioural expression. For many freelancers, that expression is a spending spree—small or large—that feels rational in the moment but often leaves guilt or instability in its wake. *The problem is not moral weakness; it is chemical miscalibration.*

What makes this dynamic more dangerous is the feast-famine pattern that defines much of self-employed life. Months of tight spending, delayed gratification, and cancelled plans accumulate into a backlog of suppressed desires. When income eventually flows in, it's not just money being released—it's a torrent of unmet psychological needs. The result is often not strategic spending, but compensatory consumption: items purchased to reclaim a sense of normalcy, status, or control. This can range from justifiable splurges (a dinner with friends, new equipment) to unanchored escapism (a last-minute holiday, a designer coat, tech upgrades with no real utility). In each case, the spending *feels* necessary. That's the core danger. Because dopamine rewards pursuit rather than outcomes, purchases made during these moments may offer little post-purchase satisfaction, leading to the urge to spend again just to recapture the original high.

Traditional financial advice offers little help here. "Make a budget," "stick to your plan," "separate needs from wants"—these are cognitively sound suggestions, but they ignore the *neuro-emotional drivers* of freelance behaviour. They treat impulsive spending as a knowledge gap rather than what it often is: a strategy for emotional regulation under conditions of uncertainty. The freelancer doesn't overspend because they're irresponsible. They overspend because their income patterns have trained their brain to be on high alert for fleeting windows of opportunity. Money becomes not just a tool but a trigger. And if that trigger is not understood and managed, it will quietly erode even the best financial architecture.

What, then, is the solution? Certainly not perfection. Trying to eliminate all impulsivity is unrealistic and, paradoxically, counterproductive—it leads to suppression, which increases the intensity of the eventual dopamine rebound. The more sustainable approach is to introduce intentional *interruptions* in the stimulus-response loop between income and spending. Not barriers—interruptions. These are friction points that disrupt the automaticity of the impulse and give the rational brain time to re-engage.

One effective strategy is the 24-Hour Rule—a forced pause between desire and purchase. When a large payment hits your account and you feel the urge to "treat yourself," allow the idea but delay the action. Write it down. Let it marinate. Often, the strength of the desire weakens not because the item becomes less appealing, but because the chemical urgency dissipates. What remains is a clearer sense of value: *Do I still want this after the dopamine fog has lifted?*

A more structural intervention involves pre-committed disbursement plans. Freelancers can automate a split of incoming income: a portion immediately into tax savings, a portion into personal pay, and a portion into discretionary or "fun" spending. This not only aligns with the "pay yourself first" principle but introduces *ritual* into the flow of money. Ritual, in behavioural science, is a known method of reducing impulsivity—it creates predictability, emotional detachment, and a sense of earned indulgence. Rather than every pound competing for your attention the moment it arrives, each pound is given a role. This narrative shift—from "I got paid" to "this portion is for joy"—makes spending both more contained and more satisfying.

Another powerful tool is gratitude-based spending journals, which are different from traditional budget trackers. Instead of listing expenses by category, freelancers write a single sentence after each discretionary spend: *Why did I choose this? What did it give me? Do I feel good about it now?* Over time, patterns emerge—not just of what you buy, but *why*. And the repeated act of reflection reduces the emotional impulsivity of future spending. You begin to recognise the difference between a dopamine chase and a meaningful investment.

It also helps to remember that impulsive spending is often *not about money at all*. It's about identity maintenance under economic volatility. A freelancer might spend £200 on a new outfit not because they "need" it but because the gap since their last project made them feel invisible, behind, or lesser-than their peers. The purchase becomes a form of identity repair. Recognising this motive doesn't invalidate the spend—but it does invite a more compassionate analysis. The question becomes not "Was this dumb?" but "What am I trying to restore?" With that lens, even poor decisions can become portals to self-awareness, and awareness is the only path to sustainable control.

Social media amplifies this problem. Freelancers live in a constant comparison economy. Every time another creative posts about their new laptop, business class flight, or co-working retreat in Lisbon, it creates a false norm. The freelancer's dopamine system—already sensitised by irregular income—is further destabilised by curated abundance. Here, one of the most effective antidotes is *personal norm-setting*. That is, explicitly defining what "enough" looks like for you. This might include limits like "one high-ticket personal item per quarter" or "no new software unless it replaces an old one." These are not moral constraints—they're clarity anchors in a blurry marketplace of desire.

In this context, *discipline is not about deprivation*. It is about *deciding once, to avoid deciding constantly*. This is especially relevant to freelancers who suffer from decision fatigue, which is common when one's role includes both creative labour and business logistics. Every decision consumes energy. Every unplanned purchase competes with more strategic uses of cognitive bandwidth. By setting parameters in advance, you preserve energy for better uses—and paradoxically, *you enjoy your indulgences more, not less.*

Ultimately, breaking the feast-famine dopamine loop requires redefining the freelancer's relationship to time, not just money. When income is irregular, there is a temptation to compress gratification into narrow windows—to spend now because the next drought may be coming. But if you believe your financial future is expansive, you stop chasing high-friction highs in low-visibility moments. You build toward stability not because it's virtuous, but because it's more pleasurable. The delayed reward becomes a *richer* one, not a lesser one. This is the dopamine economy's greatest secret: when you learn to defer impulsive pleasure in favour of chosen fulfilment, the reward isn't smaller—it's deeper. And in a world where freelancing already demands so much resilience, *deep pleasure is the only kind worth paying for.*

Chapter 11
Pricing and Power

Every price tells a story. For freelancers, that story rarely concerns purely market forces or economic logic—it is a narrative woven from identity, perceived worth, fear, and influence. Economist Mariana Mazzucato reminds us that "Price is not the same as value," yet for many independent workers, the two are inseparable. What you charge often feels like a verdict on your own worth. Consequently, undercharging is less a numerical miscalculation than a misreading of oneself. The invoice becomes a proxy for self-respect, belonging, and creative legitimacy. Pricing, more than budgeting or taxes, carries a psychological weight few other freelance skills rival.

The roots of underpricing run deep and are often invisible. Freelancers—particularly those transitioning from traditional employment or creative fields—frequently succumb to what might be called imposter pricing. Rates are lowered "just to get the work," rationalised as "temporary," with over-delivery intended to convey value absent from the bill. Over time, this behaviour solidifies into habit. The logic seems protective: lower prices shield against rejection, criticism, or confrontation over labour costs. Yet this insurance carries a hidden premium: burnout, resentment, and stagnation.

Undercharging is rarely about arithmetic. It is pre-emptive fear. Freelancers anticipate a "no" if they charge fairly, so they say it first themselves. This self-denial deprives clients of the chance to recognise true value and distorts the market. Low prices ripple outward, affecting peers, competitors, and the perception of what the work is worth. Pricing is ecological, not merely personal. Undercharging diminishes not only your own position, but also reinforces a culture of undervaluation that affects the entire sector.

Reclaiming pricing, therefore, is both strategic and psychological. Freelancers must disentangle price from approval, fee from friendship, negotiation from insecurity. You charge not to placate clients but to ensure your work is sustainable, your time respected, and your business structurally viable. A robust price reflects four factors: the tangible costs of your work, your income goals, the value delivered to the client, and prevailing market benchmarks. None of these can be ignored. Together, they form what might be called the Pricing Equation—a method to replace guesswork with reasoned, adaptable logic.

Logic alone is insufficient. Pricing must be paired with communication. Freelancers often quote rates apologetically, hedging with qualifiers or nervous inflections that telegraph doubt. This pre-emptive undermining is emotionally draining and commercially damaging. The remedy is precision, not aggression. Knowing how to articulate your price, respond to pushback, and—importantly—walk away from misaligned projects demonstrates strategic maturity. Negotiation is calibration, not combat. Confidence, not charisma, makes a price feel deserved rather than arbitrary.

Pricing is also evolutionary. Even a well-set rate must adapt as skills, reputation, and demand grow. Many delay adjustments, fearing the reaction of long-standing clients or disruption to workflow. The solution is neither secrecy nor abrupt increases, but systematic restructuring, transparent communication, and advance notice. Done thoughtfully, raising rates reinforces relationships, signalling a shift from transactional supplier to strategic partner, and prompting clients to reassess the value of both output and collaboration.

This discussion is not simply about charging more. It reframes pricing as a signal of integrity, a vehicle for sustainability, and a container for the human energy freelance work demands. Pricing well is not greed—it is clarity. Underpricing chronically is not humility—it is unsustainable. Discovering your pricing voice unlocks power: it safeguards energy, enlarges opportunity, and nurtures a marketplace where respect and remuneration coexist.

This chapter dismantles the myths that keep freelancers small, illuminates the patterns that erode profit under the guise of politeness, and presents a principled framework for setting prices that are ambitious yet aligned. Whether early in your freelance journey or seasoned but under-optimised, the guidance ahead is not about charging what you can get—it is about charging what sustains both you and the work only you can perform.

Why Most Freelancers Undercharge

Ask a freelancer what they charge, and you'll often hear hesitation wrapped in justification—"It depends," "I try to keep it accessible," "I'm still figuring it out." Pricing, for freelancers, is rarely just a numeric decision. It's a statement of self-concept, a mirror to their perceived legitimacy, and often an uneasy negotiation with their own sense of worth. Despite working in economies that prize autonomy, craftsmanship, and innovation, many independent professionals still chronically underprice their services—not because they undervalue the work itself, but because they fear the personal consequences of valuing it too highly.

This fear is not irrational. Freelancers operate without institutional validation or salary scaffolding. Every price they quote feels personal because there is no HR department, brand equity, or legacy reputation to act as insulation. The discomfort is intensified by the proximity of feedback—price too high and the client ghosts, price too low and they may say yes too quickly, revealing that you've left money on the table. *The risk of rejection becomes psychologically inseparable from the number itself.* And so freelancers lower the number not to match the market, but to minimise the emotional exposure.

But fear of rejection is only one part of the picture. More insidious is how self-worth becomes entangled with financial worth. In salaried roles, value is set externally. Even if someone is underpaid, they can anchor their identity in their title, employer, or job function. Freelancers lack that scaffolding. They're not "head of" anything; they are simply themselves. This fusion of self and service makes every rate feel like a referendum on personal value. As a result, freelancers often price to avoid shame rather than to ensure sustainability. The client's approval substitutes for internal confidence. If someone agrees to the number without protest, it feels safe—*even if it's unsustainably low.*

This psychological landscape is further distorted by cultural scripts that teach us to equate humility with worthiness. In many creative and knowledge industries, money remains a taboo metric, quietly distrusted as a sign of compromised values. Artists, writers, designers, and therapists are particularly vulnerable to this narrative—the implicit belief that if you're truly good, you won't care about getting rich. Such moral posturing, however well-intentioned, keeps many freelancers in cycles of overwork and under-earning. It rewards self-sacrifice while penalising sustainability. *To charge more is often framed not as a strategic move, but as a character flaw.*

There is also a subtler behavioural pattern at play: the pre-emptive discount. Freelancers frequently reduce their rates before the client even asks, justifying it as generosity or goodwill. But this habit often masks a deeper discomfort with assertiveness. Rather than negotiating with confidence, many pre-empt the confrontation by collapsing their margin. The logic is protective—"If I make it cheap enough, they won't object." But this approach sabotages long-term viability and inadvertently teaches clients to expect high-quality work at below-market prices.

And then there's the myth of portfolio building. Especially for newer freelancers, the instinct is to take on underpaid or unpaid work "just for exposure." But exposure is not a business model. It's a marketing tactic that should be wielded selectively, not used as a rationale for chronic devaluation. If a freelancer does not clearly define the boundary between strategic visibility and exploitation, they risk spending years in the shadow economy of pseudo-professionalism—busy, booked, and still broke.

Social comparison compounds the issue. Freelancers often operate in isolation but exist within saturated online communities where pricing is rarely transparent but always implied. Scrolling through Instagram testimonials, LinkedIn announcements, and freelance platforms, it's easy to assume that others are doing better—charging more, earning more, growing faster. In the absence of real benchmarks, many freelancers price based on perceived peer success, which often leads to further underpricing, not because others are actually charging less, but because the public-facing façade suggests they're thriving on lean margins. *Comparison corrodes pricing integrity when it's based on incomplete information.*

Moreover, many freelancers confuse being "affordable" with being "accessible." They lower prices in an attempt to be inclusive or client-friendly, forgetting that undercharging limits their ability to reinvest in quality, time, and service. There is nothing accessible about burnout. There is nothing client-friendly about work that's rushed, reactive, or resentfully delivered. Sustainable pricing *serves* clients—it allows the freelancer to show up consistently, do their best work, and stay in the game long enough to become excellent.

It's also important to interrogate the freelancer's default frame for pricing. Many anchor their fees to hourly rates, which artificially caps both income and perceived value. Hourly pricing rewards time spent, not outcomes delivered. It penalises efficiency and obscures the true worth of expertise. A senior consultant who delivers a breakthrough in 30 minutes has not done "less work" than someone who flounders for three hours—they've delivered *more value in less time*. But freelancers anchored to hours often feel guilty charging for speed, unaware that what they are really selling is not time, but results, clarity, and risk reduction.

So why do these patterns persist? Partly because freelancers lack structured training in pricing psychology. Universities and bootcamps rarely teach negotiation or value articulation. Most freelancers learn to price through trial, error, and discomfort. But without a framework, the emotional noise becomes too loud. Fear of no becomes a pricing strategy. Shame becomes a filter for decision-making. And the freelancer is left guessing in a game they were never taught to play.

The solution isn't merely to "charge more." That advice is as unhelpful as telling someone to be taller. What freelancers need is a new lens: pricing as strategy, not supplication. They need to internalise that higher prices are not arrogance but alignment. That saying no to underpriced work is not elitism but *a boundary of integrity*. That charging for value, rather than time or volume, is not exploitation but *a form of mutual respect*.

To get there, freelancers must do inner work as well as market research. They must separate their self-worth from their pricing logic, view negotiation as a dialogue rather than a confrontation, and build internal metrics that support sustainability over scarcity. They must learn to identify clients who see pricing not as a test of power, but as a sign of professionalism. And perhaps most critically, they must believe that *pricing courage is not optional—it's the only way freelancing becomes freedom, not fragility*.

Undercharging is not a benign error. It's an invisible tax on the freelancer's future. It saps their time, erodes their margins, and ensures that growth remains an illusion rather than a trajectory. But once this dynamic is named, interrogated, and replaced with strategic pricing anchored in self-respect and value creation, everything changes. The work improves. The clients shift. And the freelancer stops surviving and starts building—on their own terms.

The Pricing Equation

If most freelancers chronically undercharge, it's not merely a question of confidence—it's a lack of structure. Without the infrastructure of a company, there is often no financial model, no department of forecasting, no pricing analyst running sensitivity tests. What exists, instead, is guesswork. Numbers pulled from peer assumptions, the whisperings of online forums, or the vague sense of what "feels fair." This unanchored approach is not only economically hazardous—it also obscures a deeper truth: *pricing is not a number, it's an equation.* One that blends personal goals with market realities, and sustainability with strategic value.

The starting point in any pricing framework is cost. Not just business expenses, but the *actual cost of staying in the game.* This includes software subscriptions, equipment depreciation, insurance premiums, taxes, and professional development—but also the hidden expenses that salaried workers take for granted: sick days, holiday time, unpaid admin, and downtime between clients. If your rate doesn't cover the full economic footprint of your work, you're not running a business—you're subsidising one. *A pricing equation that ignores cost is not conservative. It's delusional.*

Yet cost is only one side of the equation. On its own, it's a survival metric. To move beyond subsistence, freelancers must account for *personal financial goals*—not dreams, not whims, but measurable outcomes. What does it cost to fund a pension, to support a family, to take proper holidays, to build reserves? The number must factor in not only today's needs but tomorrow's obligations. A pricing model that doesn't support long-term viability is simply postponing burnout. Without these inputs—real, specific, non-negotiable—freelancers will continue to float in abstract calculations, hoping each month somehow adds up.

Beyond cost and goals lies *value to the client*. This is where many freelancers falter. They base their price on what it costs them to deliver, rather than what the result is worth to the person buying it. The distinction is pivotal. If a web designer charges £500 for a site that enables a business to generate £50,000 in revenue, the designer is not expensive—they are undercharging. Value-based pricing doesn't mean inflating figures arbitrarily. It means understanding the role your work plays in the client's outcomes. Are you helping them earn? Save? Comply? Scale? Reduce risk? Every deliverable that meaningfully shifts a client's results is a business asset—not a task-for-hire.

Of course, this presumes the freelancer has done the work of *client education*. Most buyers, especially in commoditised markets, will default to price unless shown a clear correlation between cost and impact. This doesn't mean pitching with aggressive ROI claims. It means asking better questions: "What's the cost of not solving this problem?" "What happens if this stays unresolved six months from now?" "Where does this project sit in your business priorities?" Clients don't want cheap; they want clarity. If a freelancer can link price to consequence, cost to context, they reframe the negotiation—not as an expense to be minimised, but as an investment to be evaluated.

Still, no pricing equation is complete without the fourth variable: *the competitive landscape*. Not because the freelancer should copy what others charge—but because they need to understand their relative positioning. Pricing in a vacuum is as dangerous as pricing by consensus. A freelancer charging enterprise rates in a consumer market will struggle, no matter how much value they provide. Equally, charging below-market rates in a high-skill, low-supply niche is not noble—it's a failure to benchmark. The question is not "What is everyone else charging?" but "Where do I sit in the value spectrum—and does my rate reflect that positioning?" Competitor awareness is not about imitation; it's about *strategic calibration*.

When brought together, these four components—cost, goals, client value, and market context—form a complete pricing framework. But even a sound framework is vulnerable to distortion if not underpinned by self-awareness. The freelancer must regularly interrogate their assumptions: "Am I adjusting my price based on logic or fear?" "Have I accounted for the non-billable hours required to sustain this income?" "Is this price based on what I need—or on what I think they'll tolerate?" These are not soft questions. They are operational ones. *A pricing model without self-examination is a house built on shifting ground.*

This becomes especially relevant when freelancers juggle multiple services or client types. A blanket rate rarely serves all contexts. A client requiring high responsiveness, strategic input, and confidentiality should not pay the same as one outsourcing tactical execution. Likewise, a rush project that disrupts your workflow should carry a premium. Just as airlines charge differently for peak vs. off-peak, window vs. aisle, freelancers must learn to *segment their services*. Not all work is equal in impact—or in cost.

Importantly, this pricing equation is not static. It requires regular revision. As your skill grows, so should your rate. As your client base matures, your positioning should elevate. As you accumulate testimonials, processes, and domain fluency, you become not only more efficient—but more valuable. Yet many freelancers fail to update their prices accordingly, stuck in the inertia of early-stage rates. Pricing is not just a number to set. It's a system to *maintain*. Treat it like a dashboard—one that needs tuning, not just installation.

Some resist this level of intentionality. They fear that structured pricing feels "cold" or "corporate." But clarity is not callous. It's respectful. When a freelancer prices with logic, transparency, and fairness, the client feels reassured—not pressured. The relationship becomes one of aligned incentives, not adversarial haggling. There is immense dignity in saying, "Here's what it takes to do this well, here's how I've calculated that, and here's the value it creates for you." That's not arrogance. That's professionalism.

There is also a subtler benefit: *mental freedom*. Freelancers who price arbitrarily live in a constant state of second-guessing. Every client call feels like a negotiation. Every invoice stirs unease. But those with a robust pricing framework walk into conversations with calm conviction. They're not selling—they're stating. They're not hoping—they're leading. And this shift, while invisible, transforms the business. It signals to clients that this is a real operation, not a side hustle or favour exchange. It says: *You can trust me—because I trust the value I bring.*

Pricing, then, is not just a business mechanism. It's an existential posture. It asks the freelancer to reconcile their ambition with their boundaries, their economics with their ethics. It demands fluency not only in numbers, but in narrative. Because what a freelancer charges is never just about money. It's about what they believe—about their work, their worth, and the world they want to build through both.

So the pricing equation is not a tool to memorise. It's a discipline to practise. And those who practise it with consistency, courage, and self-respect don't just earn more—they build businesses with the integrity to last.

Negotiating Without Apology

The moment a freelancer states their rate is the moment they risk being misunderstood—not because the price is wrong, but because the confidence to stand behind it is often brittle. Negotiation, in the freelance world, is less about economics and more about *psychological posture*. It is not merely a dance of figures—it is a declaration of professional identity. And when that identity is insecure, the entire conversation tilts toward apology. Freelancers soften their numbers, speak in conditionals, and use phrases like "If that works for you" or "Happy to be flexible." They behave as if quoting a fee is a favour they're asking, rather than a boundary they're setting. The damage isn't just financial. It's reputational. *A price offered without conviction undermines not just what you charge, but how you are perceived.*

To understand the anatomy of unapologetic negotiation, one must begin with *internal alignment*. A rate can only be asserted externally if it is first believed internally. This belief is built not on arrogance, but on arithmetic and self-knowledge. A freelancer who has done the work of pricing strategically—factoring in overhead, goals, value creation, and market positioning—walks into negotiations with clarity. They are not guessing; they are articulating. This clarity is not rigid. It allows room for contextual flexibility—but it is not born from fear. *Confidence in pricing is not a performance. It's a byproduct of doing the math.*

And yet, even with internal clarity, many freelancers stumble when faced with pushback. A client questions the rate. Pauses. Says it's "a bit higher than we expected." The freelancer flinches. The instinct is to offer a discount, truncate the scope, or justify the price in breathless detail. This reflex is not strategic—it's emotional. It stems from the *false equivalence between self-worth and acceptance*. But professional services are not popularity contests. Not every client is a fit. And pushback is not rejection—it is part of the process. *When clients challenge a price, they are not attacking the freelancer's character; they are testing the boundaries.*

Handling that test requires both preparation and poise. A useful mental model is to treat objections not as threats, but as *invitations to educate*. When a client says, "That's more than we were thinking," the freelancer might reply: "That makes sense—many of my clients initially expect something closer to X, until we map out the full impact of the work. Would it be helpful if I walked you through the structure of the quote?" This is not defensiveness. It's leadership. It reframes the conversation from price to value—and it shifts the client's role from sceptic to partner in the discussion.

Sometimes, the issue is not misunderstanding—it's mismatch. The client genuinely cannot afford the rate, or their budget simply doesn't align with the scope. This is where many freelancers default to unearned compromise. But not all compromises are virtuous. A better approach is to offer *controlled flexibility* rather than spontaneous discounting. For example: "To stay within your budget, we'd need to reduce scope—perhaps focus only on phase one this month, and revisit the rest later." Or: "I work with a few early-stage clients at a reduced scope in exchange for delayed delivery timelines—would that be something worth exploring?" This maintains the rate's integrity while offering structural solutions. *It signals that the freelancer's price is considered—not arbitrary.*

The phrase "negotiating without apology" does not mean negotiating without empathy. It means *holding the line without drama*. Clients are not villains for having budgets. Nor are freelancers heroes for setting boundaries. It is not a contest. It is a mutual evaluation of fit. If the fit doesn't work, the freelancer must learn the rarest skill in negotiation: *the graceful walkaway.* Not the bitter exit, not the passive-aggressive fade, but the direct, respectful no: "It sounds like we're not aligned on scope or budget at this stage. I appreciate your time—and I hope we can work together when circumstances change." This is not a closing door. It is an open invitation—delivered with integrity.

To develop this presence, freelancers must divorce their pricing from their identity. Many hesitate to assert a rate because they confuse the rejection of a quote with the rejection of self. But this is category error. A rate is a commercial boundary. It does not define your worth. It defines your *business's terms*. A surgeon doesn't apologise for the cost of an operation. A pilot doesn't offer a discount on safety. In fields where value is taken seriously, pricing is proportionate—not performative. Freelancers must step into that same mindset: that *professionalism includes the courage to be unaffordable to the wrong client.*

For those who want language to practise, consider the following scripts—simple, honest, and effective:

> "That rate reflects the time, skill, and results this project requires. I'm confident it delivers strong value."
>
> "If budget is a concern, I'm happy to explore adjustments to the scope—but the rate itself reflects the level of work."
>
> "I don't offer discounts on the rate, but I can offer options that reduce the total cost if we structure the project differently."
>
> "I understand if this isn't a fit at the moment—should circumstances change, I'd be glad to reconnect."

Note the tone: clear, respectful, non-defensive. This is not about memorising scripts—it's about *embodying clarity*. Scripts are training wheels; the real fluency comes when the freelancer no longer views price as a negotiation to survive, but as a professional reality to express.

One subtle but critical practice is *speaking the number and stopping*. Many freelancers, uncomfortable with silence, fill the space with qualifiers: "I usually charge £3,000, but that's negotiable depending on your needs, and I'm open to discussion, of course, so..." This signals uncertainty. A better method is to state the number plainly: "For that scope, the fee is £3,000." Then stop. Let the silence work for you. It gives the client time to process—and positions the freelancer as someone who *expects the price to be accepted.*

It's also important to remember that clients read tone more than terms. A freelancer who wavers in confidence signals not flexibility, but instability. And clients don't pay premium rates to feel like they're subsidising your self-esteem. They pay for competence, clarity, and trust. Those qualities are conveyed not just through portfolios or testimonials, but in *the very energy of the pricing conversation*. If you act like your rate is negotiable by default, it will be. If you treat it as reasonable and rooted, it invites respect.

Ultimately, negotiating without apology is not a trick. It's a transformation. It requires a shift from approval-seeking to partnership-seeking, from scarcity thinking to strategic clarity. When a freelancer truly understands the value they deliver, they stop fearing pushback—and start expecting alignment. They move from chasing clients to choosing them. From hoping for agreement to *inviting investment.*

Because in the end, negotiation isn't about getting what you can. It's about standing for what you're worth—without flinching, without flattery, and without apology.

Raising Rates Without Losing Clients

Few moments in a freelancer's career provoke more unease than the decision to raise rates. It is a pivot that feels as psychological as it is financial, where one must reconcile economic necessity with the fear of perceived arrogance.

Many freelancers delay these conversations for months—sometimes years—not because their value hasn't grown, but because they believe that doing so might sever trusted relationships, destabilise their income, or expose them to rejection. This hesitation, while emotionally understandable, is strategically hazardous. *Stagnant pricing is not client loyalty—it's operational erosion.* The longer a rate remains untouched, the more misaligned it becomes with reality: costs rise, expertise deepens, inflation marches forward. Failing to adjust pricing is not politeness—it's quiet self-sabotage.

To raise rates effectively and preserve relationships, the freelancer must adopt a dual posture: *professional detachment and narrative clarity.* The first allows you to treat pricing as a structural update—not a favour to ask or a favour to grant. The second equips you to communicate the change in a way that maintains trust, reduces surprise, and positions the increase as part of a shared professional trajectory. Most importantly, the conversation must begin from a place of earned legitimacy. You do not raise rates because you feel like it. You raise rates because your work now warrants it. *You've delivered value, refined processes, expanded capabilities—and your fees must reflect that evolution.*

The most stable way to introduce a rate increase is through *value signalling before price signalling.* Months before you send a new proposal or invoice, begin shifting the client's perception of your role—from executor to partner, from task-performer to strategic contributor. Ensure they see not just what you do, but the *results that flow from it.* Keep them informed about what your work has enabled—whether that's lead conversions, user engagement, design coherence, brand consistency, or operational efficiency. These conversations do not require pomp or data overload. They require presence: "Just flagging that last month's content series tripled our average click-through—worth noting for upcoming budget planning." This doesn't merely flatter. It educates. It primes the client to expect—and accept—more ambitious terms.

When the moment comes to raise rates, don't surprise your clients. *Professionalism is upstream of pricing.* Send a courteous but firm advance notice—ideally 30 to 60 days in advance—that explains what is changing, when it takes effect, and why it's occurring now. A rate increase that is announced with clarity and lead time feels deliberate and respectful. A sudden price jump, however justified, can feel reactive and opportunistic. The tone matters as much as the content. Avoid emotional hedging ("I hate to do this, but...") or over-justification. State it plainly: "As part of my annual review cycle, I'm adjusting my rates to better reflect the current scope of work and the market value of comparable services." The message must be calm, clear, and unapologetic—not aggressive, not defensive, not tentative. *Your tone telegraphs your self-perception.*

The most effective rate increases are often paired with *package restructuring*. Rather than simply raising the number attached to the same deliverables, rethink what the client receives. This is not upselling for its own sake—it is an opportunity to tighten value alignment. For instance, if you previously charged £1,000 for four blog posts, consider restructuring to £1,500 for a strategic content bundle that includes one strategy call, four posts, and keyword research. Not only does this better reflect your strategic role, it reframes the conversation. *Clients tend to compare value before they compare numbers*. By elevating the offer, you shift the focus from cost to outcomes.

In other cases, especially with retainer clients, rate increases can be softly tiered. Introduce the new rate as part of a phased plan—perhaps maintaining the current rate for three months, then adjusting. This gives the client breathing room and demonstrates partnership. You are not simply demanding more—you are managing the transition. Alternatively, offer *grandfathered pricing for a fixed term*: "For long-term clients like yourself, I'm honouring current rates through the end of the year, with the new structure taking effect in January." This expresses loyalty, while making the future terms non-negotiable. The timeline acts as a boundary; the gesture acts as goodwill.

Yet no matter how carefully framed, some clients will hesitate. The key is to distinguish between *genuine budget constraints* and *habitual resistance to paying more*. The first warrants compassion; the second demands discipline. If a client truly cannot afford the new rate, offer scaled-down options. Reduce frequency. Simplify deliverables. But *never dilute the rate itself.* Once a freelancer walks back a quoted increase, credibility fractures. Clients learn to push again next time. To preserve your own positioning, hold the rate—but adjust the structure: "We could reduce from weekly to fortnightly delivery if that helps align with budget." This is respectful, not retreating.

Where there's resistance that stems from entitlement—"But we've always paid this!"—you must remember that pricing loyalty is a convenience, not a contract. The value of your work is not frozen in the past. A professional who grows must occasionally re-negotiate the terms of legacy arrangements. *You are not running a charity for long-standing clients.* You are running a business. If a client cannot acknowledge your growth, you must consider whether the relationship still serves both parties. A healthy business requires margin, not just continuity. Sometimes, the best move is the firm goodbye: "I understand if this new structure no longer fits your model. I've appreciated the collaboration and would be happy to support the transition to a new provider."

It is worth noting that *not all price increases should be uniform*. Some clients, especially those who are high-maintenance, deadline-drifting, or energy-draining, may warrant a steeper increase. Others—those who are efficient, respectful, and low-lift—might receive a lighter touch. Price is a proxy not only for time and scope, but *emotional bandwidth*. Use increases as a calibration tool. This is not discriminatory—it is strategic.

For those seeking a benchmark cadence, consider reviewing rates annually, and increasing selectively based on inflation, demand, results, and professional growth. A 10–20% increase is often digestible if justified and well-timed. Larger jumps should come with deeper structural changes or repositioning. Remember, *pricing is not static*. If you do not revisit it periodically, the market will eventually force you to—and by then, it may be too late to do so from a place of control.

The psychological hurdle, of course, is rarely the number. It is the fear of destabilising relationships built on perceived generosity. But generous pricing is not the same as generous service. You can be warm, responsive, committed—and still raise rates. *Boundaries and empathy are not opposites; they are complements*. Clients respect professionals who advocate for their own sustainability. In fact, many will quietly expect it. They'll wonder why you haven't done it yet. Because serious clients don't want a cheap freelancer. They want a stable one.

Ultimately, raising rates without losing clients is not a negotiation tactic. It is a strategic rite of passage. It is the moment a freelancer steps into true stewardship of their practice—balancing financial health with professional integrity. When done right, it strengthens—not severs—the relationship. Because it says: *I respect my work enough to charge what it's worth. And I respect you enough to be transparent about it.*

That is the kind of professionalism that invites trust, commands respect, and secures longevity—not just with clients, but with the business itself.

Chapter 12
The Freelance Finance Toolkit

The difference between a thriving freelance practice and one that constantly teeters on the edge of overwhelm often comes down not to talent or effort, but to infrastructure. Most freelancers are not undisciplined—they simply rely too heavily on improvisation. Finance, in particular, is where improvisation quietly compounds into chaos. When money management depends on mental post-it notes, emotional guesswork, or scattered spreadsheets, it siphons off the bandwidth needed for higher-value decisions. The objective is not to become an accountant; it is to prevent your business from behaving as though it lacks one.

The real challenge for freelancers is not complexity—it is friction. Many financial tools are designed for organisations, not individuals who juggle creative work with executive decisions, production with planning. Tools intended to streamline finances often demand precisely the resources they should preserve: time, focus, energy. A cumbersome bookkeeping platform is not a solution—it's a second job. A tracker requiring daily updates is not empowering—it's performative guilt. Effective tools must accommodate cognitive load rather than amplify it.

In freelancing, the hallmark of a good financial system is sustainability without heroic self-discipline. If a tool fails when consistency falters, it has already failed its purpose. A resilient toolkit functions under stress: during busy client periods, illness, travel, or burnout. This chapter curates systems that meet freelancers where they are, not where they "should" be.

Rather than cataloguing every possible app, this chapter offers a framework for intentional tool selection. Every recommended system meets three criteria: it reduces decision fatigue, demands minimal weekly upkeep (under fifteen minutes), and generates clarity faster than it consumes time. These tools are selected not only for functionality but for psychological fit—designed for real-world freelancers with irregular income, finite hours, and low tolerance for friction.

Spending visibility systems, for example, enable you to detect drift without micro-tracking. The objective is not to account for every coffee; it is to cultivate a reflexive sense of burn rate, so adjustments can be made before panic sets in. Overspending rarely stems from recklessness; it stems from a narrow visibility window. Minimalist dashboards that highlight essential outflows—rent, tools, subscriptions, tax set-asides—are more powerful than intricate budgets that remain unopened.

On the income side, automation is essential. Invoice generators, recurring payment systems, and expense classifiers save time while shielding emotional energy. Chasing late payments, manually tagging expenses, and remembering quarterly tax deadlines exact a cumulative, corrosive toll. Systems that trigger reminders or automatic categorisation do more than reduce labour—they reduce cognitive strain, helping you stay operational without becoming emotionally entangled with administration.

The centrepiece of this chapter is the construction of a personal money dashboard—a single interface, digital or analogue, presenting income, expenses, taxes owed, upcoming invoices, savings progress, and buffer levels. This dashboard is more than a tracker; it is a narrative. It reveals inflows, outflows, and emergent patterns. Unlike reactive budgets, a dashboard is architectural: it informs upstream decisions about new clients, rate increases, hiring, or taking time off.

This dashboard does not need polish—it needs honesty. A simple Notion page, linked Google Sheet, or weekly-updated whiteboard suffices. Sophistication matters less than habit. Visibility without overwhelm is the goal. A five-minute glance should leave you informed, not shamed.

One subtle lesson: no single tool can fix a dysfunctional relationship with money. No app can resolve avoidance, no spreadsheet correct under-earning, no template create self-trust. What tools can do is reduce the friction that impedes better behaviour, lowering the activation energy required to act. When chosen wisely, they transform financial management from an avoided chore into a neutral, even empowering ritual.

Crucially, financial tools are not isolated hacks; they are part of business design. Your invoicing platform shapes cashflow rhythm, which affects your capacity to invest in growth. Your expense tracker influences your sense of financial security, which in turn affects pricing confidence. Each tool carries narrative consequences, reinforcing or undermining your sense of capability.

This chapter covers practical systems, including:
- Tax-prep companions that convert quarterly filing from crisis to checklist
- Payment schedulers aligning client timelines with cashflow needs
- Digital spending visualisers revealing silent subscriptions and seasonal drift
- Multi-account banking setups segmenting income by purpose without daily micromanagement
- Budgeting approaches tailored to variable income
- Dashboards integrating with calendars to synchronise decisions with reality

More than tools, this chapter delivers a mental posture. It reorients freelancers from reactive jugglers to proactive stewards, challenging the belief that money management is inherently hard or uncreative. It offers an alternative: a lightweight, functional system aligned with your time, cognition, and tolerance for complexity.

Successful freelancers are not those who do everything—they are those who automate the repeatable, ritualise the essential, and build financial systems around how their minds actually work, not around textbook theory. This chapter is a toolkit—and a permission slip—to abandon the notion that chaos is a badge of creative honour, and to cultivate a freelance practice grounded in structure, clarity, and confidence.

Tools That Work With You, Not Against You

The digital tools landscape for freelancers is paradoxically both abundant and underwhelming. For every flashy financial app promising liberation from spreadsheets, there are five more that add friction, complexity, or cognitive burden disguised as "features." What most freelancers need is not more software. They need *better filters*. A tool is not effective because it is popular, nor because it boasts integrations. It is effective because it works with your *real cognitive patterns*—the ones that show up under stress, during a deadline week, or when motivation dips. *If a tool requires you to become a different person to use it consistently, it's not a tool. It's a tax.*

The central failure of most financial software is that it is built for corporate workflows and ported—awkwardly—into self-employed life. Business bank accounts demand documents freelancers don't have. Accounting apps ask for double-entry inputs most solo professionals neither need nor understand. Expense trackers flood inboxes with categorisation alerts long after the original receipt has faded from memory. *The wrong tool does not just waste time; it subtly erodes your trust in your own ability to stay on top of your money.*

The correct frame, then, is not "Which app should I use?" but rather: *What do I actually need to know—and when?* Good tools are not exhaustive. They are *timely*. They surface what matters when it matters, and stay silent otherwise. Consider a basic spending awareness system. Most budgeting apps fail freelancers because they operate on a fixed-income logic: assign every dollar a job, track every pound of spending, and expect stability month to month. But freelance income is episodic, often back-weighted in the year, and rarely consistent. What works instead? A weekly glance at average daily outflows. A visual cue that flags when your discretionary spend is drifting up. A digital envelope system where buffer funds are *pre-allocated*, not retroactively justified. Simplicity wins—because simplicity scales.

For many freelancers, a single shared Google Sheet (or Notion database) beats an entire subscription suite. Why? Because it's flexible, customisable, and frictionless. You can set up views that match *your* thinking: upcoming tax liabilities, overdue invoices, average monthly income from key clients. You can colour-code for visibility without needing to dig through tabs. *Control is not complexity. It is clarity.* And tools that allow you to build clarity with minimal upkeep will outperform feature-rich platforms every time.

Of course, not everything should be manual. *Automating the repeatable* is essential, particularly around invoicing, payments, and tax preparation. For instance, using a tool like **Xolo**, **FreeAgent**, or **QuickFile** (UK), or **FreshBooks**, **Bonsai**, or **Wave** (US/Canada), allows freelancers to send branded invoices that follow up automatically, accept digital payments, and tag expenses by category without requiring a degree in finance. The most important advantage of these platforms is not "time saved"—it's *emotional insulation*. You're not chasing payments; the system is. You're not manually transposing receipt data into ledgers; the tool is. This matters because *emotional labour compounds faster than technical labour.*

Reducing the number of small, avoidant, stress-inducing money tasks each month is a design priority, not a luxury.

There's also an overlooked power in having *asymmetric simplicity*. That is, separating your tools by frequency and load. Your daily-use tools should be featherlight—bank apps that allow instant categorisation, mobile spending trackers, or dashboard widgets. Your monthly or quarterly tools can afford more density—such as spreadsheets that collate revenue trends, dashboards that compare estimates to actuals, or deeper audits of profit margins. Trying to use the same heavy-duty tool every day just breeds avoidance. *Rhythm matters more than rigour.*

And then there is the question of *interface trust*. Freelancers often find themselves trapped between two options: highly polished software that abstracts too much, or raw spreadsheets that demand ongoing vigilance. The optimal path lies in the middle. Tools that are transparent in logic—where you can trace where the numbers come from—help build financial confidence. For example, tools like **Tiller Money** (spreadsheet-powered budgeting with bank syncing) allow you to see every formula, every link, and every trend with perfect transparency. There are no "black box" metrics. You know what you're looking at, which makes your decisions sturdier.

On the flip side, there's also merit in using *single-purpose tools* that enforce discipline through design. Apps like **You Need A Budget (YNAB)**—though originally built for salaried users—have adapted well for freelancers by focusing on "ageing your money," encouraging freelancers to spend from last month's income, not this month's invoices. Or consider **Fathom**, which doesn't try to be a bank, a budget, and a tax planner in one—it just helps you see what's profitable and what's not. These tools act like filters, not encyclopaedias. They strip noise, not add to it.

But even the best tools are only as good as the *habits they support*. That's why tools must be embedded into workflow, not exist as destinations. A calendar nudge to check your dashboard each Friday. A Slack reminder to categorise expenses every 10th of the month. A Zapier integration that tags all incoming Stripe payments to a "Revenue In" column. *The fewer decisions you need to make to stay on track, the more likely you are to stay on track.*

Finally, a word on pricing. Many freelancers avoid paid tools out of principle. "I should be able to manage this on my own." But this logic often backfires. Paying £10 a month for a system that eliminates three hours of emotional fog is not indulgent. It is leverage. The mental cost of using clunky, free tools is often higher than the actual cost of switching to something fit for purpose. *Time is not your only limited resource—so is attention, decision quality, and mental availability.*

So, what should you expect from a financial tool as a freelancer? It should *simplify your decisions*, *shorten your feedback loops*, and *reduce your emotional drag*. It should help you see faster, decide cleaner, and act with more confidence. If it adds visibility without stress, it's working. If it works *with* your behaviour, not against it, it's worth keeping. Anything else? Delete it. You do not need more features. You need less friction.

Spending Trackers That Don't Drain You

Tracking spending is one of the most frequently abandoned financial habits among freelancers—not because it's unimportant, but because most tracking systems are designed for the wrong kind of user. They assume stable income, consistent categories, and a willingness to input data daily. None of these assumptions hold true in self-employed life. Freelancers don't need granular, accountant-style budgets. They need *visibility with minimal intrusion*. The goal is not forensic-level categorisation, but *pattern recognition with low friction*—and the right systems can deliver that clarity in under fifteen minutes per week.

The psychological resistance to tracking often stems from the misperception that it requires perfection. But the value of a spending system is not precision; it's *awareness*. You don't need to know where every penny went. You need to know whether your fixed costs are creeping up, whether your discretionary spending is spiking after a client payment, or whether your quarterly tax savings are quietly eroding. *Tracking is not about guilt; it's about noticing.* The moment it becomes a chore, it ceases to serve its purpose.

Traditional budgeting apps often break under the demands of freelance reality. Tools like Mint, Emma, or Money Dashboard rely on predefined income streams and encourage strict monthly categorisations. For someone whose revenue varies wildly, and whose expenses follow a feast-or-famine rhythm, this becomes counterproductive. A quiet month may make the app scream "over budget," even if you're well within your personal cash flow range. Conversely, a high-income month may falsely indicate surplus. *Budgeting systems that don't understand context give dangerously misleading signals.*

Instead, what works is *trend-based visibility*. A system that tells you whether your overall discretionary spend this month is higher than your three-month average. A simple bar chart showing how your coffee shop expenses fluctuate relative to your project wins. An alert that flags when your tax buffer account drops below a preset threshold. These are not budgets in the classical sense—they are *awareness tools*. And awareness drives behavioural stability.

At the core of any effective spending visibility system is a single, elegant question: *How little effort can I expend while still staying meaningfully informed?* That means designing for *automation first, review second*. You want a system that tracks in the background and requires no more than a quick weekly glance to remain calibrated. Bank-integrated apps like Snoop (UK), Copilot (US), or Monarch give this kind of overview with less than 10 minutes of setup. Once linked, they categorise automatically, highlight anomalies, and surface trends without requiring you to manage a single spreadsheet column.

But if you prefer manual tracking—and many freelancers do, because it fosters more mindful engagement—the system must be equally lightweight. The most sustainable analogue method is a *five-minute Friday habit*: once a week, open a personal Google Sheet or Notion database and input your outflows from memory or from your bank statement. No need to categorise beyond three buckets: **Fixed Costs**, **Work-Related Spend**, and **Discretionary**. You're not trying to itemise—you're trying to *observe*. Once the numbers are in, glance at the month-to-date totals. That's it. If the discretionary number feels bloated, you know to pause. If the fixed costs are inching upward, you know to investigate. *Awareness without over-analysis is the sweet spot.*

The most elegant tracking systems also *foreground insights rather than data*. For example, using a simple visual dashboard that overlays income against spending trends helps you spot not just overspending, but under-earning. It allows you to ask more strategic questions: Am I pricing correctly for my energy outlay? Am I spending more when I'm creatively depleted? Am I confusing investment with indulgence? When the tracking interface connects directly to behavioural reflection, it moves from being a tool to being a guide.

Freelancers also benefit from *event-based rather than calendar-based tracking*. In traditional jobs, budgeting is monthly because paycheques are monthly. But when income is sporadic, a calendar loses relevance. Instead, consider setting up *project-based tracking blocks*: for every major payment received, track your spending until the next payment arrives. This "income cycle" model gives a clearer picture of how long each payment sustains your lifestyle—and whether your spending rhythm matches your earning rhythm. You begin to notice not just what you spend, but *how long it takes to spend it.*

To make this work seamlessly, some freelancers use a split-account structure. They route all freelance income into a "holding account," then pay themselves a fixed weekly or biweekly transfer into a personal spending account. This pseudo-paycheque approach stabilises spending patterns and makes tracking far simpler. Instead of monitoring dozens of income spikes and card charges, you're watching one clean stream. You only track what enters your spending account—and how fast it leaves. It's minimalist financial design, and it works.

Another overlooked but powerful approach is *emoji budgeting*. Yes, seriously. In platforms like Notion or even digital journaling apps, some freelancers tag their daily spend using emoji to track mood-linked or impulse-driven transactions. 🌩 for stress spending, 🍷 for indulgent meals, 🧠 for skill-related expenses. It takes seconds, but over a few weeks, patterns emerge. You begin to see when emotional triggers override your best financial intentions. And because the system isn't rigid or numerical, it bypasses shame. *It turns tracking into storytelling, not surveillance.*

Critically, your tracking system must also respect your *cognitive energy*. Many freelancers suffer from decision fatigue—not just in their work, but in their money management. After a day of pricing, pitching, and negotiating, few people have energy to categorise six different subscription charges. So the tracking process needs to be *self-updating*. Rules-based systems—where transactions from a certain vendor are auto-categorised, or transfers above a certain threshold trigger reminders—create consistency without demand. Every time you touch the system, it should feel like a relief, not a request.

Ultimately, spending trackers that don't drain you operate on one principle: *less detail, more direction*. You are not trying to build a perfect record of every expense. You are trying to steer your ship with enough visibility to avoid icebergs. A well-designed tracker reminds you, gently, when you're drifting. It lets you feel in control, not controlled. And it frees your attention for what matters most—creative focus, strategic growth, and personal peace.

In short, your spending tracker should not be a second job. It should be a quiet advisor, speaking only when needed, always in your language, and never louder than your life. If it takes more than 15 minutes a week, it's probably doing too much. Strip it back. Clarify your questions. Let the tools respond, not dictate. That's how tracking becomes sustainable. And sustainability is the only metric that matters.

Tax and Invoicing Shortcuts

Few aspects of freelance work feel as uncreative, unbillable, and unpleasant as the administrative back-end of tax and invoicing. And yet for many freelancers, this back office inefficiency becomes a slow leak in their business model—eroding time, delaying payments, and introducing unnecessary tax burdens. What's worse is that the dominant cultural message around financial administration tends to fall into two extremes: either outsource it entirely (which isn't always feasible or affordable), or "just be disciplined," as if good habits alone can compensate for inadequate systems. *What freelancers truly need is infrastructure that reduces cognitive friction and increases clarity—not more advice to try harder.*

The right tools do not just simplify tasks. They *transform the relationship* freelancers have with their money. A payment that used to involve multiple emails, clunky PDFs, and calendar reminders becomes a smooth, automatic experience. A tax return that once triggered anxiety is now built from already categorised expenses and logged earnings. Freelancers do not need enterprise-grade software or CPA-level sophistication. They need *minimalist tools that think like they do*: flexible, efficient, and built for flow.

The first and most essential shortcut is the *modern invoice generator*. Gone are the days when freelancers needed to build invoices in Word, manually calculate tax, and hope they didn't forget to number it correctly. Tools like **Faktura (EU)**, **Zoho Invoice (global)**, **Rounded (Australia)**, **Xolo (UK/EU)**, and **Bonsai (US)** offer plug-and-play invoicing that integrates seamlessly with freelance workflows. These platforms auto-fill client details, apply recurring line items, generate sequential invoice IDs, and embed tax logic according to jurisdiction. With a few clicks, freelancers can send out a professional-looking invoice with automated due dates, late fees, and payment links—without ever touching a spreadsheet.

This may sound cosmetic, but it's not. *The faster an invoice is generated and delivered, the sooner it gets paid.* More importantly, fast invoicing prevents the psychological lag that often occurs when freelancers delay billing—out of perfectionism, procrastination, or avoidance. A tool that lets you create and send an invoice within 90 seconds is not just efficient; it's behavioural design. It makes it more likely that the action will happen consistently.

The next frontier is *automated payment scheduling*. Many modern invoice tools integrate directly with payment platforms such as Stripe, PayPal, or GoCardless—allowing clients to pay instantly through the invoice link. More advanced tools also offer recurring payment options. This is a game-changer for freelancers on retainers or subscription-based services. Instead of chasing monthly payments with reminder emails, the freelancer sets up a pre-approved auto-debit system. It professionalises the relationship and eliminates the admin burden. Clients are far more likely to honour a set-it-and-forget-it payment structure than one that depends on their inbox vigilance.

Beyond invoicing and payments lies the often-dreaded terrain of *bookkeeping*. This is where most freelancers start to feel out of their depth. They worry about double-entry accounting, balance sheets, and VAT thresholds. But the truth is, for a majority of solo operators, traditional bookkeeping software is overkill. They don't need QuickBooks Enterprise or Sage Intacct. They need a *streamlined, category-driven system* that tracks income, flags deductible expenses, and prepares reports that can be handed directly to an accountant—or plugged into a tax portal.

This is exactly where tools like **FreeAgent (UK)**, **QuickFile**, **ZipBooks**, or **Hnry (NZ)** stand out. They are designed with the assumption that their users are *not accountants*. Interfaces are simplified, tax codes are preloaded, and workflows mirror the natural cadence of a freelance business: invoices sent, payments received, expenses uploaded, end-of-year summaries generated. Hnry, for example, goes further by withholding tax and submitting returns automatically—effectively bundling tax compliance into every invoice. It's a full-stack simplifier for freelancers who would rather never think about their tax filings again.

It's worth emphasising that the most powerful tools are *not just digital*. A single-page monthly finance dashboard—built in Notion, Airtable, or even a basic Google Sheet—can act as a real-time control panel. Link it to your invoicing app, pipe in data from your bank feed (or input key figures manually once a week), and you suddenly have visibility over your total income, average invoice lag, expected tax liability, and outstanding receivables—all in one place. The best part? You only need to glance at it once every few days. *Finance systems should not interrupt your creative rhythm. They should sit quietly until summoned.*

But perhaps the most overlooked shortcut of all is *template logic*. Every recurring freelance engagement tends to follow similar contours: the same deliverables, the same structure, often the same pricing. Instead of rebuilding invoices or tax logs from scratch, create modular templates that reflect your typical projects. Template your invoice line items. Template your expense log categories. Template your communications around payment reminders. Most freelancers are not underperforming in finance because they lack insight; they are underperforming because they repeat low-value administrative tasks manually. Templates eliminate this.

On the tax side, one further shortcut deserves attention: *real-time deduction tracking*. Tools like **Expensify**, **Shoeboxed**, or the expense logging feature within **Xero** allow you to snap a receipt the moment a work-related expense is incurred. It's then OCR-scanned, categorised, and logged in your books within seconds. Over the course of a year, this removes the need to reconstruct deductions from memory—or worse, to miss them entirely. If linked with a business credit card, the entire process becomes passive. At year-end, your deduction log is already complete. No spreadsheets. No chaos.

A modern freelancer's finance toolkit should reduce mental friction to the point where the system is almost invisible. If it takes more than five clicks to send an invoice, the system is too complex. If it takes more than 15 minutes a week to track taxes and payments, it's too demanding. *Your administrative systems should feel like assistants, not assignments.*

Ultimately, tax and invoicing do not need to be feared, resented, or postponed. With the right shortcuts in place—simple invoice generators, auto-scheduled payments, intelligent bookkeeping, and real-time deduction capture—the entire process becomes manageable, even forgettable. That's not laziness. That's efficiency. And for a freelancer whose time is their most finite currency, *efficiency is the most ethical form of self-respect.*

Building a Personal Money Dashboard

Clarity in freelance finance is not a luxury—it is an operating necessity. Without it, freelancers drift. They either overestimate their earnings or underestimate their obligations. They forget invoices, misjudge tax liabilities, or confuse busy months with profitable ones. The challenge is not just informational—it is psychological. *When money becomes opaque, it becomes stressful.* Freelancers are not inherently disorganised, but they are systematically underserved. Their income flows are irregular, their costs are mixed, and their time is fragmented. The solution isn't to become an amateur accountant. It's to build a single source of truth—a personal money dashboard that renders the financial state of your freelance life immediately visible, digestible, and actionable.

The best dashboards don't aim for completeness. They aim for *relevance*. This is where many freelancers go wrong: they attempt to track too much too soon, layering in excessive detail that quickly becomes noise. They build complex spreadsheets or download finance apps filled with features they don't use. A dashboard isn't meant to be a miniature accounting system. It's meant to answer a recurring set of high-value questions with minimal friction. Am I earning enough to meet my target? How much am I owed? What are my fixed monthly costs? How much can I safely set aside—or afford to delay? These questions should not require a calculator or a phone call to your bookkeeper. They should be answerable at a glance.

A personal money dashboard is a visual interface—a window into the health and mechanics of your freelance financial engine. It's usually built in a no-code environment like Notion, Airtable, Google Sheets, or a dedicated app with custom widgets. But more important than the software is the *design logic*. A good dashboard does not start with aesthetics. It starts with function. What specific insights do you need to run your freelance business with confidence? Not in theory—*in practice*. There are typically four categories that matter: income, expenses, cash flow timing, and obligations. Let's look at each with sharper granularity.

First is *income tracking*. Not just total revenue but a breakdown by client, project type, and payment status. The point is not to stare at large numbers—it's to notice patterns. If most of your income is coming from one client, your risk is high. If your highest-paying client is also your slowest payer, you may need to renegotiate terms. Freelancers often operate in an anecdotal fog, relying on memory and instinct. A dashboard replaces guesswork with data. It helps you anticipate issues rather than react to them. At minimum, your income module should display invoices sent, payments received, outstanding balances, and average time to payment. Some freelancers also tag each item with a category: retainer, one-off, consulting, teaching. This surfaces which revenue streams are stable and which are opportunistic.

Second is *expense visibility*. This is where discipline meets design. A functional dashboard does not track every coffee. It tracks recurring costs, contractual obligations, and scalable expenses. Think software subscriptions, outsourced help, taxes owed, and equipment amortisation. You do not need to categorise every line item for tax purposes—that's the job of your accountant or year-end tools. What you need is a contextual awareness of your *cost floor*. How much money must come in monthly to keep your operation solvent? How much flexibility do you have above that baseline? Freelancers who skip this layer of insight often panic unnecessarily or take on low-margin work because they have no clear sense of whether they can afford not to. Visibility begets strategic calm.

Third is *cash flow cadence*. Income and expenses are not static—they're temporal. It's not enough to know what you're earning or spending in aggregate. You need to understand *when* money moves. A well-constructed dashboard maps inflows and outflows across a monthly or quarterly calendar.

This lets you anticipate crunch periods and surplus periods with precision. If you know a large invoice is due mid-month but a tax instalment lands first week, you can bridge the gap with a short-term buffer rather than dipping into long-term reserves. A cash flow timeline also prevents the dangerous misinterpretation of bank balance as available funds. Many freelancers "feel rich" in months when three invoices land at once, forgetting that some of that money is already spoken for. A dashboard that shows time-based cash dynamics removes this illusion.

Fourth is *obligation management*. Taxes, subscriptions, savings transfers, software renewals, business filings—these are the often-forgotten tasks that don't appear in daily work but wreck mental clarity when ignored. A money dashboard should act as a reminder hub. What's due this week? What tax quarter are you in? When does your annual licence renew? Rather than storing this information in your inbox or relying on memory, embed these obligations as dynamic elements in your dashboard—colour-coded, date-stamped, and updated in real time. It prevents last-minute chaos and allows you to batch admin work during your least cognitively demanding hours.

The beauty of a dashboard is that it grows with you. A new freelancer might start with three columns: invoices sent, income received, expenses paid. That's enough. As sophistication increases, the dashboard can absorb more nuance—tax buffers, revenue projections, client churn tracking, savings-to-expense ratios. But it never loses its core purpose: to clarify. *Not to overwhelm, not to archive. To surface exactly what matters, when it matters.*

What tools should you use to build it? The best choice is the one you'll *actually maintain*. Google Sheets offers maximal flexibility with minimal friction. Notion adds aesthetic control and links well with project dashboards. Airtable provides database functionality for freelancers with complex service mixes. More structured options like YNAB (You Need A Budget) or Monarch can also work, but only if they're easily customisable. Avoid tools that require more input than insight. If updating your dashboard feels like a chore, the design is flawed.

The real power of a personal money dashboard is psychological. Freelancers often suffer not from objective scarcity but from perceived uncertainty. They *don't know* if they're financially safe, so they operate from a defensive crouch—undercharging, overworking, or avoiding necessary risks. A dashboard counters this with *informed confidence*. It becomes the financial equivalent of a map: a way to see where you are, where you're headed, and where you need to adjust. It transforms finance from a source of anxiety into a domain of agency.

Ultimately, your dashboard is not just about tracking—it's about perspective. It's a mirror and a compass. It holds you accountable without judgement, and it guides you without micromanagement. For a freelancer whose income is self-directed and whose security is self-engineered, that clarity is not optional. It's a prerequisite for sustainable freedom.

Chapter 13
Designing a System You'll Stick To

A financial system does not succeed because it is elegant; it succeeds because it is actually used. It sounds self-evident, yet it runs counter to how many freelancers approach money. There is a persistent temptation to design for the best-case scenario—steady income, flawless compliance, uninterrupted discipline—rather than for the messy reality of human life. Complexity masquerades as sophistication, but in practice, it often becomes brittleness. The spreadsheet is built, the app installed, the workflow mapped... and then abandoned. Not from laziness, nor disorganisation, but because the system never accounted for fatigue, distraction, or discouragement. The true test of a good system is whether it holds when you are at your most human.

This chapter begins with a somewhat unsettling premise: most money systems fail not because freelancers lack knowledge, but because of behavioural friction. The data itself is rarely the problem; the issue lies in interacting with it consistently. Tools are not inherently deficient—it is their integration, or lack thereof, into daily decision-making that determines success. Many freelancers can recite the rules: weekly expense reviews, monthly revenue targets, quarterly tax prep. And yet, that knowledge sits inert. Repeated lapses cultivate quiet self-reproach: "I'm inconsistent," "I'm not a numbers person," "I just need to try harder." But willpower is a poor long-term strategy. Endurance comes not from trying harder, but from designing smarter.

Freelance life demands a systems approach that acknowledges volatile income, uneven workload, and the psychological toll of solo decision-making. Rigid routines break under these conditions. What works instead is rhythm—flexible, repeatable check-ins aligned with your natural work cadence. Not a rigid Tuesday 10 a.m. calendar notification, but contextual cues: end-of-project debriefs, pre-invoicing reviews, Sunday evening planning. Rhythm accommodates life's nonlinearity; routine punishes deviation.

A concept too often neglected is designing for the fallback state: what happens when the ideal system fails? Is there a minimalist version that still delivers core value? For example, if your full monthly review tracks revenue, updates projections, categorises expenses, and reconciles transactions—but life intervenes—can you complete a five-minute version that simply answers: "Did I earn more than I spent this month?" This is not compromise; it is resilience. Systems that only function under ideal conditions are inherently fragile.

Behavioural psychology offers insight. BJ Fogg's research on tiny habits demonstrates that sustainable behaviour emerges less from motivation than from ease and reinforcement. A sixty-minute review that leaves you drained is inferior to a six-minute check that produces confidence. Yet many freelancers impose industrial-era expectations on themselves, ignoring psychological friction. If reviewing finances is taxing, it will be delayed, and each delay compounds the sense of disorganisation. This is not a moral failing—it is a design flaw.

A well-crafted money system begins with a friction audit. Identify what you avoid, which tasks are repeatedly delayed, which habits feel punishing. These pain points are data, not deficits. Solutions might involve fewer categories, visual rather than numerical cues, or voice-based updates instead of screens. Design for your specific brain, moods, and work rhythm—not abstraction.

Habit stacking is another powerful tactic. Attach new financial behaviours to existing actions. For instance, each time you send an invoice, update your income dashboard for a minute. After completing a project, log expenses. Following a newsletter or portfolio update, review projected income. These anchor points eliminate reliance on fresh motivation. If a system requires constant vigilance to function, it is poorly designed; a strong system activates itself.

Emotional energy also shapes financial behaviour. Money carries judgement, anxiety, and shame. A system that demands constant confrontation with "what should have been done" exacts a psychological toll. Instead, design for small, visible wins: a weekly pulse showing "invoices sent," "paid," and "overdue" offers clarity and momentum far more effectively than nested reports. Start small; let competence cultivate confidence.

Visibility is not engagement. Sleek dashboards, income summaries, and net-worth graphs mean little if they do not inform action. A system's worth lies in the decisions it enables: quoting accurately, declining poor-fit clients, adjusting pricing. If it doesn't influence behaviour, it is decorative. The purpose of a money system is directional—it should make you a better operator, not merely a more informed one.

Ultimately, designing a system you will maintain requires treating yourself not merely as an employee, but as a user. Systems fail because designers overestimate user consistency. You are both. Allow yourself iterative growth. Begin with systems that are barely sufficient and improve them over time. Make friction visible, victories frequent, and embed your tools into your natural workflow. A system becomes self-sustaining not through perfection, but by respecting the unpredictable, personal, and adaptive nature of freelance life.

This chapter offers principles and tools—not a prescriptive method—to craft a money system you will not just tolerate, but rely on. Quietly. Confidently. Imperfectly, yet resiliently.

Because success lies not in flawless execution, but in functional durability under pressure.

Why Most Money Systems Fail

The most common failure in personal financial systems is not that they lack precision, but that they demand too much of the person maintaining them. An elegant spreadsheet that accounts for every category of expenditure and projects income scenarios across multiple tiers is intellectually satisfying—but utterly useless if it sits unopened. Systems break not because people are lazy, but because they are *human*. And most systems are designed for machines.

It's tempting to assume that the problem lies in the person rather than the system. If you'd just been more consistent, more organised, more disciplined—surely it would have worked. This is not only untrue; it's corrosive. *A system that collapses under normal human inconsistency was never robust to begin with.* The error is structural, not moral. The culprit is not a lack of financial literacy or commitment, but a design assumption that human beings can operate with mechanical precision, uninterrupted energy, and stable schedules. This is especially untenable for freelancers, whose income, workload, and mental bandwidth fluctuate weekly, sometimes hourly.

One of the most common structural failures is overcomplexity. Many freelancers, driven by the same perfectionism that serves them well in client work, try to construct financial systems that account for every possible scenario: tax buckets, percentage allocations, quarterly projections, emergency flags, performance trends. The intention is good. The result is paralysis. Complexity introduces cognitive friction. Every interaction with the system becomes a micro-burden, a moment of silent negotiation: *Do I really have the energy for this right now?* Eventually, that hesitation becomes inertia. And the system stops being used—not because it failed to deliver insight, but because it demanded too much attention to produce it.

Another reason financial systems break is misalignment with actual cashflow rhythm. Traditional budgeting models—monthly expense tracking, quarterly goal reviews, weekly reconciliations—presume regular income and stable timelines. Freelance income is neither. One month might bring in five invoices; the next, none. Payments often arrive late or unpredictably. Yet freelancers frequently impose rigid structures meant for salaried employees onto a lumpy income landscape. It's like using a metronome to organise a jazz improvisation. When the timing is off, frustration builds. The freelancer begins to feel behind, even if they are technically solvent. This emotional misfit leads many to abandon the system, not because it isn't logical, but because it makes them feel perpetually disorganised.

There is also the matter of emotional burnout. Financial systems require not just cognitive engagement but emotional resilience. Money management, especially for freelancers, is often laced with identity: *Am I earning enough? Am I successful yet? Why is this still so hard?* A system that relentlessly reflects these anxieties—by constantly surfacing shortfalls, late invoices, or unrealised goals—can quietly become a source of stress rather than clarity. Instead of feeling like a control panel, it begins to feel like a diagnostic report card. The emotional weight accumulates. Many freelancers start avoiding the system, not because they lack interest in their finances, but because they fear what it will show. *This avoidance is not irrational. It is a self-protective response to a poorly designed feedback loop.*

Even well-intentioned automation can fail under these conditions. Tools that aggregate transactions, auto-categorise expenses, or forecast cashflow are helpful only if they are interpreted regularly and acted upon. Many systems automate the *input* but do nothing for the *interaction*. Freelancers end up with pristine dashboards and unread reports. The real failure isn't in the data; it's in the lack of engagement. If your system isn't making decisions easier, it's a distraction. If it isn't changing behaviour, it's decoration.

There's also a psychological factor that gets too little attention: the *moralising of money habits*. Many systems are built with an implicit judgement—what you *should* spend, what you *should* save, how often you *should* check in. This "should"-based architecture can feel prescriptive and punitive, especially when things are tight. It frames deviation as failure. But freelance life is not a laboratory—it's a moving target. The point of a system is to *adapt to reality*, not to shame you into compliance. Systems that ignore this principle quickly lose relevance and emotional permission to be used.

Perhaps most subtly, many money systems fail because they are *too front-loaded*. That is, they require a significant initial investment of setup, categorisation, templating, syncing—and promise that once this effort is completed, everything will become simple. But this logic is backward. Systems should offer immediate, visible benefits from the first interaction. A system that only becomes useful after it is fully built is a project, not a tool. For most freelancers, the difference between a working system and a failed one is not design polish—it's *activation energy*. Systems should feel easy to start, even if they evolve to be more powerful over time. The best ones create an immediate sense of traction, a small win that builds trust.

There's also the issue of *identity fragmentation*. A freelancer is often wearing multiple hats: creative, project manager, marketer, administrator, and finance director. When a financial system treats these roles as separate rather than integrated—when invoicing is over here, budgeting over there, tax prep in another place—it reinforces compartmentalisation. This leads to fragmented attention, duplicated effort, and the constant sense that something is falling through the cracks. *A system must serve the whole operator, not just one of their hats.*

Finally, many systems break simply because they aren't reviewed. This sounds tautological, but it's foundational. A money system is not a static dashboard. It's a living interface with your financial reality. If it isn't reviewed regularly—if it isn't *seen*—it ceases to function, no matter how well it was designed. And yet review practices are rarely built in. There's no rhythm. No prompt. No moment of friction that says, *Now is the time to check in*. This is not an issue of commitment. It's an issue of design scaffolding. Systems must be embedded into workflow, not floating beside it. The ones that endure are those that anchor themselves to existing routines: sending an invoice triggers a review; closing a project triggers a forecast update; a weekly planning ritual includes a 90-second budget glance.

What, then, does a resilient money system look like? It is simple at the core, adaptive at the edges, and emotionally neutral. It acknowledges inconsistency and builds for it. It delivers frequent, low-friction wins that build confidence. It relies on rhythm over rigidity, clarity over control, and engagement over elegance. Most of all, it feels *usable in the worst weeks*, not just the best ones.

The takeaway is not to abandon systems, but to abandon the myth of the perfect system. If your financial setup isn't working, the answer isn't necessarily more effort. It might be *less*. Fewer categories. Less friction. Simpler rituals. The goal is not perfection, but *persistence*. And persistence, in money as in all things, is rarely the product of discipline alone. It's the product of design that makes the right behaviour easier, not harder. That's the system worth building. And the only kind worth keeping.

Tiny Habits, Big Stability

The illusion that financial security requires massive action is one of the most persistent myths in personal finance. While windfalls and income breakthroughs certainly help, what sustains wealth-building over time is not scale, but rhythm. Most people fail to build consistent financial systems not because they lack information, but because the systems they attempt to build are too large, too ambitious, or too disconnected from their actual behaviours. The root problem isn't laziness or ignorance—it's friction. *And friction is conquered not by force, but by design.*

This is where behavioural psychology offers profound insight. BJ Fogg, a behavioural scientist at Stanford, proposed a deceptively simple model for behaviour change that has transformed the way habits are taught: *make it tiny, make it easy, and anchor it to something you already do.* What matters most in the early stages of habit formation is not duration or depth, but consistency. A 30-second habit done daily is more powerful over time than a weekly commitment that's repeatedly postponed. In Fogg's model, success comes not from motivation—which is volatile—but from environment and architecture. *The habit isn't built by trying harder; it's built by needing less effort to begin.*

This principle has particular relevance to financial behaviour, especially for freelancers. Irregular income creates irregular attention. Some weeks you're flush with new clients and feel hyper-organised. Others you're in feast-famine mode, scrambling for invoices and questioning whether the spreadsheet you built in January still reflects reality. What you need isn't a massive system reboot every quarter. You need *a few durable, low-friction habits that act as behavioural anchors—even during chaos.*

Start with the simplest meaningful unit: noticing. A freelancer who opens their financial dashboard for 20 seconds after sending an invoice is building a neural connection between action and reflection. That action, though tiny, reinforces visibility. It reduces avoidance. It keeps the system emotionally familiar, rather than alien. This is what Fogg would call a "starter habit"—not impressive in its own right, but effective because it keeps the circuit warm.

The genius of tiny habits lies in their compound effect. Take a freelancer who, every Friday, writes down the week's three largest expenses on a sticky note and leaves it next to their laptop. That's it. No budget analysis. No spreadsheet entries. But over eight weeks, a pattern begins to emerge—*you keep forgetting to cancel that software subscription, or your food spending spikes after deadline deliveries.* Without intending to, you've begun tracking your behaviour in a way that creates self-awareness without judgment. That awareness can lead to natural behaviour correction—not by discipline, but by design. *The system becomes part of you, because it works with your instincts instead of against them.*

The challenge, of course, is that financial culture tends to idolise optimisation. People often don't trust habits unless they're measurable, trackable, or maximally efficient. This is a false benchmark. *What matters most is not whether your system is sophisticated, but whether it is alive.* A 2-minute Monday review that becomes part of your cognitive rhythm is more valuable than a perfect quarterly spreadsheet that's never opened. A habit's power lies in its persistence, not its perfection.

Fogg's model also introduces the concept of *anchoring*—connecting a new habit to an existing behaviour. This is especially helpful for freelancers, whose schedules vary but whose workflows contain repeating tasks: submitting proposals, responding to client emails, sending invoices. These are ideal anchors. Attach a habit like "check outstanding balances" or "log last payment received" to one of these moments, and you now have a micro-behaviour riding the momentum of something you were going to do anyway. *You don't create new time—you repurpose existing motion.*

Consider the case of Ellie, a freelance UX designer. Like many, she struggled to stay on top of her cashflow. Her earnings were strong, but her money tracking was erratic. After reading about behavioural anchoring, she attached a 15-second habit—updating her project tracker's payment status—to her task of closing project folders in her task manager. It was already a moment of closure; she simply linked it with a financial update. No spreadsheet. No reminder app. The trigger already existed; she just built a new habit into it. Within three months, her visibility improved dramatically, without any added complexity.

The beauty of this approach is that it's emotionally sustainable. Traditional budgeting often collapses under the weight of its own ambition. When you miss two days of tracking, it feels like failure. So you delay restarting until you "have time," which never arrives. Tiny habits reverse this: *the threshold for success is so low that there's no excuse not to begin again.* This flexibility matters more than we acknowledge. Habits that require perfection die quickly. Habits that tolerate inconsistency survive.

Moreover, tiny financial habits can serve as *emotional checkpoints*, not just operational ones. The freelancer who takes 60 seconds on Sunday night to write one sentence—"How do I feel about money right now?"—is building a practice of emotional self-audit. This is not fluff. Most money dysfunction is emotional in origin: anxiety, shame, uncertainty, guilt. A weekly sentence is not therapy, but it is awareness. And awareness precedes choice.

That said, tiny doesn't mean trivial. The idea is not to reduce ambition but to *right-size it for continuity*. Think of these habits as stitching—a repeated loop that binds larger structures together. One freelancer may build stability through the micro-habit of transferring £20 into a long-term fund every Friday morning. Another may develop the rhythm of glancing at upcoming invoices every time they open their project management tool. Neither is impressive. But both create momentum. And momentum is the precursor to system integrity.

What about motivation? Fogg's work suggests that motivation is unreliable as a starting point. We assume that if we just care enough, we'll act. But most freelancers already care—they're simply overwhelmed. *The habit must not rely on willpower. It must be easier to do than to ignore.* That's why BJ Fogg encourages immediate positive reinforcement: celebrating even small actions. This is countercultural in finance, which tends to reward stoicism. But celebration increases the likelihood of repetition. When a micro-habit feels good, it gets encoded faster.

Designing your own set of tiny habits means choosing simplicity over spectacle. You are not building a financial identity to impress others. You are engineering behaviours that quietly preserve sanity. A freelancer who checks their bank balance every Monday before their first client call is not "doing finance." They are *building fluency*. Over time, this fluency becomes resilience. And resilience, not genius, is what carries you through dry seasons, late payments, and high-stakes decisions.

Of course, not all habits will stick. That's part of the process. But the low cost of experimentation means failure isn't fatal. If a habit doesn't work, you haven't lost much. You tweak the anchor, reduce the frequency, or shift the context. The best systems aren't the ones that require loyalty—they're the ones that earn it by being frictionless to maintain.

Ultimately, financial success for freelancers isn't about building one perfect system. It's about layering dozens of small behaviours that stabilise your attention, increase your awareness, and minimise regret. *Tiny habits may not look powerful—but over time, they create the mental scaffolding that allows bigger financial architecture to stand.* They are the quiet infrastructure of freedom. And the most important ones are the habits you don't even notice anymore—because they've become part of how you move through the world.

Rhythms, Not Routines

One of the most persistent illusions in personal finance—especially among freelancers—is the idea that discipline equals rigidity. That if your finances aren't built on perfectly scheduled routines, they're doomed to chaos. But for people whose lives are structured around irregular projects, shifting deadlines, and fluid workloads, routines break not because the individual is lazy or undisciplined, but because *routines are a mismatched tool.* In contrast, *rhythms*—those adaptable, recurring patterns that move with your natural workflow—offer a far more resilient approach. They are not fixed; they are responsive. And for freelancers, they may be the only structure that lasts.

Traditional financial advice often leans heavily on predictability: "Review your budget every Monday," "Track your spending daily," "Close your books at the end of the month." This advice assumes a degree of temporal stability that simply does not exist in many freelance lives. Some weeks are back-to-back with client work and Zoom calls; others are contemplative and quiet. Monthly revenue may swing by 30% or more. Against this backdrop, the idea of maintaining a static routine quickly becomes demoralising. The consequence is not just missed reviews or unchecked budgets—it's shame, avoidance, and a collapse of the system altogether. *The system fails not because it's bad, but because it's brittle.*

Rhythms, on the other hand, begin with observation. They take into account *how* you work, not just what you intend to do. A rhythm is something you learn from, not impose. You may notice, for instance, that most of your invoicing happens in the second half of the month. Rather than resisting that pattern, you align your review process to it—say, a quick cash flow snapshot on the 25th of each month, when you're already thinking about money. Similarly, if you tend to feel mentally clear at the start of the week, that might be the best time to conduct a 10-minute review of recent spending, not because it's "Monday" but because *you are alert and available.* A rhythm listens first, then adapts.

The first step in shifting from routines to rhythms is letting go of calendar perfectionism. Financial stability for freelancers is not about never missing a review. It's about *having touchpoints that repeat often enough to preserve awareness, but flexibly enough to accommodate reality.* Think of your financial rhythm not as a checklist but as a cycle—weekly, monthly, quarterly—each with a distinct role.

Weekly reviews function like heartbeat checks. They are brief, high-frequency touch-ins designed to answer the question: *What just happened, and is anything urgent?* This is not where you balance budgets or forecast projections. It's where you note whether a client has paid, whether your card expenses jumped, or whether your subscription to that software you no longer use just auto-renewed. The rhythm matters more than the detail. If you miss one week, you don't spiral—you return the following week without guilt, because *the pattern is designed to absorb imperfection.*

Monthly audits are your deeper scans. These aren't audits in the traditional tax-preparation sense—they are moments of financial reflection. What patterns emerged this month? Did your spending align with your current goals or values? Are you slipping into convenience-based costs that no longer serve you? Do you need to adjust how you forecast your savings or tax reserves for the coming cycle? The monthly rhythm invites strategic thinking without the burden of overhauling everything. *You're not judging past behaviour—you're learning from it.* And because these reviews happen regularly, no one moment needs to be dramatic or definitive.

Quarterly resets are where rhythm becomes renewal. Every three months, a freelancer should zoom out: review contracts, renegotiate rates, re-evaluate tools, and track net worth or cash runway. This is not just tactical—it's philosophical. Quarterly reviews are when you ask bigger questions: *Is the structure of my financial life still fit for purpose? Is my work supporting the kind of life I want, or is it merely surviving?* The quarterly rhythm lets you catch slow drifts before they become deep dysfunctions.

What unites these three rhythms—weekly, monthly, and quarterly—is not just their recurrence but their emotional neutrality. They are invitations, not obligations. If you miss a week, nothing breaks. If you delay a reset by a few days, you haven't failed. *This is what makes rhythms so powerful: they operate below the shame threshold.* That alone increases adherence dramatically. A system that doesn't punish deviation is one you're more likely to return to.

Importantly, rhythms can be uniquely yours. One freelancer may prefer a Sunday night check-in as part of winding down for the week. Another may do theirs Thursday afternoon when client demand is low. Some may prefer physical journaling; others use Notion dashboards or apps like YNAB. What matters is not the method—it's the momentum. *Does this rhythm keep you close enough to your money that you don't avoid it, and flexible enough that you don't resent it?* That is the central design question.

There's also a physiological wisdom to rhythms. Human attention and energy follow cycles—circadian, weekly, seasonal. Freelancers who align financial habits to their actual energetic states—not arbitrary rules—gain something profound: *ease.* A quarterly review during your lowest energy week will always feel like friction. But if you plan around your own creative highs and admin-friendly lows, the process begins to reinforce itself. When you work with your energy rather than against it, the habits stick not out of duty, but because they fit.

This principle of rhythm over routine becomes even more essential in times of volatility. When your work life is uncertain—clients cancel, markets shift, illness interrupts—you won't be able to maintain a rigid sequence. But if your financial system is rhythmic, it will *catch you*. You may miss one review, but the next one is coming. You may skip a monthly check-in, but the quarterly reset still offers you a structural re-entry point. There is no system that avoids disruption entirely, but a rhythmic one is *more forgiving*, and therefore more durable.

Consider also that financial rhythms are not just about reviewing past actions—they create forward-looking intention. A freelancer who does a 15-minute reset at the start of each month will be exponentially more attuned to opportunities and risks. They are not "behind" on their finances; they are *in conversation* with them. That ongoing dialogue, made possible by consistent rhythm, allows for intelligent improvisation. You can shift spending based on a slower month without panic, because you were already watching the curve.

It's worth stating clearly: rhythms do not require discipline in the conventional sense. They require *careful architecture*. The design of your weekly, monthly, and quarterly touchpoints should reduce friction, not introduce it. A review that takes 45 minutes and requires six tools is not sustainable. A review that fits into your workday with minimal disruption is. You don't need perfect data. You need repeated attention.

Ultimately, what makes a freelancer financially resilient is not whether they follow every budgeting tip or investment guide. It's whether they *return to the conversation with their money often enough to make adjustments*. Rhythms make that possible. They're built on responsiveness, not rigidity. And in the chaotic, creative, deeply human world of independent work, that responsiveness is not a compromise—it's an asset.

Making Finance Part of the Work, Not a Distraction

For many freelancers, finance lives in a separate mental folder—one labelled "admin," "later," or more honestly, "avoid." It is something to be tackled between projects, in a rare moment of calm, or under duress: tax deadlines, cash shortfalls, unpaid invoices. This is not merely a logistical oversight; it's a structural flaw in how independent professionals conceptualise their work. The reality is that finance is not a parallel track to creative or client work—it is embedded within it. Income does not arrive in spite of financial systems; it flows through them. The health of a freelance business is shaped not just by how brilliant the output is, but by how seamlessly money is tracked, invoiced, allocated, and reflected upon. *Treating money management as a distraction is, in practice, treating your business as optional.*

The more sustainable model is to see finance as a design element of your work—not an interruption but an integrated function, much like quality control is to product design or editing is to writing. It's not what you do after the fact; it's what shapes the outcome. The freelance economy is replete with brilliant people who undercharge, mismanage cash flow, or miss tax deadlines—not because they lack skill, but because they've mentally separated "work" from "finance." The challenge, then, is not only to learn the mechanics of money, but to *embed those mechanics into the natural arc of your workflow.*

Consider, for example, how time-tracking often exists in a grey zone between client accountability and personal data. Done consistently, it yields insight into which clients are profitable, how your attention is spent, and where your pricing model may be misaligned. Done sporadically, it offers little but guilt. Now ask: what would it look like to treat this tracking not as an external task, but as an extension of your project execution? When time logging happens *within* the same tool where you write, build, or design—automated, tagged, and reviewable—it becomes less a chore and more a feedback loop. *The financial awareness is not postponed; it's embedded.*

This integration becomes even more critical when considering cash flow. Many freelancers only "check the money" when something goes wrong—when a payment is late, when rent is due, when the bank balance shocks. But if you build a system where every completed deliverable automatically triggers an invoice draft—using templates, workflow triggers, or pre-scheduled reminders—then invoicing ceases to be a separate job. It becomes part of finishing the work. Likewise, when payments are reconciled with a few clicks inside a platform you already open daily (e.g., a dashboard that combines banking, invoicing, and project status), the cognitive cost drops sharply. *It's not about working harder—it's about reducing the context-switching that fractures attention and fuels avoidance.*

One of the most powerful shifts a freelancer can make is to move from reactive to proactive financial visibility. This doesn't mean forecasting every penny, but it does mean *designing visibility into the systems you already use.* For example, if your calendar shows meetings and deadlines, why shouldn't it also display expected payments? If your project board reflects tasks in progress, why not add a column for invoice status? These aren't just visual cues—they are behavioural nudges. The more you *see* your financial reality alongside your work, the less likely you are to defer or disassociate from it.

Part of this re-integration also involves redefining what constitutes "productive work." Many freelancers are unconsciously biased toward visible outputs: writing, coding, designing, delivering. Financial tasks, in contrast, feel invisible—admin, overhead, non-billable. This dichotomy is misleading. An hour spent raising your rates, implementing a better payment system, or scheduling your tax set-asides is arguably more *leverageable* than an hour spent editing slides for a low-paying client. Financial work *is* real work when it enhances your margins, reduces your stress, and protects your time. *If your business can't scale or stabilise without it, then it belongs at the centre of your professional identity—not the edge.*

This shift is as much emotional as it is logistical. Freelancers often struggle with guilt when they take time away from billable tasks to work "on" their business instead of "in" it. But mature businesses are not built solely on delivery—they are structured, resilient, and aware. Making space for money work during your prime attention hours—rather than relegating it to late-night catch-ups—sends a clear internal signal: *this matters.* And when it matters, it improves.

What's more, integrating finance into your workflow does not require a full suite of tools or a radical overhaul. It requires *habitual placement.* For instance, if you already have a project kickoff process, include a pricing review: are you charging enough? Is this scope aligned with your financial goals? If you run a closeout checklist at the end of each engagement, add a line: has the invoice been logged and the payment tracked? These are not new tasks—they are enhancements to tasks you already perform. And their compounding value is immense.

Integration also has philosophical implications. When you think of your financial systems as a separate "function," you unintentionally devalue their creative potential. But pricing is not just maths—it's a reflection of values, positioning, and self-awareness. Budgeting is not restriction—it's *design.* A well-integrated financial system doesn't just help you avoid problems—it helps you think better, choose better, and grow deliberately. In this sense, finance becomes not just a mechanic of survival but a tool of self-authorship. You begin to shape not just how you earn, but *why*, and on whose terms.

Importantly, embedding finance into your freelance process is not about perfection. There will be late invoices, missed reviews, overspent months. The goal is not to eliminate imperfection—it's to reduce the consequences of it. Systems that live in daily motion are far more forgiving than those you only check quarterly. Visibility is half the battle. When your workflow includes regular, low-friction checkpoints—"Is this client profitable?" "Is my reserve account funded?" "Is this expense aligned with my goals?"—then you are no longer navigating blind. *And in freelancing, blindness is expensive.*

The deeper truth is that financial integration enhances *agency.* It reminds you that your work is not being done *to* you, but *by* you. Each invoice sent, each tool reviewed, each budget line calibrated is an act of authorship. It says: *I run this business, this business doesn't run me.* And in the often-chaotic landscape of self-employment, that sense of authorship is the most renewable energy source available.

In the end, the distinction between work and finance is artificial. There is only the system—or lack of one—that governs how your effort becomes income, how your income becomes stability, and how your stability enables freedom. The sooner you embed finance *into* your workflow—not as a nuisance, not as a side task, but as a form of mastery—the more intelligent, calm, and confident your freelance life becomes. Not because you're flawless, but because your systems *serve your reality.* And that, in itself, is a mark of professional maturity.

Chapter 14
Earning Without Burning Out

Somewhere along the way, freelance culture absorbed a pernicious myth: that exhaustion signals excellence. Long hours, constant pitching, endless deliverables—these came to be seen as proof of ambition, of worth. Yet this belief, quietly pervasive, is quietly destructive. It transforms effort into a treadmill and burnishes burnout as a badge of honour. The irony is stark: autonomy, the very reason people go freelance, is traded for the illusion of productivity. Time-in equals money-out—a neat equation, if only it were true. In reality, it is a trap.

Sustainable freelance income is rarely about volume. It is about precision. Selecting projects with high return on effort, working with clients who respect boundaries, and structuring income models that scale without constant presence—these are the levers that matter. This chapter invites a shift: to measure success not by hours worked, but by energy preserved, attention protected, and recoverability maintained. True wealth is not how much you earn in a week, but what remains of you once the work is done.

Central to this framework is the concept of marginal burnout. Like diminishing returns in economics, each additional hour worked yields progressively smaller gains. That sixth or seventh hour of client work might be billable, but it rarely advances strategy. Instead, it displaces reflection, creative recharge, and decision-making for the following day. The danger lies not in fatigue itself, but in decision fatigue, boundary erosion, and the slow corrosion of clarity, profitability, and self-trust.

To avoid this spiral, freelancers must evaluate work through a return-on-energy lens. Which clients drain rather than energise? Which projects demand disproportionate handholding, endless revisions, or emotional labour? Which tasks, while profitable, leave you disengaged? These questions are qualitative, invisible in a spreadsheet, yet central to sustainable practice. Ignoring them transforms income into a stress loop masquerading as success.

Diversifying income is not a theoretical exercise—it is a protective strategy. Relying exclusively on high-intensity, synchronous work—tight deadlines, frequent check-ins, heavy customisation—builds a system that punishes rest. Introducing retainer clients, licensing, affiliate structures, productised services, or low-lift consulting creates breathing space. Such streams do not replace focus work; they balance it. They permit strategic choices without financial panic, allowing for recuperation and intentionality.

Yet strategy demands sacrifice, and herein lies the freelancer's hardest skill: saying no. Not merely rejecting the disastrous project, but turning down the merely acceptable. Good-but-not-great work, tasks that pay decently but fail to grow your brand, assignments that are easy yet emotionally costly—these require discernment. Saying no is not instinct; it is premeditated. A values-based filter ensures that attention flows to work aligned with long-term objectives, not reactive urgencies.

Saying no is relational as well as financial. Boundaries must be communicated with clarity, warmth, and firmness. Scripts are not crutches; they are instruments of professional maturity. They preserve energy, maintain trust, and prevent burnout masquerading as politeness. Without them, the default becomes obligation, guilt, or the illusion of busyness.

This chapter does not advocate minimalism nor glorify passive income. Its aim is discernment. More work may sometimes be right—but it must be chosen consciously, not by default, panic, or performative necessity. Incorporating energy as a metric shifts the calculus: success is measured not in hours logged, but in resilience maintained. Projects are no longer survived; they are selected and navigated.

Practically, this approach involves assessing the energetic footprint of projects, structuring the week to protect strategic whitespace, auditing client lists without emotional reactivity, and diversifying income even as a solo operator. These methods reintroduce clarity into a culture that too often rewards clutter. Burnout should not be the norm; discernment should.

The world does not need more exhausted freelancers. It needs freelancers who are awake—creatively, financially, energetically, and strategically. When busyness no longer masquerades as progress, you design a business that serves you rather than extracts from you. From that vantage, earning is no longer a threat to well-being; it becomes a reflection of it.

More Work ≠ More Wealth

A curious paradox lies at the heart of modern freelance life: the assumption that the solution to any financial shortfall is simply to work more. More projects, more clients, more hours. It's a logic that seems irrefutable—until lived experience shatters it. Freelancers, particularly those in their early to middle earning years, often come to discover that there is a ceiling not just to how much they can work, but also to how much they should. The idea that *time input equals money output* oversimplifies the reality of human energy, creative cognition, and emotional bandwidth. This is where the concept of *marginal burnout* becomes essential. Just as economists speak of diminishing returns, freelancers must come to grips with the law of diminishing resilience: that beyond a certain point, each extra hour of effort doesn't just produce less—it actively erodes future capacity to earn.

Marginal burnout differs from general fatigue in that it's deceptive. It doesn't announce itself as total collapse. Instead, it creeps in subtly—missed emails, curt client replies, reduced creative sharpness, increasing time to complete familiar tasks. These aren't signs of laziness or inefficiency. They're the biological and psychological costs of sustained overextension. In environments without built-in rest cycles, like freelancing, the marginal cost of that one extra gig, that "quick" weekend project, accumulates silently until the floor gives way.

This is particularly pernicious because the freelance economy lacks clear external feedback loops. In traditional employment, boundaries are externally enforced: paid leave, contracted hours, HR policies. In contrast, freelancers operate within self-governed ecosystems, where hustle is glorified and rest is often perceived as weakness or luxury. The result is a culture in which many intelligent professionals gradually train themselves to ignore the body's warning systems, rationalising it as entrepreneurial grit. Yet grit, untethered from discernment, corrodes. It turns ambition into compulsion.

If earning more doesn't always mean working more, what then becomes the freelancer's true lever for increasing income? The answer is *value per hour*, not *hours worked*. And that value hinges not just on technical skill, but on clarity of mind, strength of judgement, quality of communication, and the energy to execute—all of which are degraded under chronic overload. The modern freelancer's challenge is no longer scarcity of work, but scarcity of energy. Protecting that energy is not indulgent; it's strategic.

One way to navigate this is to think in terms of *Revenue-Energy ROI*. Traditional return on investment focuses on money. But in knowledge work, time and energy are often scarcer—and more precious—than cash. A client who pays well but drains your bandwidth with vague briefs, erratic timelines, or moral dissonance may, in reality, be less profitable than a smaller client who's efficient, aligned, and consistent. Most freelancers, if asked to map their past six months of income against their emotional state during each project, would immediately spot the outliers—work that paid well but extracted too much, or work that paid modestly but ran smoothly. The mistake is assuming those trade-offs are fixed. In reality, *every yes creates a hidden no*: a better client not pursued, a side project delayed, sleep shortened, relationships neglected.

To move from chronic effort to conscious earning, freelancers must shift from reactive to strategic engagement. This involves more than tracking hours—it means tracking vitality. This could be as simple as journaling weekly emotional energy levels alongside income, or using tools like retrospective project scoring, where each job is graded on profitability, enjoyment, stress, and client rapport. Over time, patterns emerge, and informed boundaries become possible. One discovers that not all income is equal; money earned with resentment costs more than it deposits.

Another crucial distinction is between *productive work* and *emotional labour disguised as productivity*. Many freelancers—particularly those in creative and client-facing roles—spend significant time in ambiguous tasks: rewording emails to avoid sounding "too direct," over-researching out of insecurity, or repeatedly rechecking work already done well. These aren't just habits; they're often symptoms of anxiety and undercharging. When one's rate feels unjustifiably low, the instinct is to overcompensate through overdelivery, in an unconscious attempt to validate one's worth. Ironically, this reinforces the underpricing trap, creating a cycle where more work is done to justify less pay.

Breaking this cycle requires not just better pricing, but better self-concept. Emotional boundaries must mature alongside financial ones. Saying no is not only about workload—it's about saying yes to strategic rest. And strategic rest is not passive. It's the soil in which future creativity grows. As studies in cognitive neuroscience have repeatedly shown, downtime is essential for complex problem-solving, lateral thinking, and idea synthesis—all core to high-value freelance work. In this light, burnout is not a badge of honour; it's a warning light that your earning engine is misfiring.

So how does one escape the trap of marginal burnout while maintaining income? It begins by identifying the inflection point where output stops scaling with effort and starts eroding resilience. For some, that line is 30 hours a week; for others, it's not a fixed number but a ratio of project types. The goal is not uniform restraint, but intelligent calibration—knowing when intensity is an asset and when it's a liability. This calls for systems, not willpower.

One approach is to adopt cyclical planning models, such as 6-week sprints followed by 1-week resets, or quarterly reviews that assess workload against physical and mental health indicators. These practices help freelancers escape the tyranny of constant hustle and reframe time as a finite, high-value asset—not an endless resource to trade for money.

Ultimately, the belief that more work equals more wealth is not only outdated—it's dangerous. It seduces intelligent people into sacrificing their core advantage: the ability to think clearly, choose wisely, and work sustainably. In a freelance economy defined by autonomy, the most powerful metric is not hours billed, but value generated per unit of wellbeing preserved. Master that equation, and you'll not only earn more—you'll endure longer, create better, and live more fully in the process.

Revenue vs. Energy ROI

In a market that champions productivity and monetisation, freelancers often find themselves measuring success in revenue alone. But earning power, when decoupled from energy management, becomes a deceptive metric. A client who pays £5,000 for a short-turnaround project that demands late nights, emotional strain, and communication acrobatics may not be more "valuable" than one who pays £2,500 consistently with clarity, trust, and room to breathe. *Revenue without energy awareness is a false signal of profitability.* What matters, ultimately, is not just what you earn, but *what's left of you after you earn it.*

The concept of Return on Investment (ROI) is well understood in financial terms—but vastly underapplied in human terms. What is the return on your *time*, your *focus*, your *mental bandwidth*? Financial ROI is only one layer of the real calculus freelancers must make. Energy ROI—how much of your personal resourcefulness is consumed versus replenished—is often the better predictor of sustainability, satisfaction, and long-term earnings. And unlike financial capital, which can be leveraged or replenished through external resources, personal energy is finite. When it's gone, it's gone. The freelancer who underestimates this cost wakes up to find that even a thriving client list can become a trap rather than a triumph.

There is a kind of moral clarity that comes from recognising energy as a non-renewable currency. It forces you to scrutinise not just how much you're paid, but *what that payment costs you.* Is it project clarity—or chaos? Respect—or second-guessing? Reasonable timelines—or creeping scope creep that siphons your weekends? A sophisticated freelancer evaluates projects on multiple axes: financial return, emotional friction, communication latency, and energetic drag. The worst clients rarely look like villains—they're often polite, prompt, and high-paying. But the hidden toll is a fragmented week, chronic inbox tension, or the slow erosion of one's creative core.

Some of this stems from legacy thinking. In salaried environments, effort and output are bundled under the illusion of consistency. You're paid to show up, regardless of how energetically efficient the work feels. But freelancing disaggregates that equation. You are no longer just trading hours for income—you're trading hours, presence, and your ability to focus deeply again tomorrow. Every new client must now be interrogated through that lens. The myth of "it's just a few extra hours" collapses under the weight of accumulated fatigue. What begins as a simple task can metastasise into a pattern: persistent overcommitment that leaves little room for restoration.

To calibrate your energy ROI, you need a friction audit. Begin not with rates, but with resonance: which clients leave you feeling energised, trusted, and respected? Which drain your attention even when you're off the clock? Notice your post-call physiology—does your body tighten or relax? Keep an internal ledger: not just of who pays on time, but who *leaves you on time*—mentally and emotionally. Consider assigning an "Energy Cost Multiplier" to each client, project type, or workflow. A client might be financially generous but carry a 1.8x energy multiplier due to their indecision, poor briefs, or entitlement. Another may pay modestly but score a 0.9x—reliable, precise, low-friction. The more honest you are with this accounting, the clearer your earning reality becomes.

Energy ROI also intersects with the concept of "margin." Many freelancers mistakenly see margin as the leftover after costs—but few include energy as a line item. They track software subscriptions and transaction fees but fail to account for the 90 minutes lost recovering from a toxic feedback loop or a disorganised handoff. *Margin isn't just money. Margin is the space in your week not filled by repair, resentment, or recovery.* The best clients don't just pay you—they protect your margin. They enable you to work in your zone of competence without making you a project manager, therapist, and telepath simultaneously.

This is not to suggest that high-energy-demand projects are inherently bad. Some are thrilling. Some stretch your creative ceiling and generate a kind of productive euphoria. But those projects must be *selected*, not accumulated. One or two per quarter may be strategic; five simultaneously is unsustainable. Similarly, short-term high-stress gigs can sometimes be worthwhile if followed by deliberate decompression. The problem arises when intensity becomes the default rather than the exception—when your entire income depends on adrenaline, endurance, and after-hours anxiety.

Modern freelancers often mistake busyness for progress. But busyness without clarity is entropy. Every invoice you send must be balanced not just against hours worked, but against energy spent, recovery required, and your ability to remain creative for your next client. Burnout rarely announces itself with a single crisis; it arrives disguised as success, dressed in deliverables, riding a string of "yeses" that felt reasonable in isolation but reckless in aggregate.

Energy ROI is ultimately about choosing your clients and projects through a more mature lens—not just what pays today, but what preserves your ability to perform tomorrow. It reframes the central question from "Can I do this?" to "Can I do this *again and again without erosion*?" The better you become at this calculus, the more resilient your freelance business becomes—not because you're working more, but because you're working *wiser*.

The freelancer who understands energy as an economic variable gains leverage that transcends pricing. You start saying no not out of scarcity, but out of clarity. You design workflows around renewal, not depletion. And your income stabilises—not just because you've charged more, but because you've stopped leaking value in unseen places. You've aligned earnings with endurance. You've stopped confusing hustle with health. And that, in the long run, is what real profit looks like.

Designing an Income Mix

The freelance economy does not reward the most talented; it rewards the most structurally intelligent. You can be an exceptional designer, writer, strategist, or consultant—but if your income model is built entirely on one-off projects, you are effectively reconstructing your business every month. It is a treadmill disguised as a career. *Sustainable freelancing is not about charging more per project; it's about designing your income like an ecosystem—not a single harvest.*

An income mix is more than diversification for its own sake. It is a deliberate strategy to balance volatility, increase long-term earning potential, and protect against energy depletion. This means thinking beyond the next invoice and building a system that can generate cashflow across three temporal zones: *short-term (urgent and active), mid-term (recurring and stabilising), and long-term (scalable and detached from time).* The blend is not about doing everything—it's about doing the right things at the right tiers of effort and payoff.

Short-term income is the freelance comfort zone. It includes project-based work, emergency contracts, quick consults, or rush jobs—anything that gets booked and billed quickly. This stream is indispensable. It keeps the lights on. But if it becomes the only stream, the result is a reactive business. You are only as secure as your next deadline. Worse, your schedule is perpetually full of other people's priorities. The paradox is that short-term gigs often feel productive because they generate fast money, but they rarely generate compounding value. They demand time, but they don't *buy* time.

That is why mid-term recurring income is the freelancer's antidote to panic. Retainers, ongoing content packages, subscription-based services, or fractional roles (e.g., part-time CFO or UX lead) are examples of this middle layer. They stabilise income through predictable, periodic billing and reduce the emotional tax of monthly revenue resets.

Importantly, they create margin—mental space and time capital—that allows for long-term planning. Many freelancers mistakenly assume clients won't pay for ongoing access, but in practice, businesses crave continuity more than they crave novelty. A retainer is not just a billing structure; it is a *trust contract.* Clients agree to pay not just for output, but for readiness, consistency, and context retention.

But even a well-crafted blend of project and retainer income can keep freelancers trapped in a time-for-money loop. That's where the third layer—scalable income—enters the frame. This includes assets that can be sold repeatedly with minimal marginal effort: ebooks, online courses, templates, design systems, licensing agreements, affiliate revenue, paid newsletters. These streams do not require passive effort—they require *asynchronous effort.* You work once and sell many times. But unlike popular myth, scalable income is not magic. It's labour—just front-loaded. You don't earn while you sleep until you've first worked while others were playing.

Critically, scalable income is not inherently digital. A photographer who licenses images, a copywriter who creates branded content kits, or a coach who offers group intensives is participating in this layer. What matters is that the income is *decoupled from hourly presence.* Over time, the freelancer who invests in scalable assets builds leverage—earning capacity that compounds without commensurate exhaustion.

The most robust freelance income systems contain all three layers—each serving a different role in the financial architecture. Short-term income feeds liquidity. Mid-term income buys breathing room. Scalable income builds freedom. Think of them not as separate businesses, but as different settings on the same dial. You don't need to be perfect at all three simultaneously—but you do need visibility across the whole spectrum. Otherwise, you are a craftsperson without a portfolio: excellent at execution but fragile in cashflow.

To design this mix, begin not with ambition, but with data. What percentage of your past year's income came from each stream? Map your revenue to effort. Which clients paid most *per hour of actual energy spent*? Which projects created new inbound opportunities? Where did you over-invest emotionally without corresponding returns? This is not simply an accounting exercise—it is an energetic audit. Financial strategy is not only about money. It is about meaning. The ideal mix is not just what pays—it is what *sustains*.

Then layer in philosophical alignment. Not all income is equal in how it makes you feel. There is money that builds your identity, and money that blurs it. Some work leaves you sharper, more centred, more referable. Other work erodes confidence, burns nights, and yields no compounding effects. A £10,000 project that isolates you, depletes you, and yields no future leads may be worth less than a £2,000 project that energises, showcases your unique method, and leads to scalable product ideas. In that sense, designing an income mix is as much about *moral economy* as it is about money. The question becomes not just "What can I sell?" but "What deserves to be part of my business model?"

Importantly, income mix is seasonal. In the early years of freelancing, you may be 80% short-term work simply to survive. That is not failure—it is *foundation*. As you grow, your goal should not be merely to "earn more," but to *earn differently*. Transition a percentage of your calendar from production to creation, from reactive work to proactive value. Shift one-off clients into subscription offers. Turn your FAQs into a paid guide. Package your method into a process you can license. Build scaffolding around your talent.

The mistake many experienced freelancers make is waiting too long to build their income infrastructure. They get caught in operational excellence—delivering outstanding work, pleasing every client, staying "booked out"—but they forget to architect a business. Eventually, the body says no. Burnout is not always the product of bad clients. Often, it's the result of *good work inside a brittle income model*. One with no compounding. No redundancy. No time-insensitive upside.

Designing your income mix is an act of maturity. It is recognising that your work is not merely a service to be traded but a system to be built. It is the difference between being a gig worker and being a freelance founder. It requires intention, pattern recognition, and a willingness to say no to money that pulls you away from your long game. But the reward is elegant: a business that earns while you sleep because you worked awake, aware, and aligned.

Saying No Without Regret

Freelancers do not burn out from hard work alone. They burn out from *misaligned work*—the kind that depletes energy faster than it replenishes income. Saying yes to every opportunity may feel productive in the short term, especially when invoices are inconsistent, but over time, it quietly corrodes your confidence, your boundaries, and your business model. *The ability to say no without guilt is not a personality trait—it is a professional discipline.*

Too many freelancers believe that rejecting work is a privilege reserved for the fully booked, the elite, or the lucky. In truth, saying no is not a luxury; it's a system of filters designed to protect your capacity for meaningful, profitable, and reputationally aligned work. And like any system, it improves with practice, data, and language.

Most regrets in freelance work are not about what we turned down—they're about what we accepted too quickly. The underpaid rush job that ballooned into a multi-week headache. The vague favour that morphed into unpaid scope creep. The "great exposure" project that drained your weekends and taught you nothing new. These are not isolated mishaps; they are symptoms of a missing filtration system.

A good filter asks not just, *Can I do this work?* but *Should I?* This is a higher bar, rooted in energy economics, not fear of scarcity. Every yes costs something: time, emotional bandwidth, creative focus, opportunity cost. A sustainable freelance business treats "no" as an investment in future capacity, not a rejection of generosity or ambition.

To apply this mindset practically, consider a three-part test:

1. Strategic Value: Does this work build toward your long-term positioning, skillset, or visibility? Will it open doors you care about, or deepen mastery in your field? Will it generate portfolio material that attracts more of the clients you want?

2. Emotional Load: How much stress, uncertainty, or client management friction is likely? Past experience is often the best predictor—if a client shows red flags in communication or timelines, trust your data. If you leave the first call feeling heavy, listen to that signal.

3. Financial Efficiency: What's the true hourly rate after factoring in edits, communication, learning curves, or delays in payment? Low headline fees are sometimes fine if the work is clean and quick. But high-paying projects that hijack your calendar or peace of mind can be costlier than they appear.

If a prospective project fails two out of three of these filters, it's almost always worth declining. But how you say no determines whether the act preserves your reputation or damages it. This is where freelancers often falter—not in decision-making, but in delivery. They over-explain, apologise, or backpedal. The result is awkwardness or guilt where there should be clarity and professionalism.

A clear, graceful no respects both parties. It communicates boundaries without shame. Here are several scripts that strike the right tone, depending on context:

The values mismatch:

"Thanks for reaching out. I'm currently focusing on projects that align more closely with [area of expertise or focus], so I'm not the best fit for this request. Wishing you success in finding the right partner."

The bandwidth issue (without implying you'll say yes later):

"I appreciate the offer, but I'm at full capacity and unable to take on new work without compromising current commitments. I hope we can stay in touch for future opportunities."

The budget disconnect:

"Thanks for the details. Based on the scope, my rates start at [£X] for this kind of work, which I understand may not align with your current budget. If things change, feel free to reach out down the line."

The high-risk client (polite but firm):

"After reviewing your request, I don't think I'm the right partner for this particular project. It's important that both sides feel fully aligned, and I want to respect your time by stepping aside now."

These responses are not formulas—they are *calibrated closures*. They allow you to exit without burning bridges. And they serve a second purpose: they train your prospective clients. Over time, the market begins to reflect your standards. People learn how to engage with you. Saying no is part of your branding.

Critically, saying no is also a form of financial hygiene. Just as you wouldn't fill your calendar with untracked expenses, you shouldn't fill it with untracked emotional labour. A clean "no" reduces future resentment, overcommitment, and underperformance. It creates space for high-quality yeses—projects that align, compound, and respect your professional maturity.

The deeper challenge, however, is internal. Many freelancers struggle to say no not because they lack the words, but because they fear what the silence might mean. What if no more clients come? What if I was ungrateful? What if this was my only chance? These are scarcity scripts, often inherited from earlier stages in a career. But they don't serve a sustainable practice.

To counteract them, it helps to build a record of good nos. Keep a private document of "declined projects" that later affirmed your choice—when you saw the client ghost another freelancer, or heard the scope changed midstream, or realised you would've missed out on something better. This is not a practice in schadenfreude. It's data-gathering for your intuition.

Another tool is the *future-facing yes*. When you say no, plan what you'll do with the time. Write a pitch for a dream client. Work on your product. Follow up with a warm lead. Build your portfolio. Use your rejection as leverage for action. Saying no *is* a kind of yes—to your strategy, your values, your calendar, your energy. But only if you fill the space intentionally.

Finally, remember this: saying no is not the absence of generosity. It is the *organisation of generosity*. It says, I am building something worth protecting, and I want to serve in a way that is sustainable. Freelancing is not a waiting room for employment or a side hustle on steroids. It is a business. And no is one of its most powerful operating tools—not for pushing people away, but for pulling the right ones closer.

Chapter 15
Wealth Is a System, Not a Number

Security is often imagined as a number: a figure in a bank account, a lump sum tucked away, a portfolio hefty enough to withstand turbulence. For freelancers, however, that arithmetic view falls short. When income fluctuates not just month to month, but sometimes week to week, "enough money" is a mirage. What protects the self-employed is not a balance—it is infrastructure. A structure that delivers visibility, consistency, and clarity of choice, no matter how chaotic the outside world may feel.

In this context, wealth transforms from passive possession into a dynamic relationship. It is a dance between earnings and outgoings, risk and margin, uncertainty and rhythm. Freelancers quickly realise that high income alone does not bring peace of mind, nor does frugality on its own confer control. What delivers confidence is command: knowing what is coming in, what is going out, and which levers are available when the unexpected arises. This command is not a spreadsheet artefact—it is a lived habit. It is a system.

Traditional employment lulls us with the illusion of stability: fixed paycheques, automated benefits, predictable tax handling. It also detaches us from financial thinking, leaving the architecture of money to the employer. Freelancing flips that script. Suddenly, you are CFO, compliance officer, operations lead, and sales engine all at once. Without a system that makes finances visible and decisions repeatable, the business can feel perpetually one crisis away from collapse—even when revenue is healthy.

System-building need not be intimidating. A freelance finance system is modular and grows with your practice. Early on, it may be nothing more than a weekly revenue check, a simple savings rule, and a threshold for accepting projects. Later, it may expand to automated tax buffers, quarterly profit reviews, and cashflow scenario planning. Complexity is not the goal; coherence is. The system must reflect your rhythms, tolerances for risk, and strategic ambitions.

Measurement forms a core part of this architecture—not for obsession, but for insight. It anchors reality. Vague anxiety turns into tangible feedback. A freelancer who feels "broke" may discover that 70 per cent of cash is tied up in receivables. One who thinks they "don't earn enough" may find they misallocate across lifestyle costs. Numbers don't carry intrinsic truth; they illuminate patterns we might otherwise ignore or rationalise.

The aim is not micromanagement. Like an athlete monitoring performance to avoid burnout and sharpen timing, freelancers track finances to detect drift. Audits serve as diagnostics, not judgment. Many resist this engagement because it feels tedious or overly corporate. Often, this resistance signals a deeper belief: that money is inherently stressful, or that systems are antithetical to creativity. The truth is the opposite. Systems create space for creative risk. They absorb shocks, reduce decision fatigue, and let the mind focus on innovation instead of survival. Far from suppressing artistry, they sustain it.

This chapter is a call to financial self-leadership. Not mere budgeting, but architecting. Not reacting to cashflow chaos, but imposing cadence. Weekly visibility, monthly audits, quarterly reviews—not as rote corporate rituals, but as strategic acts of sovereignty. Rhythm here is resilience, not rigidity. It is what allows a freelancer to keep showing up, even when pipelines thin or invoices are delayed.

The benefits compound. Operating from system rather than scramble transforms wealth from accumulation into agility. It is not the six-figure year that matters most—it is the capacity to take a sabbatical and return with momentum. It is the courage to decline a misaligned client, confident that your finances can sustain the choice. It is the freedom to build scalable offerings while day-to-day work continues to cover living costs.

This level of freedom is tangible. Financially fluent freelancers do more than react—they design. They master irregularity rather than relying on luck, viral clients, or relentless overwork. Their systems are small, repeatable, and customised, and therefore durable. Money doesn't merely land in an account—it flows through a structure they own.

This chapter is not a checklist. It is a reframing, a synthesis of what precedes it. You need not become an accountant to feel financially capable, but you must become a system builder. In the freelance life, wealth is never a final destination. It is a structure, cultivated deliberately—a way of operating that opens room for possibility, not someday, but now.

Rethinking Security in a Freelance World

The traditional definition of financial security—usually anchored in the idea of a stable income and an ample savings account—was constructed for a world built around formal employment. It assumes predictable paydays, fixed benefits, and the quiet promise that, if you stay within the system long enough, the system will take care of you. But the freelance world operates on a different physics. It doesn't offer a straight line to stability. It offers volatility, agency, and exposure. In that landscape, the old markers of security fall apart. *A freelancer can earn £15,000 one month and nothing the next. They can close three new clients and still feel broke if the payments are delayed. They can hit a financial milestone yet remain anxious because they lack visibility, not liquidity.* The essential truth is this: in freelance life, security is not a number—it is a system.

This is a difficult shift for many independent workers to make, especially those conditioned by decades of employment to associate peace of mind with accumulating savings. Savings matter, of course. But they are not security in and of themselves. A large balance with no strategic structure around it is merely a cushion—useful for absorbing shocks, but not for preventing them. *True financial security comes from clarity, control, and repeatability.* It comes from knowing not only what you have, but how your financial system behaves under pressure: how fast invoices are paid, what your minimum margin is, where your spending thresholds lie, and what you can adjust in a down month without spiralling into panic or paralysis.

Without that infrastructure, freelancers are perpetually reactive. When money is abundant, they overextend. When money slows, they contract suddenly, making emotionally driven decisions—undercutting their rates, hoarding work they shouldn't accept, or cancelling strategic investments that would have returned long-term value. This is not a character flaw. It is the inevitable result of operating without a system. When you don't have rules, rhythm, or visibility, fear fills the vacuum. And fear, unchecked, makes security impossible—even when the account balance looks healthy.

What does a system look like in practice? It begins with intentional friction: a separation between the business and the self. Many freelancers conflate the two. Their income flows directly into a personal account; their expenses blur with personal spending. The first corrective step is to build boundaries. A business account, even for sole traders, is not cosmetic. It is the scaffolding for financial clarity. When money lands there, it is not yours—it is the business's. You decide how much to pay yourself, how much to allocate for tax, how much to reserve for operations. That act alone transforms your posture from passive recipient to active steward. *Control is born from separation. Separation allows discernment.*

Next is cadence. You cannot manage what you only glance at. Yet most freelancers avoid their numbers until something breaks—a bounced payment, an overdraft warning, a quiet month that stretches longer than expected. Regular financial rituals counteract this. A weekly check-in to review incoming invoices, chase late payments, and update balances. A monthly review of income and outgoings—categorised not by software but by intentionality. A quarterly audit to assess profitability per client, not just aggregate income. These rituals are not administrative burdens. They are trust-building exercises. They rewire your brain to see finances not as chaos, but as information. And when the numbers are visible, the anxiety often fades. *Uncertainty doesn't disappear, but it becomes legible.*

Still, clarity without action is insufficient. The system must be responsive. If a client pays late, how do you handle it? If you exceed your spending threshold one month, what adjustments will you make the next? If a large project falls through, how will your reserves support you, and for how long? Most people ask these questions during a crisis, not before. But the freelancers who build robust systems write the answers *in advance.* They automate buffers. They define their non-negotiables. They decide what spending flexes and what remains fixed. That decision-making framework—made during calm, not chaos—is the ultimate source of confidence. *When you know your own rules, panic becomes unnecessary.*

Of course, systems are not static. They evolve with your business. In year one, your system may be basic: a savings buffer, a cash tracker, a recurring tax set-aside. By year three, it may involve income smoothing, diversified revenue, and forward-looking forecasts. But its essence remains constant: *structure in service of sovereignty.* The point is not bureaucracy. The point is to create a container strong enough to hold your ambition without leaking your energy.

This reframing of security matters because many freelancers carry a quiet shame around their financial instability. They internalise irregularity as personal failure. They believe that if they were smarter, more disciplined, or more "business-minded," their income would be consistent and their anxiety would vanish. But that belief misplaces the problem. *Freelance income will always be irregular. The problem is not income volatility. The problem is system absence.* Systems absorb irregularity. They create buffer, anticipate dips, and make the irregular feel navigable, not existential.

There is also a broader cultural context to this conversation. As the workforce fragments and more people enter freelance, contract, and creator roles, the burden of financial infrastructure is being pushed downward. The social safety nets and institutional scaffolding that once provided external security are being eroded. In their place, individuals must now construct their own ecosystems. Freelancers are the early adopters in this shift. What they learn about building security through systems—rather than through static savings targets—will increasingly be relevant to others navigating the new labour economy.

The freelancer who internalises this lesson becomes something more than a skilled worker. They become a financial architect. They stop chasing a mythical sense of "enough" and start engineering conditions for stability—conditions that hold even when cashflow wobbles or markets stall. They invest not just in revenue, but in repeatability. Not just in savings, but in visibility. Not just in buffers, but in behaviour.

And the long-term payoff is profound. When your finances operate within a system, your brain becomes free to focus on strategy, not survival. You can say no to a client who drains you, because your margins are mapped. You can plan a sabbatical, because your reserves are structured. You can reinvest in growth—courses, marketing, collaborators—because you know your burn rate. *This is what security looks like in the freelance age: not a magic number, but a dynamic system you trust.*

In the end, confidence is not gifted by the market or manufactured by positive thinking. It is earned—incrementally, repeatedly—through the practice of financial clarity and control. It is built not by having more, but by knowing what you have, what you need, and how to navigate the gap. For freelancers, that shift is not optional. It is foundational. And once made, it becomes irreversible. Because once you experience the stability of a system, you will never again confuse it with the false promise of static success.

What Gets Measured, Stays Real

The human brain is brilliantly adaptive, but also conveniently selective—especially when it comes to numbers that make us uncomfortable. Freelancers, even the most intelligent and well-meaning among them, often live in a paradox: they are willing to work harder than most employees, yet remain curiously reluctant to look directly at the mechanics of their own money. This avoidance isn't always rooted in laziness. More often, it's an unconscious self-defence strategy. If one doesn't measure the month's income, the shortfall can't officially disappoint. If savings are left unchecked, the imagined balance remains intact. If time spent working isn't tracked, overwork can continue undisturbed. But *avoidance is not a neutral act*—it compounds risk. And over time, it quietly erodes the very clarity and confidence that financial independence demands.

To measure is not to obsess. It is to acknowledge reality, and in doing so, reclaim agency. Most people think of measurement in terms of spreadsheets and accounting software. But at its core, measurement is a practice of *honesty*. Not performative self-tracking. Not perfectionism. Just deliberate observation of key patterns: what's coming in, what's going out, and what's being built—or eroded—in between. In the freelance context, where income is irregular, expenses are self-directed, and boundaries between work and life blur constantly, this observational discipline is not a luxury. It is the only way to maintain financial coherence in a landscape that lacks built-in structure.

The danger of operating without measurement isn't merely logistical; it's psychological. When income ebbs and flows unpredictably, the brain tends to overemphasise recent data. A good month feels like evidence of growth—even if it followed two bad ones. A late invoice feels catastrophic—even if the overall quarter was profitable. In behavioural finance, this is known as recency bias: *a cognitive distortion that warps judgment in environments without formal feedback loops.* Regular tracking creates those loops. It replaces guesswork with grounded information. It reduces emotional volatility by anchoring perception in broader patterns, not momentary extremes.

This does not require an elaborate system. What matters is rhythm and consistency. Weekly snapshots of cashflow: invoices sent, payments received, current bank balance. Monthly reviews of profitability: revenue earned, expenses incurred, and net margin. Quarterly check-ins on savings: how much is allocated for taxes, for emergencies, for planned investments. The metrics themselves aren't exotic. But their power lies in *continuity*—in their ability to create a stable dashboard from which better decisions can emerge. And those decisions, over time, compound into stability.

It's easy to misinterpret this practice as tedious self-surveillance. But the aim is not control for its own sake. The aim is clarity. *You cannot design an intentional life—financially or otherwise—if the numbers stay vague.* Freelancers often say they want more freedom. More time. More spaciousness. But when their numbers remain opaque, their actions are shaped by anxiety, not strategy. They say yes to the wrong clients. They underprice their work. They neglect savings—not because they're irresponsible, but because they haven't mapped their reality clearly enough to know what's truly possible. Measurement is the prerequisite to that mapping.

There's a second benefit, less discussed but equally vital: measurement fosters *integrity*. When you know your numbers, you can hold yourself accountable. You can't claim you're too broke to hire help if your discretionary spending tells another story. You can't complain about overwork if your time logs show six hours of actual client work per day. Self-measurement isn't punitive; it is clarifying. And clarity, while sometimes uncomfortable, is deeply empowering. It lets you separate fact from feeling. It sharpens your intuition over time. And it helps you grow in a way that is not just reactive, but reflective.

Critics of quantification argue that too much tracking reduces life to data points. And it's true—obsessive measurement can backfire. When every hour becomes monetised, or every coffee scrutinised, the system collapses under its own weight. But what's being proposed here is not maximalist. It is minimalist. Track what matters most. Let go of the rest. *The goal is not to mechanise your life, but to illuminate your blind spots.* For freelancers, those blind spots are often where money leaks, time slips, and stress builds unnoticed until it breaks something essential.

Consider a practical example: a freelance writer with five active clients. She earns £7,000 in a good month, £3,500 in a slow one. Without tracking, those numbers remain anecdotal. She feels "busy" and "broke" at the same time. She assumes she's earning enough, but she's unsure where the money goes. She thinks one client is her anchor, but hasn't calculated their actual margin after all the revision time. When she begins tracking, she discovers that the high-paying client consumes 60% of her time but only delivers 40% of her profit. Another client, with modest fees, yields much higher returns per hour. This insight isn't academic—it's catalytic. It lets her renegotiate, reprioritise, or redesign her service mix based on *data, not emotion*.

The same applies to spending. Many freelancers resist budgets because they feel restrictive. But tracking spending isn't about cutting back—it's about becoming conscious. If you know that your average monthly outlay is £4,200, you can reverse-engineer your required income more precisely. If you see that your software subscriptions quietly ballooned to £300 per month, you can trim without guesswork. If you realise that your quarterly tax bill is consistently higher than anticipated, you can adjust your reserves in real-time. *Measurement replaces vague worry with specific information.* And that shift, over time, is what enables sustainable financial self-leadership.

Measurement also reveals *behavioural patterns* that influence finances as much as numbers do. Do you spend more after a tough client call? Do you neglect your books during periods of creative flow? Do you avoid your accounts entirely after a lean month? These are not just quirks—they are clues. Patterns in behaviour often drive patterns in income and expense. By noticing them, you can begin to *interrupt automaticity* and replace it with intention. The goal is not to eliminate all irrationality—humans are not spreadsheets—but to reduce the number of blind reactions that silently sabotage your goals.

Importantly, this discipline must be framed not as a burden but as a *practice*. Like stretching or journalling, its benefits are cumulative, not instantaneous. You won't feel transformed after your first audit. But over months and years, the compounded effects of measurement—clarity, responsiveness, confidence—create a baseline of financial fluency that most freelancers never reach. And from that baseline, bigger moves become feasible. You can raise rates with logic. Decline bad-fit work without panic. Invest in growth without gambling. Because you're not operating from hope or fear. You're operating from understanding.

This is the hidden power of measurement. It makes your financial life *real*. Not abstract. Not theoretical. Not based on vibes or assumptions. Real. And reality, no matter how imperfect, is always a more powerful foundation for freedom than fantasy.

So if your finances feel blurry, start not with a grand system, but with a small commitment: 15 minutes a week to look. Then 30. Then a monthly review. Then a quarterly reset. Don't aim for perfection. Aim for visibility. *Because what gets measured, stays real. And what stays real, can be changed.*

From Chaos to Cadence

Most freelancers begin with a vision of freedom, but quickly find themselves shackled not by clients or competitors, but by unpredictability. Their days are peppered with delayed invoices, unplanned expenses, and the emotional noise of financial ambiguity. They adapt, as humans do, by developing a reactive rhythm—scrambling to catch up, stretching to make ends meet, and deferring long-term clarity for short-term survival. But over time, *reaction becomes routine*, and the very autonomy they sought starts to feel indistinguishable from instability. Mastery, in this context, begins not with working harder or earning more—it begins with creating *cadence*.

Financial cadence is not about rigid routines or standardised formulas. It's about designing a durable system that supports clarity, flexibility, and forward movement even when external conditions shift. It's the difference between bracing for each month as a unique financial crisis, and stepping into each cycle with foresight and structure. For freelancers, whose income naturally fluctuates, cadence is the antidote to chaos—not by eliminating variation, but by containing it within thoughtful systems.

Those systems are built from the very principles that have surfaced across this book: track what matters, plan around volatility, prioritise value over volume, separate emotion from execution, and build systems that serve the work—not distract from it. The culmination of these ideas is not a universal blueprint, but a framework adaptable to individual rhythms. *Cadence is personal, but never accidental.*

Start with awareness. The difference between a reactive freelancer and a financially sovereign one often begins with visibility. What are your average earnings? What's your minimum viable income to meet obligations? Which clients are delivering consistent value—not just in revenue, but in creative and emotional ROI? Cadence begins when these metrics are not just known, but consulted. Not obsessively, but reliably. *You cannot lead your financial life if you are too afraid to look at it.*

Next comes architecture. Financial cadence is underpinned by structure that flexes but does not collapse under strain. This includes a calendar of financial behaviours—not just a spreadsheet of targets. Weekly reviews to check cash flow, send invoices, and note red flags. Monthly audits to assess margin, reallocate budget categories, and plan for tax obligations. Quarterly resets to revisit rates, realign client rosters, and reinvest surplus intentionally. These are not time-consuming tasks. Done well, they take minutes. But they create alignment across time scales—so that what happens this week still maps meaningfully onto what you want next year.

Perhaps most overlooked, yet most transformative, is the emotional cadence of financial self-leadership. Surviving irregularity demands stoicism. Mastering it requires *emotional pacing*. Too many freelancers live in a feast-or-famine loop not just financially, but psychologically. They overcommit during abundant periods, burn out, then disengage entirely during quiet ones—only to panic and scramble again. Cadence means *de-linking your identity from your income*. It means creating internal steadiness that doesn't rise and fall with each project or payment. And that steadiness is fortified through rituals: reflecting after high-income months without euphoria, reviewing lean months without shame, and building rituals of check-in that reduce financial amnesia.

An essential part of cadence is learning to think in *cycles*, not emergencies. Emergencies force improvisation; cycles allow iteration. Cycles acknowledge that some months will underperform—but that's not failure, it's fluctuation. A well-designed system doesn't treat a single slow week as a threat to solvency. It absorbs it, adjusts, and continues forward. This is what freelancers often lack: a built-in feedback loop that prevents one offbeat note from derailing the entire melody of their business. Cadence protects against overreaction. It offers perspective over panic.

Systems built for cadence are also characterised by *modularity*. The more every element of your freelance business can be updated independently—rates, offers, client tiers, savings buffers—the easier it becomes to adapt without dismantling everything. A chaotic freelance practice requires a complete reinvention with each pivot. A cadence-based practice can shift gear with grace. That modularity extends to income design as well: when short-term projects are balanced by retainer work, and complemented by scalable or passive streams, financial stress doesn't concentrate in one failure point. This diversification is not just an income strategy—it's a resilience strategy.

But cadence is not just about numbers. It is about posture. Freelancers stuck in chaos often feel like they are being dragged by their work. Those in cadence *lead their business*.

They know their capacity. They set parameters. They are not afraid to say no because they understand what a yes costs in time, energy, and momentum. Cadence gives permission to prioritise rest, recalibration, and strategic pause—not as a luxury, but as part of the work itself. *Sustainability is no longer negotiable.*

One of the clearest indicators of cadence is how a freelancer makes decisions. In chaos, decisions are rushed, reactive, emotionally loaded. In cadence, decisions are contextualised. A freelancer in cadence knows if they can afford to take a sabbatical because they have tracked their surplus. They know when to raise rates because they understand client-level margin. They know when to let go of a project—not because they feel overwhelmed, but because the numbers confirm misalignment. *They trust their system because they built it deliberately.*

None of this means perfection. Cadence does not immunise you from uncertainty. But it gives you tools to respond without regression. When a client disappears, a cadence-based system prompts a reallocation—not panic. When a month underperforms, it is seen in light of a 12-month view, not a 12-day spiral. Chaos creates confusion. Cadence restores context.

Ultimately, what this chapter—and the book more broadly—has invited is not just better budgeting or higher rates, but *a reframe of freelance finance as a form of self-leadership.* Financial sovereignty is not built by reacting to the world faster; it is built by stepping back, seeing your patterns, and designing with intention. You do not need to be perfect. You need to be consistent. You do not need to control everything. You need to be able to *recover well.*

The final synthesis, then, is deceptively simple: measure what matters, design systems that reflect your actual rhythm, and let go of the idea that irregularity must equal instability. There is no one-size-fits-all freelance plan. But there *is* a common trajectory: chaos gives way to cadence when information becomes insight, and insight becomes structure.

That is what mastery looks like. Not rigidity. Not constant reinvention. But *a resilient rhythm*—deliberate, adaptive, and quietly powerful. When that rhythm is in place, you don't just survive freelance life. You *lead it.*

The Next Level of Freedom

There is a subtle but decisive line between earning money and owning your financial system. Most freelancers cross the first threshold early—through hard work, reputation, or relentless hustle. But far fewer reach the second. The former can generate income, even impressive income. The latter creates *capacity*. It makes room for risk, recovery, and reinvention. *Financial fluency*, not just financial gain, is what ultimately expands freedom.

Freedom, for the freelancer, is often miscast as a lifestyle brand—a beach laptop fantasy or a rejection of conventional employment. But those aesthetic tropes obscure the deeper opportunity: *freedom as the ability to choose without destabilising your life*. To say yes to a passion project, a sabbatical, a startup pivot, or simply a period of rest—because the system you've built can hold you. That's not about passive income or early retirement; it's about being structurally sound enough to adapt without unraveling.

This level of freedom begins with clarity. Most freelancers know their revenue but not their runway. They know what came in last month, but not how long they could sustain a dry spell. They may even know they're undercharging but feel too precarious to change it. What's missing is not ambition or intelligence—it's a *clear, consistently consulted financial infrastructure*. The freelancers who feel unshakable are not usually the highest earners. They're the ones who've built a simple, adaptive map of their money: what comes in, what it must cover, what it funds next, and where it needs to grow. That clarity *is* confidence.

With clarity comes optionality. Once you know your margins—financial, emotional, energetic—you can start designing around *better returns*, not just more work. This is where fluency begins to compound. For example: a designer who has moved from hourly projects to a hybrid model of retainers, teaching, and digital products is not just diversifying income. They are diversifying *risk and rhythm*. If one stream falters, the system holds. If a new opportunity arises, they don't have to decline it out of fear. They have breathing room—not gifted to them, but architected over time.

This breathing room is what enables creative risk. Many freelancers want to write a book, launch a course, start a podcast, or experiment with a new service. But those ambitions often die in the face of cash flow panic. Not because the idea is weak—but because the system can't hold the uncertainty that comes with iteration. Without financial fluency, every risk is a threat. With fluency, it becomes a *choice*. The goal isn't reckless leap-taking. It's calculated, recoverable exploration.

And the benefits aren't only professional. *Sabbaticals, slow seasons, and sustained recovery*—these are not luxuries at the next level. They're stabilisers. Burnout is not just an emotional state; it's a structural symptom of financial systems that offer no space for recuperation. When freelancers master cadence, buffers, and pacing, rest becomes a built-in feature, not a desperate recovery plan. A well-timed sabbatical doesn't derail the business. It refuels it.

From there, freelancers can begin to scale—not just in revenue, but in *impact and identity*. Scaling doesn't mean building an agency or growing a team, unless that aligns with your vision. It means *elevating your leverage*. That might look like raising your rates because your systems have shown exactly how much each client costs you in hours and stress. It might mean shifting from bespoke offers to a productised suite. It might mean licensing intellectual property, building partnerships, or creating modular assets that decouple income from time. The path is variable. The principle is not: *scale becomes available only when the foundation is sound.*

The deeper opportunity, though, is psychological. When money ceases to be a constant uncertainty, it frees up the mental bandwidth previously spent on anxiety, overwork, or reactive decision-making. You don't just become more financially stable—you become *more strategic, more creative, and more composed*. That composure matters. It changes how you negotiate, how you market, how you select clients, and how you weather setbacks. It's not confidence as a performance. It's *infrastructure-backed self-trust.*

Crucially, the next level is not a fixed destination. It's a posture: *proactive, intentional, and self-authored.* It's the shift from "how do I stay afloat?" to "what am I building and why?" It's the freelancer who no longer treats money as the aftermath of their work, but as the architect of their opportunities. It's someone who checks their financial system not out of fear, but to align their time and energy with what matters most.

This is where fluency evolves into stewardship. You're not just tracking expenses or planning tax quarters. You're shaping your business as a tool for your life—not the other way around. That's what true financial autonomy looks like: the ability to make deliberate trade-offs, to work toward something beyond next month's invoice, to protect your energy as fiercely as your earnings, and to step away without everything collapsing.

None of this demands perfection. Fluency is not measured by zero-error budgets or flawless spreadsheets. It's measured by adaptability. *How quickly can you assess a shift? How gracefully can you recalibrate? How well do your systems absorb change without resorting to chaos?* Those are the real metrics of mastery. And they are available to every freelancer—regardless of income—who chooses to engage deeply with their numbers, their patterns, and their vision.

So the call to action is not to earn more. It's to *own the structure through which your money flows.* Audit what exists. Notice what's missing. Design around rhythm, not rigidity. And, most of all, stop waiting for permission. The tools are here. The frameworks are available. The insight is within reach. What remains is the choice to build—not just to make a living, but to make *freedom replicable.*

You are not just a freelancer. You are the architect of your own economic ecosystem. Build it like it matters. Because it does.

About the Author

Jonas Wilder has spent over a decade navigating the unpredictable terrain of freelance life—learning firsthand that making money on your own terms requires more than hustle; it demands systems, clarity, and discipline. His work is rooted in a belief that financial fluency is not just for Wall Street insiders or spreadsheet obsessives—it's for designers, consultants, writers, coders, and creators who wake up every day without a paycheck but with full responsibility. Known for his calm, no-fluff approach to money and work, Jonas blends behavioural insight with real-world practicality to help readers move from chaos to confidence. When he's not writing, he mentors independent professionals on building sustainable income and designing a life that doesn't trade freedom for instability.

www.ingramcontent.com/pod-product-compliance
Lightning Source LLC
Chambersburg PA
CBHW031338230926
51848CB00002B/286
9789371779111